David Stafford is the author of several highly acclaimed books on espionage and intelligence, including *Camp X, The Silent Game: The Real World of Imaginary Spies, Churchill and the Secret Service*, and *Roosevelt and Churchill: Men of Secrets*. A former diplomat, he is Visiting Fellow at the Institute for Advanced Studies in the Humanities at the University of Edinburgh and Project Director at the University's Centre for Second World War Studies. He is the author and narrator of several radio documentaries for both the BBC and the Canadian Broadcasting Corporation, and worked as a consultant for the accompanying BBC television series on the Special Operations Executive.

Other books by David Stafford:

Camp X
Churchill and the Secret Service
Roosevelt and Churchill: Men of Secrets
The Silent Game: The Real World of Imaginary Spies

Secret Agent

Britain's Wartime Secret Service

David Stafford

For Beth, Sonia and Michael
whose grandfather was part of the story

This book is published to accompany the television series *Secret Agent* which was first broadcast in 2000. The series was produced for BBC Television by Darlow Smithson Productions Ltd.

Executive producer: John Smithson. Series producer: David Darlow
Producers: Jonathan Dent and Jonathan Hacker, Darlow Smithson Productions Ltd.

Published by BBC Worldwide Limited, Woodlands, 80 Wood Lane, London W12 0TT

ISBN: 0 563 48811 5

First published in hardback 2000. Copyright © David Stafford 2000
This paperback edition published 2002
The moral right of the author has been asserted

Commissioning Editor: Sally Potter. Project Editors: Helena Caldon and Cath Harries
Copy Editor: Christine King. Picture Researcher: Miriam Hyman
Production Controller: Mark Sanderson

Set in Jansen and Rockwell
Printed and bound in Great Britain by Mackays of Chatham
Plate sections printed by Lawrence-Allen Ltd, Weston-super-Mare
Cover printed by Belmont Press Ltd, Northampton

CONTENTS

AUTHOR'S NOTE

This book has been written to accompany the TV series of the same title, shown on BBC2 in summer 2000. My greatest debt is to those veterans of SOE, men and women, who agreed to be interviewed for the programme and whose recollections have shaped and immeasurably enriched the story. I am also grateful to the entire production team at Darlow Smithson who conceived the series and kept me provided with transcripts and other material that has gone into the making of the book: David Darlow, Jonathan Dent, Jonathan Hacker, Dominic Sutherland, Nigel Morris, Alison Moody, Gillian Strachan, Chloe Benedictus, Bernadette Ross, Kate Shepherd, Daphne Walsh and Jan Surtees. At BBC Worldwide Sally Potter and Helena Caldon nursed it through the editorial process, while Miriam Hyman took care of picture research. Christine King copy-edited the manuscript with thankful efficiency. Andrew Lownie, my agent, did more than his fair share to help it all see the light of day. My thanks for help with translation go to Christine Haunz and Jim Hurford.

Above all I wish to thank my wife, Jeanne Cannizzo. Delivery of the manuscript by the deadline imposed by the demanding broadcasting schedule felt at times like mission impossible and would not have been accomplished without her boundless practical help, advice and encouragement. She has been my editor of first resort and has more than completed her tour of duty with SOE.

The story told here concentrates mostly on SOE's activities in occupied Europe. Even here, alas, there are gaps, such as the heroic resistance of the Poles, the partisan struggles in Italy, the quiet bravery of many Danes, and the undercover work of agents in neutral countries. But SOE also waged secret war around the globe, in the Americas, in the Near East, and in Asia, where Force 136 achieved impressive results in arduous conditions. This last area of operations indirectly touched my own life, for – as I learned only after his death – my own father, a meteorologist with the Royal Air Force, helped brief special duties flights in what was then Ceylon, now Sri Lanka, for their perilous clandestine flights to south-east Asia. It is for this reason that I have dedicated this book to my nieces and nephew who sadly never knew him but of whom he would have been immeasurably proud.

The worldwide reach of SOE should not be forgotten. Perhaps one day, in similar fashion to this, that story can also be told.

David Stafford, Edinburgh, April 2000

CHAPTER 1

'SET EUROPE ABLAZE'

It was an unlikely beginning. The St Ermin's was – as it remains – a respectable hotel on Caxton Street tucked away off Victoria Street in the heart of Westminster. But in the summer of 1940, with the Luftwaffe launching its first heavy bombing raids on London, it was hardly the most secure of places. Nor, despite its ornate central stairway and baroque Victorian interior, did its decor suggest anything special. The writer and wartime spy Malcolm Muggeridge wryly found it dim and quiet, 'suggestive of conferences to promote world government, family planning, or the practice of eurhythmics'. Nonetheless, in three gloomy rooms of its fourth floor, as Adolf Hitler planned the invasion of Britain and Winston Churchill promised to fight on the beaches, a handful of men hatched a campaign of European-wide sabotage, subversion and revolt. Soon the plotters expanded and took over the top three floors of the hotel.

Who they were, no one quite knew. If asked, they sometimes said they belonged to the Admiralty; at other times to the Army or Royal Air Force. Occasionally they claimed to be from something called the Inter-Services Research Bureau, which helped account for the variety of uniforms passing in and out of the hotel. Anyone looking for this shadowy organization's number in the London telephone directory ended up frustrated, for it was unlisted. Nor did their stationery carry the St Ermin's hotel address. But, using this modest hotel as a mysterious and deliberately confusing cover, the team became global in its span, with regional headquarters in such places as Istanbul, Cairo, New Delhi and New York. This was the first home of what history now knows as the Special Operations Executive, or SOE.

On 16 July 1940, Hitler signed his Führer Directive No. 16 for the planning of Operation Sealion, the invasion of Britain. That same night Churchill summoned his Minister for Economic Warfare,

Hugh Dalton, to a midnight meeting at 10 Downing Street. The collapse of France and the débâcle of Dunkirk had left Hitler in command of Europe. Now urgent discussions were under way in Whitehall about a top-secret organization intent on sabotage and subversion behind enemy lines, to spark revolt, and undermine Hitler's Europe from within. Churchill gave Dalton, who had been lobbying hard for the position, charge of the new agency. As he turned to leave, Churchill commanded him: 'And now set Europe ablaze.' The War Cabinet endorsed Churchill's decision one week later.

Dalton was a large man with immense energy, a powerful conviction that he was usually right, and an irrepressible urge to provoke his opponents. One of his subordinates recalled that his voice was penetrating and that when he was angry his eyes used to roll around 'in rather a terrifying way'. Nicknamed 'Dr Dynamo', he had been a vigorous opponent of appeasement during the 1930s and believed fervently in the need to use 'ungentlemanly warfare' to defeat the Nazis at their own game. He argued that Britain must organize movements in every occupied territory comparable to Sinn Fein in Ireland, the Chinese guerrillas fighting the Japanese, the Spanish irregulars who'd defeated Napoleon in Spain and – 'let's face it' – the subversive organizations run by the Nazis themselves in Europe: 'We must use many different methods, including industrial and military sabotage, labour agitations and strikes, continuous propaganda, terrorist acts against traitors and German leaders, boycotts and riots.'

This enthusiasm had made him an obvious candidate for running SOE, and he had high expectations of what he could do; but there were two problems. The first was that Churchill disliked him. The Prime Minister had witnessed guerrillas in action as a young soldier and war correspondent and was a fellow enthusiast for secret war. But he regarded Dalton with deep suspicion. Dalton's father had been the Canon of Windsor and tutor to the future Kings Edward VIII and George VI, and Dalton literally grew up in the shadow of Windsor Castle. Not surprisingly, he'd also gone to school at Eton, only a stone's throw from his childhood home. Yet Dalton's political career was built on attacking the very wealth and privilege that had nurtured him. He became an ardent socialist, a fiery lecturer at the London School of Economics, and by 1940 he was one of the most powerful men in the Labour Party. As an intellectual socialist he aroused all Churchill's dislike of the class traitor. 'Keep that man away from me,' he once said. 'I can't stand his booming voice and shifty eyes.' He was far from Churchill's first choice for the job. But as head of a coalition, the Prime Minister had to throw a bone to Labour to balance Conservative control of the Foreign Office. During the crucial period that SOE struggled to get up and running, Dalton suffered from the handicap of having no easy access to Churchill. It was testimony to his enormous determination that SOE even survived these early days.

Dalton's second problem was that he had very few weapons at hand to set Europe ablaze. Late in the 1930s Hitler's takeover of Austria prompted the Secret Intelligence Service (SIS) to create a special unit to carry out dirty tricks against the Nazis. Known as Section D ('D' for destruction) and run by a flamboyant army major named Lawrence Grand from offices at 2 Caxton Street, next door to the St Ermin's Hotel, it had devised plenty of imaginative schemes, such as destroying the Rumanian oil fields, blocking the Danube by blowing up the Iron Gates, a narrow gorge on the river, and sabotaging iron ore exports to Germany from Sweden.

But there had been few results. In the War Office a small subdivision of Military Intelligence under an inventive genius named Jo Holland had carried out research on paramilitary warfare under the designation MI(R) but had not yet moved from planning to action. And attached to the Foreign Office was a shadowy organization known as 'EH', for Electra House, which dabbled in subversive propaganda – what Dalton described as 'leaflets, whispers, rumours, secret wireless transmitters and so forth'. Subsisting on tiny budgets, lacking co-ordination, these three small secret units had barely scratched the surface of what needed doing. But they provided the unlikely building blocks of SOE.

Once in charge, Dalton moved with his customary energy. After reviewing the scene he briskly concluded that 'the selection of the right men is even more important than the creation of the right machine'. He relentlessly employed the old boys' network to form the kernel of a central staff. The main nucleus came from Section D. Many were bankers, businessmen or lawyers with international contacts who knew how to move money and fix deals. One of the most important was George Taylor, a ruthless Australian with business interests around the globe who had worked tirelessly for Section D in the Balkans. He specialized in subversion in neutral countries. Even Dalton was forced to admit he was 'always belligerent, persistent and ingenious' and 'as clever as a monkey'. Bickham Sweet-Escott, a banker from Courtaulds, played a similar role and left one of the best accounts of SOE ever to have appeared, under the title *Baker Street Irregular*. Charles Hambro, of the banking family, had powerful connections in neutral Sweden and throughout Scandinavia which SOE used to excellent effect. From the top City solicitors, Slaughter and May, came Harry Sporborg and Jack Beevor, the former to oversee operations in western Europe, the latter as SOE chief in Lisbon – a neutral capital rich in intrigue and subversive possibilities. Others came from the Foreign Office, such as Gladwyn Jebb, who proved valuable in resisting his fellow diplomats' desire to strangle SOE at birth.

Civilians accustomed to order, now this small band of warriors had disorder and chaos in Europe at the top of their agenda. Angus Fyffe, who joined SOE in 1941, recalled the atmosphere of these early days: 'Quite informal, they were all jolly lads together. You see, we must remember that at the outset SOE was composed of representatives from Courtaulds, Hambro's Bank, they were all civilians, lawyers, men of the City, and there was almost a black jacket, striped trousers, briefcase air about the place.'

Dalton chose Sir Frank Nelson as SOE's first Executive Director. After a successful career as businessman and Conservative MP, he had served as Vice-Consul at Basle, Switzerland, a post traditionally providing cover for the Secret Intelligence Service. He installed himself in a serviced flat close to the St Ermin's, spent seven days a week in his office from a quarter to nine to midnight, and single-mindedly devoted himself to building SOE from scratch. This eventually exhausted him and he was forced to quit the job after eighteen months.

But by far the most important appointment in the long term was that of Brigadier Colin McVean Gubbins, a professional soldier, as Director of Operations and Training. Throughout SOE's many trials and tribulations and behind nearly all its triumphs, Gubbins acted as the indefatigable mainspring and source of inspiration. Eventually, in 1943, he became Executive Director.

Gubbins was already in his mid-forties, a soldier with an unorthodox past. Born in Japan, he had served with the Royal Artillery in the First World War and as ADC to General 'Tiny' Ironside, commandant of the anti-Bolshevik expeditionary force to Archangel after the Russian Revolution. Then in Ireland he had encountered the guerrilla tactics of the IRA and become a convert to the power of irregular war. In 1938, working with Jo Holland in MI(R) in the War Office, he helped draft a handbook on guerrilla war and a companion text for partisan leaders, full of practical advice on how to organize an ambush and what to do with enemy informers ('kill them'). When Britain sent a military mission to Warsaw immediately prior to the outbreak of war he headed its guerrilla war and behind-the-lines resistance section. After Poland's defeat he raised special commando-style units during the Norwegian campaign. At the peak of the invasion scare he masterminded plans for behind-the-lines resistance in a Nazi-occupied Britain, the so-called 'Auxiliary Units'.

A shortish, dark man with clipped speech and a brisk mind, he made an immediate impression on those who met him. Bickham Sweet-Escott described him as 'a man of immense energy and vitality with a quick wit, and an imagination rare in a professional soldier. He enjoyed life to the full; he never forgot a face or a name, and he had a gift for inspiring confidence in those working under him. He was in fact a born leader of men.' Peter Wilkinson, his military assistant and biographer, also stressed Gubbins's power of leadership as well as his popularity among younger officers: 'He was a wonderful leader of the young, whom he inspired, and of course in SOE found his niche because resistance was essentially a young man's job. He had an imaginative temperament, really quite visionary, and was a very efficient soldier in the technical sense.'

Angus Fyffe felt much the same: 'A charming man but a very efficient and brusque officer. You didn't take risks with Gubbins because you wouldn't have got away with it, but a very highly intelligent and kind chap.'

Gubbins arrived at SOE with a concept. His military experience had brought him particularly close to the Poles. Their country was now occupied by the Nazis but already resistance was stirring. The Polish government under General Sikorski had moved to London and was talking enthusiastically of its secret army at home. Even before the Nazi invasion, Gubbins had discussed with the Polish General Staff possible underground resistance and he shared the Poles' optimism.

Dalton was a ready convert and put Poland high on his list of priorities. On a visit to the Polish Army in Scotland over Christmas 1940 he brought the roof down with a stirring talk. On the day of victory, he declared, Poland – as the first nation to stand up to Hitler while others grovelled on their bellies – should ride in the vanguard of the victory march. If SOE could equip its Home Army (as Poland's secret army was known), then it would spark a major uprising at the moment of liberation.

Not surprisingly, Poland took up much of SOE's energy in its early months. Within the Polish General Headquarters at the Hotel Rubens in Buckingham Palace Road, its VI (Intelligence) Bureau selected and trained a small group of officers who had volunteered to be parachuted back into Poland. Working closely with the head of SOE's Polish section, Captain Harold Perkins, another of Gubbins's protégés from the War Office, they planned a flight for December 1940. After two false starts, it finally succeeded on the night of 15 February 1941. A two-engined Whitley aircraft, modified to carry a special auxiliary fuel tank for the fourteen-hour round-trip, successfully dropped three Polish parachutists who safely made it secretly into Nazi-occupied Warsaw. Peter Wilkinson described the importance for SOE of this flight.

This was the first connection with occupied Europe. It was in itself an extraordinary feat to fly blind across occupied Europe at about 120 miles an hour in the depths of winter and to find a dropping zone and to get back. The whole flight took about fourteen hours and it was a notable feat of navigation and endurance. This in itself was terribly important, to find out that one could do it. Secondly it was really vital at that time to try to convince very doubting chiefs of staff and a very sceptical Whitehall that this sort of thing was feasible at all.

Dalton was elated – it fuelled his enthusiasm for supplying the Polish Home Army with vast supplies. He proposed similar ideas for the Czechs. Yet the mission in reality showed how difficult this would be. Once the dark winter nights yielded to long summer evenings, flights across occupied Europe became terribly exposed. In any event only a handful of planes were at SOE's disposal and all would have required special modifications. In fact, such a flight was not to be repeated for another twelve months. It was simply impossible to supply the Polish Home Army on the scale envisaged from bases in the United Kingdom.

Gubbins was quick to draw the lesson. If SOE were to produce results, operations would have to be closer to home and on a more modest scale. Moreover, SOE would quickly have to get hold of adequate transport to deliver its agents to the field.

Meanwhile, in October 1940, SOE moved its burgeoning staff from the modest St Ermin's to a large modern office block at 64 Baker Street, stamping ground of the fictional supersleuth of an earlier fight against evil, Sherlock Holmes. Its propaganda section, known as SO1, was based at Woburn Abbey in Bedfordshire. Twelve months later this was split off to form an entirely separate agency, the Political Warfare Executive, and played no further part in the SOE story. From now on 'Baker Street' referred to SOE headquarters.

As it expanded, its premises relentlessly colonized Marylebone. It took over Norgeby House, at 83 Baker Street, and then spilled over into the top floor of No 82, Michael House, the corporate headquarters of Marks and Spencer. Nearby streets and blocks of flats such as Dorset Square, Orchard Court, Montague Mansions and Chiltern Court housed SOE's various country and technical sections.

Sir Frank Nelson and his team continued their urgent search for staff officers and field agents. There was no real system. Advertising was out because secrecy was paramount. Instead, discreet approaches were made to the armed forces for people with foreign languages who might be interested in 'special' wartime service. Ernest van Maurik's experience can serve as an example:

I was in the Wiltshire Regiment and had been since the beginning of the war. At the end of 1940 I was on the beach at

Folkestone waiting for an invasion that one more or less knew was not going to come. I was called up to my commanding officer who said, 'I've got to send you up for an interview – it ought to be somebody with a certain amount of weapons small-arms training, you're the only junior officer. So you go, and if you don't like it, come back.'

Well, I got up to London in Horse Guards parade. There were a lot of other people being interviewed. The interviewing officer said, 'I see you've got a Dutch father, so you must speak Dutch.' Actually my mother had always discouraged my father from teaching me any real Dutch. I eventually persuaded him that I didn't speak Dutch, so he said do I speak any other language. I said French and German. They said it'll be interesting work if we select you and you will get instant promotion to lieutenant. It had been mentioned that it might be to do with training foreign troops so I thought probably it was something with the French troops who had escaped at Dunkirk, but I didn't think for a moment it had anything to do with infiltration into France, all that sort of thing.

Angus Fyffe was also unimpressed with his first interrogation about his language skills.

I went into this room with several others. We didn't speak to one another because it was so secret, didn't even say good morning. Eventually a hole in the wall opened. A young man came through and said 'Good morning, gentlemen. I'm going to give you a piece of dictation in French. I will speak very slowly. I will repeat the phrase twice and you will write down what I say, understood?' A tacit nod, that was all. I'd never had such a puerile piece of dictation that I learned when I was a wee boy in the qualifying class.

It was that sort of thing. 'Mr Crow was sitting on a tree, comma', repeated twice, 'in his beak he had a piece of cheese, comma' exploded from his lips. We had about fifteen minutes of this and then he disappeared back in his hole through the wall.

New recruits in turn suggested friends and acquaintances. This was how Francis Cammaerts, one of SOE's outstanding agents in

France, got in. A registered conscientious objector before the war, he changed his mind after his brother was killed with the RAF.

> For a number of reasons I decided I had to join in the combat with fascism which the whole of the nation was involved in. I tried to find some kind of activity in which such talents as I had might be used, of which knowledge of French was a clear one, and it was in that way that I consulted Harry Ree [a friend] who was in the intelligence services at the time and he said yes, I can get you an interview. I was told to go to a room in Northumberland Avenue in which I saw an officer. We spoke in French the whole time…

Margaret Jackson, Gubbins's personal assistant, was also recruited through personal contacts. Her sister worked as a secretary in MI(R) and mentioned her name to Joan Bright, Colonel Jo Holland's personal assistant; it also helped that she spoke French. Recourse was inevitably had to the 'old-school tie', the network of personal contacts formed by the then narrow male élite that governed Britain. Yet the sheer number and variety of agents needed by SOE guaranteed an extraordinary diversity of men and women, from different social backgrounds, religious denominations, occupations and political beliefs. While most of the Baker Street staff were British, field agents came from many other nations including most Commonwealth countries such as Canada, New Zealand and Australia, as well as the United States. Many were nationals of the target country and had dual nationality.

Such was the case with Roger Landes. Born in Paris of a French father and English mother, he was living in London when war broke out and was then called up for the Army: 'In December 1939 I was called to register for the British Army. I had my medical and I was accepted. I had to fill in a form and they said do you speak any language? I said yes, I speak French fluently and I didn't hear anything until March '41, then I received my calling-up paper to the Royal Corps of Signals to be trained as a wireless operator. The day I finished my training I was called to report to the War Office for interview.'

When he arrived in London he was interviewed by Major Lewis

Gielgud (the brother of John Gielgud the actor). Landes was surprised to find that his file was so detailed as to include the colour of his eyes.

> He said, 'We found out that you can speak French, and you've been trained as a wireless operator. We want you if you will to go to France. You'll be dropped by parachute or motor boat or by fishing boat. You've got a good chance to be arrested, tortured, maybe shot. I give you five minutes to say yes or no.' I said I will do it. He said, 'You return to your unit and we get you transferred within a fortnight. If they ask any questions why you've been called to see me, just say we wanted some information about Paris.'

Employing foreigners in itself could cause complications and slow things down. Suitable nationals of the many governments-in-exile that had taken refuge in London were in short supply and high demand. SOE quickly made contact with these governments for help with both recruitment and operations. But even when willing to help, the exiles had to tread carefully. Their own intelligence services' traditional links were with the SIS, who jealously guarded them. Here again, Baker Street often found itself resisting bureaucratic sabotage and subversion in Whitehall itself.

Women formed a significant proportion of the administrative staff but were also recruited as agents – although almost exclusively in France, where of fifty despatched some thirteen never returned. One who did survive was Yvonne Baseden.

> My mother was French and I was born in Paris. My brother and I travelled throughout Europe accompanying my father, who was an electrical engineer. We came back to England and war was declared. Because I had dual nationality I was very interested in what was happening in France as well as in England. When I heard de Gaulle speak up, I thought I'd better go and see if I can do anything. I went along to his offices and spoke to his secretary who said that he might be interested and asked me to wait. He came back and said unfortunately because my father was English, I was bi-national and they couldn't possibly employ or help me in any way to join their organization. So that was that as far as the Free French.

So I went away and had to think again. I remembered my father telling me that in the First World War he'd been not only despatch rider to start with but one of the first Royal Flying Corps pilots, and I thought I'll join the WRAF. I did work in different parts of the Air Ministry, and the secretary of the PA to the wing commander in charge of a particular department I was working for was a French woman who had been in the field working for SOE. I didn't know, I hadn't heard of SOE, but she had no doubt been told that if there was anyone that she came across who might be suitable to pass the word on. And that is how I was contacted eventually by SOE.

Another avenue was the First Aid Nursing Yeomanry (FANY), the first all-women volunteer organization formed to work with the armed forces before the First World War. It provided a recruiting ground for over a thousand agents, home-based wireless operators, coding clerks, drivers and secretarial staff. In the field, they worked mostly as couriers or radio operators, but occasionally as organizers of whole networks. Other FANYs worked at SOE training schools and on dirty tricks teams. Pauline Brockies recalls how she found herself on just such a team.

I didn't particularly want to go into a factory; a friend of mine had joined the FANYs and I liked the uniform. So I applied to join and after a lot of interviews, I was accepted. We went to a place called Overthorpe Hall near Banbury for two weeks' instruction – talking about corps history, security, nothing appertaining to SOE. I just thought it was a natural induction course that everybody went into when they joined the Services. Then I was directed to go to Norgeby House in Baker Street. I didn't know anything about what was going on. We were taken round the back of a restaurant to what was Michael House and went up the stairs into an office. There's a man in civilian clothes and he gave us a piece of paper to sign; I signed it and he said to me, 'Have you read what you've just signed?' Well, I hadn't. He said, 'Because if you divulge anything while working for this organization, you'll be stood up against a wall and shot!' Well, when you're eighteen, that is a bit scary.

SOE was organized into country sections which took care of much of their own recruiting. This haphazard method was eventually replaced by a formal interview board composed largely of psychologists who, over several days, probed the characters and capabilities of would-be spies. For early recruits life in Baker Street sometimes possessed a surreal quality. In the meantime, however, everything seemed to be on hold.

Not surprisingly, SOE was regarded with considerable suspicion by the regular armed forces and other government departments in Whitehall. As Angus Fyffe recalled:

It was working from day to day and holding one's fingers in one's mouth, hoping it would be all right because we were very much an embryonic organization, not very popular among the other organizations, the senior branches, you see, not very popular with them. We were upstarts and we were going to indulge in not very nice warfare. Anthony Eden didn't like us at all, not at all. Dalton was the one who saved SOE. No, it was a hand-to-mouth organization for quite a long time and we had lots of difficulties in overcoming opposition from various quarters.

They claimed to be secret warriors but had little military expertise. Operating in foreign fields, where were their diplomatic skills? Acting as a 'secret service', what clandestine arts did they know? It was all made worse when SOE inevitably had to seek their help. Could the Admiralty provide boats to carry its agents across the Channel? Could the Army supply weapons and ammunition? Could the Air Force help with dropping supplies and agents? Could the Foreign Office assist with subversive operations in neutral countries? The answers to these questions were usually an instinctive 'no'. Gubbins later recalled that among the established organs of government, 'at the best SOE was looked upon as an organization of harmless backroom lunatics which, it was hoped, would not develop into an active nuisance. At the worst, it was regarded as another confusing excrescence…as a whole it was left severely alone as a somewhat disreputable child.'

Peter Wilkinson, used to the tight little nucleus of Whitehall, found that the physical location of SOE in Baker Street didn't help, nor did the ultra-secrecy assist in his efforts to squeeze supplies from other government departments.

> You were separated from the mainstream of Whitehall. It was too far for example to go and lunch at one's club where one met one's friends and maintained relationships on a much easier footing and was rather an essential part of conducting the sort of activities we were attempting. One way and another it was an uphill fight because it was top secret. I remember going down to try and cadge some arms from a member of my old regiment and rather laughingly, when he was asking what it was for, I said, 'My lips are sealed,' and he said, 'So are the doors of the armoury.' Altogether there was a general feeling that, well, to put it quite shortly, SOE was a racket.

This distrust, combined with loathing, was most severe in the Secret Intelligence Service (SIS or MI6). Its director, Major-General Stewart Menzies, was known in Whitehall as 'C', after the initial of the service's founder Sir Mansfield Cumming. A powerful figure, he was dangerous to cross. His officers considered themselves professionals who had been in the intelligence game for decades whereas SOE were upstarts and amateurs. Menzies had set up Section D, and so could control it. But after SOE absorbed Section D, Menzies became unhappy. SOE and SIS had very different and often conflicting interests. 'C''s intelligence networks flourished in peace and quiet. SOE's sabotage operations were by definition noisy and attracted the attention of the Germans. Wilkinson recognized this, although doing so didn't make life easier: 'It stood to reason that the activities of SIS that involved the recruitment very often of large groups of people and the blowing up of buildings or bridges were directly inimical to the work of the Secret Intelligence Service which depended for its effect on melding into the local population and being invisible. Understandably they took a rather gloomy view of our activities.'

The Broadway Buildings, Menzies' headquarters opposite the St James's Street underground – and just around the corner from the St Ermin's Hotel – was thus regarded with great suspicion by Baker Street. The feeling was mutual.

SOE's 'charter' – the founding document proved in July 1940 by the War Cabinet – had anticipated the problem by ordering it to 'co-ordinate' its activities with relevant agencies. But the well-established SIS was in a powerful position to veto or severely limit Baker Street's plans. Not long after Gubbins arrived Menzies turned his thumbs down on plans by SOE to infiltrate its agents into France by sea because this would seriously disrupt his own secret networks across the Channel.

The Admiralty supported Menzies. Ironically, the Director of Naval Intelligence, Admiral John Godfrey, was a strong supporter of SOE and 'dirty tricks'. His personal assistant Ian Fleming later armed James Bond, his fictional secret agent, with many of the skills and gadgets he learned about through his knowledge of SOE. But given his dependence on Menzies' men for the collection of much naval intelligence, Godfrey felt compelled to agree that SIS intelligence should be given precedence over SOE subversion – 'now and in the future'.

Menzies exerted power over Nelson's Baker Street irregulars in another significant area – wireless communication. Agents in the field needed wireless transmitting sets, codes and ciphers, frequencies and home receiving stations. All these were controlled by 'C', and SOE messages had to be submitted to Broadway, who had the right to accept or reject them. This unwelcome dependence generated resentment and suspicion. Was SIS using its ability to read SOE signals to interfere with Baker Street's plans? Only in June 1942 did SOE finally acquire the right to build its own sets, use its own codes, and run its own networks and home stations. At its peak, SOE ran four receiving stations in Britain employing 1500 W/T operators and cipher clerks keeping a round-the-clock watch for messages coming in from several hundred agents scattered behind enemy lines. Likewise, until 1942, SIS also kept a tight control over clandestine forgery and was able to restrict the quantity of forged papers available for SOE agents.

Six months after Churchill's rousing order to Dalton to set Europe ablaze, Baker Street had little to show for its efforts. In occupied Europe the Nazis were tightening their grip and even isolated incidents of resistance were few and far between. For the most part the occupied populations were too shattered and cowed to do more than concentrate on survival. In October 1940 Nazi troops entered Rumania, and the Balkans came under heavy German pressure. Hitler met Mussolini at the Brenner Pass and declared, 'The war is won.' The Italian dictator struck at Greece. In Poland, forced labour began and Jews were herded into ghettos; twenty miles across the English Channel, in occupied France, they were given specially marked identity cards. In the Atlantic U-boat wolf-packs began to wreak havoc on British convoys to North America. The Luftwaffe began its night-time blitz of London and other British cities, and in November devastated Coventry in a raid that flattened the city centre and killed hundreds of civilians. Four days after Christmas, in a massive German raid, a fire engulfed the City of London and destroyed or severely damaged the Guildhall and seven Wren churches.

It was London, not Europe, that was ablaze. SOE was under mounting pressure to produce results. Baker Street was growing in leaps and bounds while costs were escalating. But where were the results? Frank Nelson gave Bickham Sweet-Escott the task of drafting a weekly progress report. 'In the winter of 1940,' recalled Sweet-Escott, 'the meetings were grim, and we all looked forward to Wednesdays with a sinking feeling.'[1] In a 'Most Secret' paper circulated to key Whitehall officials Baker Street insisted that it was impossible to produce 'an army' at a moment's notice: 'To send out *untrained* men is far worse than useless – it merely puts everything back and exposes our plans to the enemy.' The conclusion was obvious. For the moment *'we are simply not in a position to effect any major sabotage operations in Western Europe'*.

But things were about to change. Gubbins had been strenuously at work on his training schemes and the first agents were now poised for action.

NOTES
1 Bickham Sweet-Escott, *Baker Street Irregular*, p. 48.

CHAPTER 2

KINDLING THE FIRE

Days after SOE's move to Baker Street, Gubbins arrived as Director of Operations and Training. But space was already tight and he and his small staff found themselves housed nearby in two gloomy flats in Berkeley Court, across from the Baker Street underground station. To the stern professional eye of Peter Wilkinson, Gubbins's military assistant, who'd transferred with him from MI(R), it was all rather makeshift.

> Everything was very improvised, I mean instead of the nice army trestle tables covered by a blanket, which of course we'd all been used to, our offices were furnished with pretty nasty furniture from the cheaper end of Tottenham Court Road, and instead of the stud-nosed Humbers which we'd used for our staff cars there was a fleet of sleek black Pontiac limousines driven by chauffeurs in uniform and peaked caps – which was really very inappropriate for future brigands and *condottieri*. The whole thing was run in a very civilian and rather unsuitable way to begin with.

Also housed in Berkeley Court were the Polish and Training sections. Head of the latter was Jack Wilson, a former deputy police commissioner in Calcutta who one day, as Wilkinson remembered, had a bad shock as he stepped into the lift: 'We only had two floors, and Jack Wilson was coming back from lunch one day and getting into the lift, and found himself whooshed up to the fifth floor and confronted by a group of grinning Japanese. It was only then discovered that the floor above our requisitioned flat was occupied by some department of the Japanese embassy, so that was highly undesirable and they had to be cleared out.'

But the main problem with Berkeley Court was its physical separation from Baker Street, even though it was only five minutes' walk away. The largely civilian group in Baker Street was at first wary of Gubbins's military approach and background and their separate housing only highlighted this. Wilkinson found the atmosphere of these early months suspicious and unhelpful.

> We were very much apart. [Gubbins's arrival] was viewed with very mixed feelings. I think there were some who suspected, quite wrongly, that it was an attempt at a military takeover and there were others who sincerely believed that subversive operations of the sort they expected to undertake were not likely to be well performed by professional soldiers who they thought were really temperamentally unable to deal with that sort of thing. There was a fair degree of hostility in the early days to Gubbins's set-up in Berkeley Court.

Baker Street quickly learned that Gubbins was far from an orthodox soldier and came to appreciate his qualities of drive, energy and leadership. These amply proved themselves in his creation of the army of secret agents able to carry out Dalton's mission. Even as he and Wilkinson were unpacking, the Chiefs of Staff issued their first directive. SOE was to co-ordinate its plans with general strategy. Its main priority was to hit the enemy's communications and supplies, and sap the morale of its troops.

For Gubbins this meant that the top priority was to get agents quickly trained in the arts of ungentlemanly warfare. There was not a long tradition to call upon, although the British Empire had often been maintained by unorthodox methods and much had been learned about guerrilla warfare from anti-colonial resistance movements. The adventures of Lawrence of Arabia behind Turkish lines in the First World War had gripped the imagination and many Army officers, including Gubbins, had fought the intelligence war against Michael Collins and his Irish nationalists.

Gubbins urgently needed training schools for his special students. Early in the New Year his energy had already produced results and two main centres were up and running. One was at Arisaig in the Scottish Highlands, north of Fort William. The other was at Beaulieu Manor in the New Forest close to the Solent.

Gubbins's mother came from the Isle of Mull, and Scotland was his spiritual second home. In this familiar terrain he found an ideal place for the 'Group A' schools for advanced paramilitary training, a complex of several houses and shooting lodges with their headquarters in Arisaig House on the rugged coast. Remote and inaccessible, the dozen or so buildings were protected from prying eyes by the lack of roads and designation as a wartime 'protected area' accessible only to local residents and visitors with special passes.

Angus Fyffe thought there was another reason Arisaig was a safe location.

It was secure because it's an isolated part of the country, sparsely populated except when the shooting season was on. The people up there, of course, from way, way back were very conscious of keeping a secret. If you cast your mind back to the 1745 Rebellion, after Culloden in 1746, Prince Charlie was tucked away in that part of the country. A price was put on his head of £30,000 by the government and nobody gave a whisper away. It's inbred, honesty, loyalty within the people up there. Nobody would say a word about SOE.

Nationalities were kept separate, each with its own accommodation and a conducting officer, or minder. Most of those who passed its three- or four-week courses found it a gruelling experience. 'A wretched, barren countryside, thinly populated; rain fell from a heavy sky that never cleared completely,' recalled one recruit, 'a most depressing place.' Here, would-be agents went through rigorous basic infantry training, handled demolitions and learned about sabotage, perfected their skills firing pistols and other small arms, picked up the rudiments of Morse code, and learned the arts of unarmed combat and silent killing. Francis Cammaerts, who went on to become an agent in France, sums up his Scottish training: 'It was an ideal place to get very fit physically, to learn quite a lot about supporting yourself in very difficult situations. We went deer stalking, we went fishing for salmon...'

Recruits were reminded, 'You will be a cog in a very large machine, and its smooth functioning depends on each separate cog carrying out its part efficiently. It's the object of this course to clarify the part you will play.'

The part Ernest van Maurik played was as explosives and demolition instructor.

I had never done demolitions before in my life and within about two weeks I was giving lectures on the use of explosives and teaching people how to use them. Why we didn't all get blown up I don't know, but after a bit I got quite competent and enjoyed it. When we attacked the Mallaig train I must say that the train drivers got to know us. If it was a successful attack, they would always lean out and give us the thumbs up. Of course we hadn't actually used explosive. One way of doing it was to put what they called a pressure switch under the rail. When the rail thumps up and down that would be enough to ignite the pressure switch. The railway drivers got quite a lot of pleasure in being blown up.

Arisaig's first commandant was Lieutenant-Colonel J. W. ('Jimmy Willy') Munn, a former instructor from the nearby paramilitary and commando training centre at Lochailort. The SOE training school's most unforgettable instructor was Major William Ewart ('Bill') Fairbairn, the silent-killing specialist, otherwise known as 'the Shanghai Buster' because of his thirty years' service with the Municipal Police in China's most chaotic and violent city. There he had learned the arts of ju-jitsu and produced manuals on self-defence for British imperial police forces throughout the Far East. One SOE agent who passed through his hands at Arisaig remarked that off duty Fairbairn's conversation was limited to two words – 'yes' and 'no' – and that when explaining human anatomy he would point and simply say 'this bone' or 'that muscle'. Another Baker Street mandarin who saw him in action noted dryly that Fairbairn had many methods to impart, all long, complicated and hard to remember. 'But each of them,' he recalled later, 'ended with the phrase: "and then kick him in the testicles".'

Fairbairn worked closely with Captain Eric Anthony ('Bill') Sykes, a crack rifle shot who'd teamed up with Fairbairn in Shanghai while working for the Remington rifle company. Ernest van Maurik recalled the unlikely team, whom he encountered while still himself a student: 'Fairbairn really played second fiddle at that time to Sykes. He was fairly nondescript, rather tough and short. Sykes was the surprise, because he was a most benevolent looking person. I mean, he could have worn a dog collar and been in your local parish church, but in fact once he got going he was pretty lethal.'

Together they invented the famous double-edged commando knife now widely used by special forces around the globe. Angus Fyffe described it:

It's a double-edged knife, an eight-inch blade with a cross piece, and it has a ribbed centre both sides. You have the hilt just covering a possible slash on your artery. It fits exactly into the palm of your hand, it's beautifully balanced and you just feel comfortable with it. I don't know exactly how they developed it except that they were spending a lot of time working out a design. Eventually, when they had decided on the length of the blade, the cross piece and the hilt nicely balanced, they reckoned this was it. So they sent this cable to London. It was simply signed FS and it said, 'See Second Kings, Chapter 18, Verse 23' or it may have been Judges. The verse runs something like 'they used the knife after their manner and the blood gushed out'.

Developed from Boer War bayonets, the knife was too dangerous for student practice – a short, thick length of rope was substituted.

Another lesson drilled into the students was how to take care of an enemy sentry who'd been disarmed. 'Kick him up the backside if you like, but hold the gun at least a foot away from his back,' insisted Fairbairn and Sykes. There were plenty of spare German helmets for use in practice sentry attacks. So successful were these techniques that German soldiers slung their rifles in such a way as to deflect the deadly attentions of SOE's silent killers. Such exercises, endlessly practised, produced results for van Maurik: 'I think the training there did give one confidence. I felt that I could cope with things much better.'

Not that practice always made perfect, as one of van Maurik's own students proved.

Michael Trotobas was in the Army, obviously quite well trained, but from the first moment he was a loner. He came from the south of England, and if I may say it, he looked almost like a spiv, but in fact he was a wonderful man. One night we set them the task of getting ready for an exercise in the mountains the next morning. It was a Saturday night and my commandant, Jimmy Young, and I took advantage of going to the local pub, having a couple of drinks and then driving back. We found the wheels of a motorcycle upside-down, still turning. We looked down into this ditch and there was Michael Trotobas. He said, 'It's bloody marvellous.' He said there were hundreds of salmon floating all over the place. He had somehow got hold of a small piece of plastic explosive and a detonator. After he'd had one or two too many drinks, he had borrowed the staff sergeant's motorcycle and experimented with this little bomb by throwing it into the pool.

Jimmy Young was a really very orthodox Scot and the idea of anybody having dynamited the salmon pool was anathema to him. We drove up to the pool. We hoped perhaps they were stunned, but no. Now we knew this would be an awful hooha with the local people. So we tried to fish them out and hide them. But next morning the inhabitants of Mora went up to church and they had to pass this pool and of course there were still a number of dead bodies all floating about the place. The trouble was that we couldn't explain that this young man was under pressure. We heard afterwards that all the local inhabitants had a very good meal of salmon that night. I always wanted to have the opportunity of going back there and telling them that Trotobas had distinguished himself. He had been captured, led a jail outbreak, and come back to England again. He'd been re-parachuted into France, then after a lot of sabotage, somebody had betrayed his hideout. The Gestapo had arrived, he'd shot dead the first man then was himself killed. I felt and knew that they would have forgiven him for blowing up their salmon.

Fairbairn taught a few other tricks of the trade: how to board and leave a train travelling at speed, how to enter a house from the second storey, how to walk up the face of a cliff using a rope. But his real legacy to SOE was the 'close combat' syllabus which was used by other training schools around the world and was eventually adopted by the equivalent of SOE, and forerunner of the CIA, the American Office of Strategic Services (OSS). It taught the agent how to fight, and kill, without firearms. Every agent in the field needed this skill, insisted Fairbairn, because there would always be a moment of danger when he or she would either be without a firearm, or unable to use one for fear of raising the alarm. The agent had to forget any notion of fair play. As the basic SOE training manual instructed: 'This is *war*, not sport. Your aim is to kill your opponent as soon as possible. A prisoner is generally a handicap and a source of danger...So forget the term "foul methods" – they help you to kill quickly. Attack your opponent's weakest points, therefore. He will attack you if he gets a chance.'

Agents did not always apply such brutal methods. But if they had to, they knew how. More than a technique, silent killing was a state of mind.

SOE was also interested in what they called 'gunfighting'; instructors aimed 'to turn out good, fast, plain shots'. Sportsmen and clay-pigeon shooters in a previous life had to be retrained and all had to think of a pistol not as a weapon of self-defence but of attack, for combat. The basic lesson was to use 'tremendous speed in attack with sufficient accuracy to hit the vital parts of a man's body, for killing at close quarters demands aggression and extreme concentration'. It also needed an innovation called 'instinctive firing'. Ernest van Maurik explained:

> In the Army, if one was given a pistol, one would have held both arms out in front and taken aim, by which time you might well have been shot yourself. They went on the principle that if you've got a gun in your hand and you point instinctively, you'll probably hit the target. Just in case you don't stop him first time, they taught us to fire twice, just to make sure. It's surprising how effective it was. That is what we taught all the people who went to Europe for SOE. They were all taught Sykes and Fairbairn shooting.

Instructors would draw a .22 Hi-Standard or a Colt .32 from the camp's armoury and set the scene for the students:

> Picture in your mind the circumstances under which you might be using the pistol. Take as an example a raid on an enemy-

occupied house in darkness. Firstly consider your approach. You will never walk boldly up to the house and stroll in as though you were paying a social call. On the contrary, your approach will be stealthy. You will be keyed up and excited, nervously alert for danger from whichever direction. You will find yourself instinctively crouching; your body balanced on the balls of your feet in a position from which you can move swiftly in any direction. You make your entry into the house and start searching for the enemy, moving along passages, perhaps up or down stairs, listening and feeling for any signs of danger. Suddenly on turning a corner, you come face to face with the enemy. Without a second's hesitation you must fire and kill him before he has a chance to kill you.

Pairs of students began by facing each other and pointing, at the instructor's command, at 'targets' such as the right eye and the left foot. This exercise was designed to provide the shooter with some 'natural' control over direction and elevation when firing. Recruits then moved on to more elaborate, and dangerous, live ammunition exercises during which they might imagine themselves outside a German beer cellar: 'You have reached the doorway of the cellar by a stealthy approach, making no sound whatever. Very quietly turn the handle of the door as far as it will go and then, preparing yourself for the effort, you kick the door open and kill your targets before they have a chance to realize what has happened.'

Beyond pistols, SOE liked its agents to be familiar with the organization's weapon of choice, the Sten gun, which it favoured over the Thompson sub-machine-gun. Recruits were assured that despite its 'rough appearance' the Sten gun was light (7lb) and fired 9mm Luger ammunition easily available on the Continent. In the field it could be quickly and easily disassembled and hidden; its working parts didn't have to be regularly oiled and, in a tight spot, the Sten gun could be fired 'dry', 500 rounds a minute. Accurate up to 175 yards, it was also, most usefully for partisan warfare, impervious to water, mud and sand. Recruits were assured that it was the perfect weapon 'for the type of work with which we are concerned'. When possible, students also had lessons on a variety of enemy arms, including the Spandau Maxim machine-gun.

Scotland housed other SOE bases. Angus Fyffe ran Inverlair House, close to Spean Bridge, a super-secret facility for 'malcontents'. These were trainee agents who proved either physically or psychologically unfit, or simply did not fit in with their fellow agents and could be a security or operational risk on their overseas missions. With all the secrets they knew, it was too dangerous to send them back to their original army units or civilian life. So they were sent to Fyffe.

The term 'malcontents' is, I think, slightly misleading and incarceration was not the right use of a word either. These chaps had fallen short of requirements – sometimes it was because their physical ability didn't match up to requirements, sometimes they were found to be mentally not suited for the job that was intended for them and sometimes they just didn't have the gumption or the guts to do the job. Eighty odd people passed through my hands in the time I was there. They were all perfectly decent chaps, they had just fallen short; maybe it was the fault of the selection committee by the country section in the first instance.

I had only one whom I would call a malcontent. He was a Dutchman who early on got drunk one night and started singing bawdy songs in Fort William High Street, in Dutch fortunately, so it didn't matter. He was a difficult chap. I was sitting with the adjutant at lunch when there was the most godawful row outside. He had bashed a Belgian in the face without any provocation or reason. This is the only place in the whole organization where different nationalities were allowed to come together under one roof. He wasn't a good type, but the rest had tried their best. My job was to employ them to such an extent that they hadn't time to sit down and grouse. We worked them quite hard.

He set up a foundry run by an Italian, a trained engineer, and here they made operational equipment for SOE missions such as grappling irons and boathooks. They also ran a cobbler's shop and repaired the boots worn out by Arisaig trainees. Even an assault course, complete with street façades, houses and moving targets, was constructed.

A complex at Aviemore was used exclusively by the Norwegian

section. Both here and at Arisaig took place the intensive training that culminated in one of SOE's greatest successes: the 1943 attack on the Norsk Hydro heavy water plant in southern Norway being used for German atomic research. But even training in Britain had its perils. During night exercises on skis in the mountains two of the Norwegians hit ice, went over an edge and were killed.

Not all agents went to Scotland, but all received basic training in physical fitness, map-reading, and small-arms handling. Courses were invariably in some requisitioned country house, usually in the south of England and within easy reach of London. All had a well-stocked bar – deliberately so. Agents who couldn't hold their drink and their tongue would be worse than useless: they could betray a whole network. These introductory courses, lasting two or three weeks, were a form of psychological testing. One of the best known was Wanborough Manor, used by SOE's French section. Francis Cammaerts, one of Baker Street's most successful agents in France, was sent there immediately he was recruited in 1942.

At Wanborough Manor, where we first spent three weeks, it was clear that we were being examined to see what we were suitable for. They were looking, it seems to me, to see what kind of person you were and what kind of work you might be prepared to undertake. Of the twelve to fifteen people who were with me then, only about three undertook the kind of work I was asked to do eventually. Presumably some of the students were regarded as unsuitable for this kind of work and they went off back to their regiments or whatever it was.

Agents who passed their first screening ended up at Beaulieu Manor, the spacious grounds of an old abbey set deep in the New Forest that was home to the Montagu family. Noreen Riols recalls her introduction to the place.

I had been working at Norgeby House in F Section with [its head] Colonel Buckmaster. Suddenly I was told, with a couple of days' notice, you're going down to Beaulieu. We didn't argue; I just went. My mother thought I was working for the Ministry of Agriculture. My father was in the Far East nearly the whole of the war. I didn't see him for nearly four years, so he didn't enter into it. My own brother was at school and I didn't see a lot of him. We didn't ask questions, people learned not to. When I first arrived it was a snowy afternoon. It was very beautiful, going through the New Forest, because we were literally cut off from civilization. Arriving there and going into this little cottage, which we three women had, cosy and a fire waiting and a cup of tea, it was all very civilized.

This was the jewel in the crown of the SOE training empire, its finishing school. John Debenham-Taylor, an instructor at Beaulieu, described what he and his colleagues were looking for when considering a potential agent:

The sort of things that we looked for were indications of how people reacted to surprise situations: whether they were taken aback by them, or whether they managed to treat the whole thing quite calmly and not give any indication of being rattled by them. Secondly, was simply the general intelligence and quickness of people to grasp what you were trying to tell them and to carry it out when they did exercises to show that they'd absorbed the lesson. Thirdly, the question of temperament and readiness to accept instructions and orders. Some people did exactly as they were told and others queried it or tended to be excessively laid back about it, as though it was unimportant. It seemed to me this was an important factor in judging to what extent you know the agent was likely to be obedient to the instructions he got. It was a bit of a hit and miss business assessing an agent, but I feel that if you applied those three maxims, you were getting near an accurate picture.

Here, carefully segregated into national groupings and isolated in various houses scattered through the estate, trainee agents now learned the finer points about their future lives behind enemy lines. What were conditions of life like in their country of destination? What identity cards did they need? How were the local police forces organized? How could they recognize their uniforms? How closely did they work with the occupying forces? What were the various branches of the German and Italian security forces? John Debenham-Taylor listed what dangers they tried to convey.

> We tried to give them every possible bit of information about the uniforms, the behaviours, or the various arms that they had to fear, be it the Gestapo, who of course operated very largely in civilian clothes, the Waffen SS and the ordinary Wehrmacht, then the collaborationist organizations, to enable students to be able to identify what particular unit or type of unit the person was from and thus to give some indication of the sort of dangers that they constituted. An ordinary Wehrmacht soldier was unlikely to be in his own right a particular risk. Indeed almost all German personnel were potentially less risky than people like the [collaborators] and to some extent the French police. Not all the French police were pro-resistance or prepared to help agents operating in the field. Many were, but many were not. Virtually any uniform, be it German or French, constituted a potential danger and one would try and impress that point upon students.

Students also received lectures on the Nazi Party, the German Army and the Gestapo, and heard from agents who had returned from Europe how to deal with police controls and interrogations. John Debenham-Taylor recalled not going into interrogation techniques too deeply.

> I think everybody who was going into occupied Europe knew perfectly well what might happen to them if they were caught; namely, torture and beatings. There was no point in trying to spell that out in great detail. The main thing we would concentrate on was in trying to impress upon them the need to stay quiet for as long as they could without giving anything away, for at least forty-eight hours, which would give their colleagues time to learn that they had been arrested and to make themselves scarce.

One of the staff members, Noreen Riols, summed up Beaulieu's role.

It was the last holding centre which the agents went to before they were parachuted. They'd gone through all the other horrendous things and Beaulieu was in a way a bit of a rest cure because there was no crawling under barbed wire at three in the morning in the pouring rain. They were trying to really test them for the final mettle, to find out if they would stand up against, not necessarily terrible interrogations, but against the ordinary little things which make up everyday life which quite often tripped them. It was the final testing ground. If they failed at Beaulieu, all the rest was useless. They didn't go.

Most of the houses at Beaulieu had been built only thirty or so years before, when the second Baron Montagu sold several ninety-nine-year leases on his vast estate to various friends. They lay hidden in extensive grounds, approachable only by private roads and tracks, out of sight of each other as well as invisible to the Montagus' family seat at Palace House. They were ideal for the job, some with only half a dozen bedrooms, others with as many as twenty. Most had been vacated at the beginning of the war, and Gubbins quickly grabbed them. 'The Rings', a rambling thirteen-bedroom 'Tudorbethan'-style half-timbered mansion, served as the headquarters. Other houses bore such names as Hartford House, The Vineyards, Boarmans, The House on the Shore, and The Drokes. Inchmery House, four miles away on the Beaulieu River and owned by the Rothschilds, was also requisitioned. Some became particular favourites for certain nationalities or groups. Boarmans, for example, was preferred by the French section, and here many of SOE's women agents were also trained.

'Jimmy Willy' Munn came south from Arisaig early in 1941 to get the complex up and running. One of his staff vividly described him as 'a young colonel of the sensible military type, as opposed to the no-nonsense military, the mystical military, and the plain-silly military. He neither barked nor advocated yoga [and] held together a shoal of pretty odd fish in a net of personal authority.'

Not least of the odd fish was the writer of those words himself, 'Kim' Philby, Britain's most infamous twentieth-century spy and Soviet 'mole'. In SOE's chequered history Philby played a small but intriguing part. Originally recruited by Section D, he'd spent hours at its sabotage training school at Brickendonbury Manor, another large country house in Hertfordshire, where a legendary figure often described as 'the founder of modern industrial sabotage', George Rheam, taught agents the vital skill of how to disable a factory with a few well-placed ounces of explosive. One important lesson he taught was that if several machines were to be destroyed, then the same part had to be destroyed on each so as to prevent repair through cannibalization. One who learned those lessons well was Francis Cammaerts.

> I went to the school in Hertford after I'd completed my first round of schools and learnt about railway sabotage, railway destruction, the blocking of railways. I learnt about the use of very small quantities of explosive to destroy very important parts of machines, the kind of parts of machines which were irreplaceable or would take a very long time to replace. Those are the kinds of things which were very important and which people like myself knew nothing about at all.

Philby drew up Brickendonbury's syllabus on basic espionage trade-craft. When SOE absorbed Section D it took over Brickendonbury, the syllabus and Philby. Gubbins sent him to Beaulieu as chief instructor in propaganda, which Goebbels had once described as 'the fourth arm of warfare'. SOE more prosaically described it as 'the art of persuasion with a view to producing action'. It was useless, they insisted, 'for our propaganda merely to persuade Frenchmen that the Boche is a swine. It must also instruct Frenchmen how to kick the Boche out of France.' Comparing advertising and propaganda, students were reminded never to say 'hunger' when 'empty bellies' was better, and that 'patriotism' was never as strong as 'love of France'.

Students and fellow staff found Philby outstanding. It was hardly surprising. He had secretly been working for Moscow since 1933 and had been trained as a spy by the Russians. Thus, ironically, some of the skills taught at Beaulieu came indirectly from Moscow. He did not stay long. Later that year he was recruited by SIS, where he rapidly rose through the ranks while continuing to report to his KGB masters in Moscow.

Among the other 'odd fish' at Beaulieu was its first Chief Instructor, Major Stanley Woolrych, a First World War veteran who claimed he 'had security in his bones'. This sprang from his army experience as both spycatcher and spymaster on the Western Front, sniffing out alleged spies and running agents behind the German trenches. Noreen Riols, one of his staff at Beaulieu, describes him thus: 'I think I was terrified of everybody at that age. He was a formidable figure but I believe a very kind man, he may even have been rather a shy man. The others called him "Woollybags", not to his face, of course. I was very much in awe of him but he was, I think, basically a kind man who didn't suffer fools gladly but who understood if you made mistakes.'

Then there was George Hill, a stocky man in his late fifties. Known at Beaulieu as 'Uncle', he was already a legend, having worked as a spy in Russia during the First World War. After the 1917 Russian Revolution he plotted with the 'ace of spies' Sidney Reilly to overthrow Lenin's regime and carried out at least one successful sabotage mission behind Soviet lines. He, too, stayed at Beaulieu only a few short months. After Hitler's attack on the Soviet Union, Churchill sent him to Moscow as SOE's liaison with the NKVD, predecessor to the KGB. Not surprisingly, they already had a bulky file on him. This did not prevent him from jointly arranging the dropping of several Soviet agents into western Europe over the next couple of years.

The most colourful of Beaulieu's early staff was undoubtedly Major R. M. ('Bill') Brooker, a powerful extrovert with little respect for pomp, pretension or position. Born in France, where his father ran the Paris office of Thomas Cook, he spoke fluent French and spent the 1930s travelling around Europe as an export salesman for Nestlé of Switzerland. A brilliant and convincing lecturer, he had an immense fund of stories he claimed came from the real lives of secret agents. Philby was particularly impressed by his inexhaustible fund of wisecracks and his rich command of criminal slang from Marseilles.

In reality Brooker's only first-hand knowledge of clandestine activity came from once smuggling blocked Nestlé funds out of Spain during the Civil War using couriers and false papers to cross the Pyrenees. The rest sprang from his fertile imagination. But it was so convincing that most Beaulieu recruits thought it was true. Both Brooker and his close colleague Cuthbert Skilbeck, who followed him as Chief Instructor, ended up at Camp X, SOE's training school in Canada. So did Paul Dehn, who succeeded Philby in teaching propaganda at Beaulieu and had a brilliant postwar career as a screenwriter for such films as *Goldfinger* and *The Spy Who Came in from the Cold*. Camp X opened its doors on the eve of Pearl Harbor, principally to train Americans. Fairbairn and Sykes also took this path. That Beaulieu's top instructors were sent there demonstrates how important Baker Street considered their American connection. Many OSS trainees were so impressed by Brooker they believed he was head of the British Secret Service.

Yet another 'odd fish' who left his mark was Peter Folliss, Beaulieu's last Chief Instructor. Like many SOE graduates, he transferred to SIS at the end of the war and set up its training school at Gosport. It was rumoured that Folliss had once been an actor, although this was almost certainly untrue. But he did teach potential recruits how to make false scars with collodion, a colourless fast-drying liquid often used for dressing wounds.

The Beaulieu syllabus also contained a module on criminal skills. For this, SOE turned to a notorious Scottish burglar and safecracker of Polish origin named Johnny Ramenski. In his mid-twenties, he'd been released for war service from Glasgow's tough Barlinnie gaol. He had a swarthy and pock-marked face and many recruits found his thick Glasgow accent indecipherable. 'Hush yer greetin,' he'd growl if interrupted during one of his impressive demonstrations of how to blow a safe so as to take out the lock but not wreck the room in which it was standing. No one knew exactly where he lived on the Beaulieu estate, and eventually he disappeared, apparently back to Barlinnie for having practised his profession out of hours. He was replaced by a Captain Green, always known as 'Killer' Green, who in turn was followed by John Debenham-Taylor.

I took over Killer Green's selection of keys and moulds for taking impressions of keys, materials for making keys, blanks and zinc plates from which we used to make Yale-type keys and all that sort of thing. The main thing with making replica keys, to take Yale keys first, was to get a decent impression of the key. The sort of tool that was used for this was an ordinary matchbox filled with plasticine with a slight groove cut in one end of the matchbox so that if you could borrow a key for long enough, you could lay it in the plasticine and then put the matchbook on and clear out. From that impression you could make Yale keys cut out of sheets of zinc. I'm not sure what the civilian use of that sort of zinc is, but it's roughly a sixteenth or an eighth of an inch thick and you could cut it out from the impression with a fretsaw. It's much easier with zinc or a soft metal like that than something hard.

As far as the other pipe keys are concerned, of course, you needed two impressions – the side and also the nose of the key for its width. There were also the various techniques that he had taught for breaking and entering, you know how to smash glass quietly, all those various dodges that burglars use. We had a sort of demonstration door fitted with a Yale lock. One of the ways of opening that type of lock is to use a sort of tiny metal pick to stick into the lock to put pressure on it. Then hold a piece of stiff piano wire under the tumbler and jiggle them up and down until eventually with luck you get them right and the thing slides just a little way from the pressure you're putting on with the pick and it will open. Our demonstration door had been opened many times and so was rather easier to do than perhaps any lock you're likely to run into anyway.

Debenham-Taylor also developed a special technique of his own for picking handcuffs.

It occurred to me that it would be perhaps useful if we could give agents some idea of the possibilities of opening handcuffs without the key. So we managed to procure two sets of handcuffs for me to experiment. One operated on a ratchet and, after experimenting with them for a while, I found that if you could locate a suitable nail in the wall and bring the cuffs up so that the nail touched on the bottom and press it, you could get this to move one ratchet at a time. Difficult but not impossible.

The other pair of handcuffs proved rather easier. They had a barrel end to them and they were closed over the person's wrist by use of a key which tightened a screw inside the cylinder. The key was rather like the ones that are used on radiators for bleeding. I found that if you got some cat gut, violin string or something like that, and wound it over something like a diary pencil and then bent it and, pushing it down the bolt of the cylinder and tightening it by holding one end in your teeth and pulling the other, you could fix it round the bottom of the bolt. Then pulling the two together would free the bolt sufficiently for the cuff to open and that did work fairly well. In fact I was finally able to do it with my hands behind my back.

Disguise was another technique Debenham-Taylor taught. The trick was to use simple techniques that could easily be altered so as not to cause suspicion. Changing clothes was easier and faster than changing facial features, so agents were urged to keep a wardrobe ranging from 'rough gardening clothes to a good lounge suit' and reminded that 'stripes downwards with a single-breasted suit make a man look taller'. Long hair could be cut short, dramatically altering the appearance of the face. If on the run, an agent could wear or change spectacles, comb his or her hair differently, button a coat in a different way. More complicated devices such as false hair or greasepaint would be dangerous, although Max Factor hair whitener for instant greying temples could be helpful even if traces of these on an agent could only rouse suspicion. For the adventurous, two small round nuts into which tiny breathing holes had been drilled, inserted in the nostrils, would distort the shape of the nose, making it very flat; while teeth could be stained with iodine.

Getting feedback from agents who'd returned from behind the lines was especially valuable. The Germans were constantly updating security regulations or identity papers, and SOE had to keep up. Fortunately, as the war progressed and methods of getting agents out of occupied Europe improved, the opportunities of learning from them increased.

For the agent it was more than a question of absorbing basic principles. It was also a matter of memorizing particular details of a country, region or city so that the agent could almost recite them in his or her sleep. What *were* conditions like in southern France in 1943? How should you dress to be inconspicuous? What would not draw attention when ordering drinks at a bar? What foods were so scarce that asking for them would raise eyebrows? Did Belgians and Italians hold and smoke their cigarettes in the same way? Which were the local black market cafés liable to be raided by the local police? Making a mistake over such small points could prove fatal. John Debenham-Taylor illustrated the point.

> One anecdote that we were given when I was a student and which I used to pass on later when I became an instructor, was the case of a chap who had recently parachuted into France. Shortly after his arrival he had gone into a café and asked for a *café noir*, black coffee, which immediately aroused the waitress's attention, because there wasn't any other kind of coffee you could have in France in those days. I don't know whether this resulted in some tragic consequence. We were not told that, but we used it when passing it on to the students as an indication of how vital anything was which indicated that you were not familiar with the area and the practices of the people living in it.

The climax of student training came at the end of their stay when they were sent off on a two- or three-day mission to a town like Southampton or Bournemouth – in some cases even as far afield as Birmingham. Surrounded by their oblivious fellow citizens, the would-be spies demonstrated their skill at shaking off someone shadowing them, making contact with an unknown person, passing a message without seeming to do so, reconnoitring a target, and even recruiting someone – in other words play-acting being a secret agent at work in the field. Sometimes Beaulieu had them arrested and interrogated to see how well they maintained their cover story. The next day, after their return to Beaulieu, there'd be a debriefing and final assessment. For suitably impenetrable reasons this was known as a 'Y9'.

This final exercise provided a unique opportunity for some of the young female secretaries. Just out of school, they spent most of their time shut away, unseen by any of the trainees, in The Rings, typing letters and answering telephones. Now they came into their own and made ideal shadows to trail the unsuspecting agents. Sometimes the roles would be reversed, with an agent trailing one of the secretaries while she tried to shake him or her off. Noreen Riols found this easy with men.

There was a big department store in Bournemouth called Plummers. I used to go into the ladies' underwear department. In the early 1940s I don't think many men would be found in the ladies' underwear department. I would linger there and find out who was lingering also. When I'd discovered which one it was, I would go nonchalantly up the stairs, press the lift button. Then when he began to come after me, also very nonchalantly, of course, I would nip down the other side very quickly. But as I was going down the other side, I would take off my hat, my coat, my shopping basket. By the time the poor man realized I wasn't taking the lift he would be looking in the crowd of shoppers for somebody with a hat and a shopping basket, who no longer was there. I used to go straight out the other door and that was it, I'd lost him.

At other times the secretaries would act as a courier, making contact at some previously agreed rendezvous and passing on a message.

Near the pier, in the Pavilion gardens, there were several benches. We'd be told that there would be a man sitting on the bench who would pass a message. So one would go and sit on the bench near the man one thought would be the one who would be passing the message. He would be reading a newspaper, which was quite normal in the middle of the afternoon. When he would decide he'd had enough of his newspaper, discard it on the bench and go, I would nonchalantly pick up the newspaper, which is another quite normal thing to do, glance through it, take the message and also go. There was a telephone booth in the same gardens. You'd see the man and so you would go and wait. When he came out, he would have left a message and he would say 'under Harris' or something like that, indicating to you what page it was on. We got awfully clever at speaking without using our mouths. You'd go in, open the telephone book, which was quite normal, see the message, pick up the phone, make a fictitious call and then leave. Nobody notices. It's extraordinary.

Nobody in Bournemouth knew what was going on under their very eyes. I suppose there must have been a bit of the actress in me. It was fun; it was a great change from being in an office.

Some of the older secretaries were assigned other delicate tasks. Noreen Riols remembered that these took place in one or other of Bournemouth's better hotels.

The agent would be there in the evening, sitting with one of the instructors and I or somebody else who'd been assigned would walk in. The instructor would say, 'Oh, how lovely to see you, I haven't seen you for ages. Come and have a drink.' So you'd say yes and you'd have a drink and he'd say, 'If you're not doing anything, why don't you join us for dinner?' Whereupon a telephone call would come for the instructor. He would come back and say, 'I'm awfully sorry, but I have to leave. Why don't you two go ahead and have dinner?' So we would trot into the dining room and have dinner. My job was to get him to talk. Mostly they didn't. I did my utmost. I remember one man saying, 'Oh no, I'm just a representative for toothpaste.' I think it was mostly the foreigners who cracked because they were so alone in England, and somebody was interested in them. They cracked, but, of course, it was finished for them.

One agent who did spill his story to Noreen Riols paid the price.

I don't think he would have said anything if I hadn't let him hold my hand and get a bit sentimental. I said, 'What are you up to, are you going to be here for long?' I can't remember the exact words. But he said, 'Well, I'm not all that I appear to be. I shall be going back into my own country, infiltrated. We're going back to form resistance groups for when the invasion starts.' I don't think I pressed him very much more because I knew that there was no point, he was into it up to his neck. He said, 'Are you free on Sunday?' We made a date to meet on the Sunday, which was pathetic. I knew that I couldn't and it was awful to have to deceive him.

The next day we had a confrontation. Colonel Woolrych

would have us in and say what happened. At which point the door opened and he brought in this unfortunate Dane. He said, 'Do you know this woman?' He just looked at me and said 'You bitch!' People didn't use strong language in those days, not in front of women, and it did upset me rather because it was a horrible thing I'd done. Colonel Woolrych was very nice to me. He said, 'Look, if he can't resist talking to a pretty face here, he's not going to resist when he goes back. It won't be only his life; it'll be many others which are put in jeopardy.' Of course he couldn't go, it was dreadful. He'd gone through all this training and just for the moonlight on a warm summer evening he'd cracked.

For some of the would-be agents there was a final test – 'Fifi'. All the secretaries seemed to know about her, for she was the ultimate Agent Provocatrice, gorgeous and enticing, who *went all the way* (at least for male trainees; what facilities, if any, were provided for the female agents remains a mystery). Significantly, none of them ever actually *met* the legendary Fifi, nor has she ever surfaced with her story. Perhaps she has passed on, or now resides in south-coast respectability eager to forget her risqué past. More likely she never existed, her slinky seductress ways merely conjured up by Beaulieu's ingenious minds as a dire warning to their students. This, certainly, will be one SOE secret never revealed.

Aspects of Beaulieu's training may now seem absurd. This was because Beaulieu itself was learning. It had no huge body of expertise to draw on. SOE has sometimes been accused of being amateurish. Noreen Riols acknowledged this: 'Of course it was amateurish, it was amateurs doing it. They were doctors, lawyers, university professors. We were all amateurs doing our best. There was nobody there who was a professional anything, except a professional burglar. It was something which was thrown together for a purpose. Nobody pretended they were going to make this their life's work. But it was pretty professional in the end. I think they had it honed to a fine art.'

It undoubtedly made mistakes and not all of its agents were as skilled as others. But it was beginning from scratch. None of its instructors – if we except George Hill and, of course, Philby – had any personal experience of operating behind enemy lines. The SIS, which itself had a scanty record of training, was unable or unwilling to help. Francis Cammaerts, who escaped being caught thanks to his care with security, can now laugh over some of his training. Nonetheless, he put it this way.

> I think they were thoughtful. I think they felt that they were trying to teach something that they didn't know, they could only guess what sort of things they were instructing us on. They couldn't really tell us how to judge someone you were going to recruit as a colleague in the resistance, that was impossible because they couldn't know. They didn't know where you were going to go, what kind of people you were going to work with. I couldn't in any way criticize them for not being able to go very far on that line.

The survival rate of SOE agents behind enemy lines in Europe was between 60 and 70 per cent, higher than Baker Street's own initial estimates of 50 per cent, and considerably better than that of Bomber Command aircrew. In the circumstances, as recognized by Noreen Riols, it was a remarkable testimony to the skills taught at Arisaig, Beaulieu and other SOE centres around the country: 'I don't think there's anything romantic in the world of spying except in books, especially the kind of spying they were doing. It wasn't cocktail parties and slinky spies with long cigarette holders seducing people. It was everyday living, and rough living, very often. No, there wasn't anything romantic about it.'

What of the unorthodox weapons of war developed by SOE? Its main 'dirty tricks' experiments were carried out at Station IX based at The Frythe, a former private hotel in Welwyn Garden City, although it also benefited from the inventive experiments carried out at The Firs, a large mansion in Whitchurch near Aylesbury run by Millis Jefferis, an explosives and devices expert who had worked with Gubbins in MI(R).

Perhaps the single most important contribution of both was to produce firing mechanisms for Baker Street's most useful sabotage tool, plastic explosive. This was already in production when SOE was formed and had been developed by the Royal Arsenal at

Woolwich. Its great advantage over more traditional explosives such as dynamite or gelignite was that it could be safely handled, cut and shaped to fit the target, and transported and stored in safety. The Firs developed the L delay, a time-delay device that allowed a striker to fire the detonator at a predetermined time.

But more commonly used was the 'time pencil', developed by The Frythe. When the agent pressed a ridge on the pencil, acid was released that ate through a wire attached to a detonator at a rate that could be carefully pre-set, thus allowing the agent to get away before the explosion went off. Twelve million were produced during the war. The Frythe also produced other useful switches, such as the 'pull switch', used for trip wires, and the 'pressure switch', which was mainly used for railway sabotage; when placed beneath a rail it was activated when the train passed over it. Likewise, trains would activate another of SOE's devices, a switch resembling a normal railway fog signal on the line that fired a detonator attached to a larger charge buried close by. The 'limpet mine', for attaching to ships' hulls, was another invention, as was the 'clam', packing half a pound of PE and for use on dry land, and the 'gammon grenade', an impact fuse attached to a couple of pounds of PE used for ambushes; such a device was used by the SOE agents who assassinated Reinhard Heydrich in Prague in 1942.

The Frythe also developed a gun suitable for discreet one-off killings. This was known as the Welrod (most of The Frythe's devices enjoyed the prefix Wel-). A single-shot weapon with a silencer, it was only eleven inches long, had a detachable butt, and could be carried on loops hidden inside an agent's clothes. The silenced version of the Sten gun also emerged from The Frythe in 1943, a valuable weapon for attacks on sentries and guards.

From The Frythe came other lethal anti-personnel devices, including the exploding rat, meant to take off the foot of the German sentry who kicked it out of the way.

The Frythe, or more accurately one of its sub-stations based at a former roadhouse, The Thatched Barn, on the Barnet bypass, also developed a refined line in exploding turds, tailoring the model to geographical or topographical need for donkeys, horses, cows – and, for the North African desert, camels. There was also the Welbike, a portable and collapsible mini-bike, and the Welman, a one-man submarine. Neither of these was much use (the bike was immediately identifiable in Nazi-occupied Europe, for example), but designing such devices kept enthusiasm and morale high among the boffins of The Frythe. They also busied themselves with developing a range of incendiary devices and came up with the highly effective abrasive grease, made with finely ground carborundum, designed to be smeared on vehicle axle-bearings. Rightly applied, it could bring trucks and trains to an inconvenient halt.

But many of the SOE agent's most basic tools were standard army issue, or else purchased elsewhere, such as the pistols carried by agents which needed to have nothing that could identify them, and thus the carrier, as British. When not using weapons captured from the enemy, these were bought from as far afield as the United States, Spain and Argentina. One of the most popular was the .32 Colt, although the .38 Super Colt was also used. For more offensive weapons, the American M1 Carbine and the Thompson sub-machine-gun also proved popular. Far outstripping the latter in popularity and use, however, was the Sten sub-machine-gun, a brutally simple weapon.

Having left training school, there was one other skill an agent needed to enter the field: how to parachute. This was taught at a house in Altrincham, near Manchester. The practice jumps took place in the grounds of Tatton Park, from aircraft based at Ringway Airport or else from a balloon tethered in the park. Ernest van Maurik was glad the balloon was unavailable.

Our chief instructor apologized that the balloon was not working, which I didn't realize at the time was jolly lucky for us because jumping out of a balloon was much, much worse than jumping out of an aeroplane. I can remember going up with the other students. The first morning we had a twenty-minute trip looking through the hole; one jumped through the hole in this old Whitley aircraft. It was the first time I'd ever been up in an aeroplane in my life. The next day we had two jumps. Once you're out of the plane you get a wonderful feeling of euphoria. You feel you can stay up there the whole time. You look down, you don't have any feeling of height or anything.

You are coming down very slowly. You think so beautiful, never seen the place look so nice in my life and then towards the end you suddenly realize you're coming down at a fair speed.

For Roger Landes, it was also his first trip in an aeroplane.

We put our parachute on the back. We were ten of us and we drew who was going to jump first. I was the last one to jump. The plane used to do one round and one man jumped. There was a hole in the plane and what you do there is to stay like that and when you get the green light you jump to attention. The parachutes open within two and a half seconds. It takes half a minute to reach to the ground. There was someone on the ground with a loudspeaker telling you, keep your legs together because the danger is to break the leg. Then we did five jumps and we were ready.

By the late winter of 1941 the first secret agents were emerging from their months of training. Baker Street's warriors were on their way.

CHAPTER 3

TRICKS OF THE TRADE

The SOE story is usually told through the exploits of its agents behind enemy lines. But another way to savour its unorthodox approach to war is through the reminiscences of those at home who worked in such experimental outfits as Station IX (The Frythe), its annexe at The Thatched Barn, and at the forgery section at Briggens near Royden in Essex (this, known as Station XIV, turned from working exclusively for the Polish section to serving SOE generally after the Secret Intelligence Service gave up its monopoly on clandestine forgery in 1942).

Here are the typical stories of three such people, each told in their words: Bert Adlington, who came from a long line of plasterers and found his métier making fakes and forgeries; Claudia Pulver, a refugee from Vienna, who put her dress-design skills to the task of creating the authentic Continental-style clothes, and Pauline Brockies, who, after joining the FANYs and being recruited into SOE, then found herself posted to Station XIV and involved in faking a variety of 'official' documents.

BERT ADLINGTON

I was offered a job at age fourteen in the Gaumont British organization, in the plasterers' shop. In 1936 I had to find another job, with a firm of architectural developers in Camberwell which was also a fibrous plastering unit and I stayed with them till I went into the Army in 1940 – I stayed with the East Surrey Regiment until 1942. We were up at Thetford under canvas and one of my friends, a sergeant-major, he said, 'Bert, get your kit laid out, you're posted.' I reported to Baker Street with my rifle, fifty rounds, my full kit and I saw Major Rawlinson who said take all this gear home. He told me to report the next morning to the old carpenters' shop at the back of the Victoria and Albert Museum and ask for Captain Wills.

Eventually I found this rickety old place up a dirty wooden

staircase and banged on the door. A little window opened and the civvy bloke said what do you want? He took me into this other room where there were some blokes mucking about with dead rats and I thought I don't want to come in this outfit very much! Captain Wills, as he was then, said I know you. We had a chat and I saluted him: 'Oh, cut that bullshit out,' he said.

The first job he gave me was to mould a knob of coal in a two-piece gelatine mould, with a plaster case. He wanted ten or twenty casts and I thought what the hell do they want lumps of coal for? I soon found out. They were going to fill them with plastic explosive and trundle them off to blow something up.

After a couple of days he asked me to go out to a big old roadhouse called The Thatched Barn, on the Barnet by-pass. A very nice place actually, very big swimming pool which was full up with filthy water, full up with frogs and newts, but we used to swim in there. I remember one of the lads dived off the board and when he came up he was ripped up from chest down to the bottom bit. He'd cut himself on something that was in the water. So Captain Wills said not only was it a health hazard, it was dangerous. He went down to one of the film studios and one of his old pals contacted the local fire service. They pumped all the water out – this bloke had cut himself on a pair of deer antlers. There was all sorts of rubbish in there. The Pioneer Corps gave the whole thing a good old scrubbing and eventually got it nice and clean where we could swim.

It was at this stage that I first saw these midget submarines. One looked like a dodgem car and two blokes sat in it in frogman suits. The other one was like a little torpedo and I can only remember one bloke sitting in that. They'd put these things in the pool for about an hour. They had a big steel plate in there. The men would fix something to this steel plate and then they'd go back into their little machine and trundle around for another half-hour. That was the first I ever knew of midget submarines.

I met the other members of the group making the benches up in what had been the squash court. That was our workshop where we did most of the plasterwork, not only coal but mangelwurzel or as you would probably say turnips. They put hand grenades in them and we cleated them together like we did the coal and stopped the joint around so that nobody could see it's ever been anything but one whole thing. Then we had ATS girls come in, they were artists these girls, and put blotches on them. When they were finished you couldn't tell the difference between a swede or a turnip, a lump of real coal.

We also made thousands of tyre bursters. These were stones that had been collected from North Africa where the Germans were in retreat and to speed the thing up they brought us the actual stones, which I moulded. We got casts out and in the casts we bedded tiny land mines. You could tread on them and they wouldn't hurt you; a tank or heavy vehicle had to go over them before they exploded. They were sent out to the Middle East. They were in great demand. The SAS I suppose would go right behind the German lines when they were retreating, scatter these on the road. As the armour went along and ran over one of these things, there was enough explosive to blow the track off a tank or it would the blow the wheel off an armoured car. This slowed down the retreat so that old Montgomery could capture more Germans than we would have otherwise.

We were brought these skittles, nine to a set with a ball. They wanted them moulded, which we did. I use the word 'we' because I wasn't the only one, there were other lads doing these. Of course they were hollow and inside each skittle went the hand grenade and inside the ball went the detonators. They were sealed up and cracks all round filled up. That's when the ATS girls painted them and stuck on caricatures of the famous Allied people – Churchill and company, de Gaulle, Stalin. They were hideous examples. They were done this way, I believe, in case a German sentry suddenly saw a car coming with a box in it – what have you got in that box? Skittles. Who are they for? Oh, they're for Colonel so and so. They'd pull one out and look at it. A picture of de Gaulle looking really horrible, and he'd shriek and hoot with laughter. As far as I know they shipped these off to Italy where the partisans wanted them. Of course, I suppose when they got them they broke them open and got the explosives out of them and used them as their back-up for blowing up the Germans.

One bloke went to Poland and inside one of our imitation logs was his transmitting set. The log had to be constructed in such a way it wouldn't rattle; the ATS girls used to pack them and they were sealed, with the radio inside, and taken off to Poland. The agent was a wood cutter; he had lots of these logs of wood all stood up. This one would go among them and nobody could tell the difference. He would transmit from these logs anything that the Allies wanted to know about the area, which was brilliant, really.

Having seen the way the log of wood was moulded, we did something almost identical with a chunk of masonry which was brought in, possibly off a bomb dump somewhere. We used to cast as near as we could in the colour that the masonry was but if you couldn't then the ATS girls would paint it to look exactly like the model. Inside that went another transmitting set.

We seldom got to know what happened to our end product but we did learn that this piece of masonry was bunged on a bomb dump in Berlin. The people in Berlin were living in bombed-out cellars. They would stick a pole up and stretch a line through and hang their washing on there. This agent did exactly the same but his line was an aerial. He used to transmit from the bomb dump or the cellars or wherever it was and hang his washing on the aerial. Nobody ever found him as far as we knew, so that was a remarkable one.

Colonel Wills came to me and said to me to come with a lump of tin. We went to London Zoo and picked up a camel shit, which we did in exactly the same way as the log of wood. A camel shit is not very thick, it's only about an inch and a half thick, I suppose, and he wanted these cast in papier mâché. I do remember Colonel Wills sent me back to the zoo to see if I could get a better one. I went in a little truck. He said to me, once you're at the zoo and you get what you want, nobody but nobody is allowed to look in. If anyone does, there's a revolver, shoot them. We're coming through Hyde Park on the way back and we're stopped by two Red Caps on motorbikes. They wanted to know what we were doing and I said I'm sorry but I can't tell you. One of them went to walk round to have a look. I said if you touch those buckles, I shall shoot you. I would have shot the bugger because we were told nobody was to see what was in the back of that vehicle.

What explosive they could put in there I just don't know, but we never saw them any more. They all disappeared and apparently whatever they used them for was very successful. Probably blowing up tanks out in the desert, because they would only want a camel shit in the desert, wouldn't they!

I'd done everything they wanted in the plaster shop and there was little more to do there. Colonel Wills said to me he wanted me to come back to London to take on some ageing. I knew what ageing was because we had a staff sergeant who was the 'ager'; but I think he wanted assistance, or he'd moved on to something else. So I got the job of ageing. The first thing I was given was a briefcase. I understood that on the Continent women didn't have shopping bags, but they all had briefcases with handles on. I thought I'd put it in a pot of boiling water but when it came out it was like a handbag! I thought old Wills was going to die of laughter. I had put in too hot water. If you used lukewarm water it softened the leather up and creases came in the leather that should be there naturally. Then you'd let it dry, this is not just one, this was quite a few. Once they were dry, you'd rub it over with fine sandpaper to take any bloom off. Then you would rub Vaseline over it with a sprinkling of what we called 'rotten stone', getting into the little cracks and crevices. You'd wipe it all off and then dust it again with rotten stone which didn't make it look like a piece of mud, it just looked like an old case. They were sent, as far I as knew, with things in them to the agents.

To make the metal parts look old I used a mixture of methylated spirits and I'm not sure if it was sulphuric acid or nitric acid, the weaker one of the two. It gave off a dense vapour which probably didn't do my chest any good, and might have helped towards TB eventually. You'd get this on a little piece of wood or an old brush and just brush it on the metal parts and wipe it off straight away. It'd take the shine off all the metal. Sometimes it took some of the plating which didn't matter. We found this system was also good for suitcases. You'd kick the suitcase up and down the workshop a few dozen times, get a few rust scratches on it, then treat it exactly the same as the briefcase. It looked really old and when the agents came they were fitted out with whatever they wanted. They selected their case and bunged their equipment in and sometimes that was the last we ever saw of them. So the ageing went down very well. In fact I don't think the ageing was ever discovered by the enemy.

We had an old tailor, an old German man, who managed to escape the Nazis and he was an absolute artist in his work. He could look at a suit and tell you where it came from – Czechoslovakia, Italy, Spain, Germany. If an agent was going off to Germany, he'd make him a suit in the German style, but it had to be aged. There were no new suits in Germany, only for the real higher ups, so the suit had to age. Sometimes we'd put that suit on and go to bed in it, keep it on for a week. It stunk to high heaven at the end of it because you never had a shower. After it had got creased naturally, I mean you put a jacket on, in two days you got crease marks, we used to get a very thin film of Vaseline, very thin, on your hand and just gently rub it over the creases. When you hung your jacket up you got a dirt mark where the creases had been. You again used 'rotten stone' to dust on them to take the newness out. On the lapels you'd use a bit of very, very, very fine sandpaper to take the gloss off, then again the Vaseline with the rotten stone. You got a suit that had only been twenty-four hours old, you got a suit that looked six months old.

Colonel Wills brought an American general into the workshop one day, just to show him around. And like most Americans they were fitted out beautifully – their clothes were marvellous. When they'd gone and we'd gone to lunch, I came back and noticed that there was a pair of yellow pigskin gloves on the end of my bench. There was no note but if anything wanted to be aged, it was put on the end of the bench with a little note, please make look two years, or six months. But there was no note and I enquired if anyone knew who had left them but nobody knew. So I made them look six months old. That same afternoon this general came back and said I left my gloves in here. I said there they are. No, no, he said, they're not mine, mine were new. I said so they were till you put them on the end of that bench! And he thought this was marvellous. He said I shall keep these gloves for ever – to remind me of this dreadful place. I bet he got a new pair straightaway, but they were his memento of Station 15A, I think that was what we used to call ourselves, didn't we?

Every article of clothing had to have all English marks removed, including zip fasteners of the flies. Underneath the zip they used to have 'Lightning Zip'. All that had to be taken out with a dentist drill with a little stone. They would have been a giveaway straightaway. If an agent was captured, they looked at everything, scrutinized everything, and if they saw 'Lightning Zip', he was in trouble. So everything had to be done absolutely methodically. If there were any British marks or numbers, size seven for instance because on the Continent there was no size seven, they had to be dealt with. It was a very, very thorough job, because a man's life depended on it.

Colonel Wills sent for me one day and sitting in the office was a group captain from the Air Force. On the table in front of him was a bundle of notes. So old Wills pulled one off and said could you age that? I said I can have a go. There was a little room, no window, with a skylight, and it had water, a sink. I had a couple of lads and a couple of girls to help me. So we were locked in this little room; there was a bloke who stood outside on guard. No one was allowed in. We filled the sink up with water, put some black aniline dye in it. It never came out black, it always came out a dirty grey. So we bundled these notes in this water with the dye in, left them in for a little while. We strung wires across the room and hung those notes out to dry. But before some of them got completely dry, we would screw them up in our hand and then open them out and hang them out. We'd fold them to make out they'd been in somebody's wallet. After a couple of days, they looked beautiful.

CLAUDIA PULVER

I came to England quite early; I was sent to a convent in Fitzjohns Avenue because I couldn't speak any English, only French. I then went back to Vienna, before Hitler, to go to an art school and, of course, had to leave very quickly. I was for a very short time in the Wyman School of Arts which closed down when the war started and then it was really entirely up to me. I was trained as a designer generally speaking, anything to do with fashion. I had very, very little training; it was all what we call *Fingerspitzengefühl*, it was all in my fingers.

I went to a number of small companies, the last of which was bombed in a daylight blitz. We came in one morning to find shards of glass sticking in the dummies. I then went to a very small refugee-run company and became their designer; they didn't have any manufacturing possibilities, but sent all their goods out to be made. Eventually we were approached by a Major Kenmore. He was a Continental but appeared in full British uniform. He came and asked my boss, whom I think he knew, whether he could set up an organization to collect second-hand Continental European goods. He didn't tell us why, but we were made to go round to a lot of the refugees to find suitcases, overcoats, some with fur collars, Homburg hats, gloves, ties, everything – mostly male things to start with. Of course we gave them new ones and they were quite delighted.

Eventually I was called up for war work and I wasn't too eager to go into a munitions factory. I suggested to my boss that perhaps we could start making garments for whoever needed the suitcases. Obviously if people were found, they would be in less danger than if they were wearing things which were shop-bought or made by British people. That was accepted and we were made to sign a secrecy document, not to talk about it. We had two large rooms, one was the cutting room and the other was the stitching and ironing room. I imagine we had two cutters, a number of machinists, some finishers and pressers. It was a proper professional outfit which got better as we went on. It was a nine to five operation, except for the times when we had to dive under the table because there was an air raid, which was quite frequent.

We started with shirts; I would imagine we made a hundred or two hundred shirts a week, all by hand and individually. We had all these lovely young men coming. I quite enjoyed all these handsome, dashing officers from France, French Canada, England, from all over the place. They wouldn't say very much, we had to guess a great deal. They came into the show room which was actually in Margaret Street, around the corner from the work room in Great Titchfield Street. We had to take their measurements. We started making shirts for them in the Continental fashion, which was quite different to anything in England. We got old shirts from the refugees again. We took them apart, we looked at the various collar shapes, looked at the way they were manufactured. We looked at the seams, and there certainly was an enormous difference between the side seams. The shape of the cuffs was different, the position of the buttonhole on the under collar was entirely different, and sometimes the plackets of a shirt were different. The width of the stand underneath the collar was different. I think the Continental were a little bit lower than the English ones, they were quite high, probably because Continental people have shorter necks than the British. They chose their own type of collar, because every man likes a different shape of a collar, but they were only allowed to choose from the Continental versions. So we made a lot of cardboard patterns of European shapes so that we would have a library for people to choose from.

Labels were taboo, my goodness, labels were taboo. I remember a pair of gloves went across and the agent came back saying you made a mistake. I turned them inside out and there was a 'Made in England' label in one of the fingers. That's really the only mistake we ever made, because we were terribly careful about labels.

They had women later on. A lot of them had been living in France and knew exactly what the fashion was in France, which we wouldn't have known any longer. We made clothes to suit whatever their style of living over there was. Violet Szabo was probably the most beautiful girl I'd ever seen and I remember making black underwear for her, God knows why she needed black underwear. We also had a lot of ladies of the brothels in Paris, they were terribly important because they had a lot of German clients. So we made the appropriate clothes, very provocative, and underwear for them, which was quite fun.

You had to be careful to be in character. I had a French countess who came across in a rowing boat. She was a very elegant lady so she was wearing more elegant clothes than a wireless operator would have done. We had an Irish girl who was quite wild and used to go around France with a wireless tucked in her bag. She was dressed quite ordinarily. When the Germans stopped her and asked her what she had in her bag, she said, 'It's a wireless, of course.' But she got away with it. She survived the war, too.

Others didn't. We had a Jewish girl who was supposed to be dropped in the south of France in some chateau, occupied partially by German officers. Because she was supposed to be a relation, we had to make riding clothes for her, but she didn't make it for very long. She managed to get a few Germans before they killed her. We had Odette Churchill. They all had different names of course, but we realized later, after the war, who they actually were. We could never, never understand that they could be as brave as they were. They were incredibly contained and distant. Somehow you felt that there was something very special about them.

Towards the end of the war, they brought me a really peculiar garment. It was terribly dirty and smelly. I said what is it? Oh, he said, this is from a man who was hanged and buried for three days. We took this kimono off him. They wanted it copied and that was more or less the last thing we did.

PAULINE BROCKIES

When I was posted to Roydon I got a big shock. I was introduced to Captain Edwards and taken into this office. I was very astonished when I found out what was going on – forging documents for the agents to take across when they went. I went to Roydon originally to type for Mr Rubens, who was a Pole. He was playing around with microdots and the idea was for me to type the work and for him to photograph it down, but I don't think very much came of that. After that I suppose I was then a technical secretary, cutting out French ration cards, using rubber stamps to stamp things with, all sorts of different things. The cover story at Station XIV was that we were a mapping research station. I think the majority of the sergeants were in the Royal Engineers, the CO was in the Intelligence Corps. The sergeants that were in the Army were obviously picked for their capabilities and what their jobs had been in civilian life, because they were all highly skilled, every one of them. They had to be. There wasn't any particular type. Nobby Clark who was one of the etchers, he played the piano beautifully by ear. There wasn't any particular type of forger.

The work docket would come down with the original documents. They would then be taken to have photostats made; and then go to the camera room. In the camera room it was decided whether they would go to the litho room or to the letterpress room. The printing had to be right, everything about it – whatever we were printing, ration cards or identity cards or birth certificates, everything had to be absolutely perfect. They were examined in some instances by the Gestapo, so they had to be absolutely bang on. I don't think we ever did make an error.

Sergeant-Major Gatwood was the person who was going to sign all those items. He was a much older man than all of us, more like a father figure. He was a very kind and gentle man. His skill was absolutely fantastic. He had the largest ink stand you've ever seen, with all sorts of coloured inks and different kinds of pens. He would sit there quietly taking half an hour to study something. I never, ever, saw him practise. He wrote straight onto the card or whatever it was he was signing, which I think is remarkable.

The *Fremdenpass* was a foreign worker's pass. It had a red, bright scarlet cover with a big black German eagle on the front of it. We eventually found that the paper was grey but it took a while to work this out because of the cross-screening. The Germans were very clever in their cross-screening. It was always difficult to find out what the colour of the paper was, and yet this was something you had to establish before you did anything. The cross-screening on it was black and red. The black would go down first and then the red would go over the top of it, or vice versa. It was highly technical to find out these things as we were working back to front, weren't we? I'd love to know what happened to them.

We printed some documents for a ship. The German officer who boarded the ship called for the papers because he'd got to sign that he'd been on the ship. When they were brought to him and he examined them, he recognized the signature of the man who'd previously examined this document or been on this ship, a friend of his, and he recognized this man's signature. But, in point of fact, they were our documents that we'd made at Roydon. They were perfect, weren't they?

CHAPTER 4

GETTING THERE

By the spring of 1941 Gubbins could point with pride to the large numbers of secret agents now graduating from the SOE schools. But how were they to get from Britain to their field of operations behind enemy lines? The postwar movie image of the silent parachute drop by moonlight immediately springs to mind. But it was far from clear during the early months of the war that this would be the way.

There was a simple explanation for this. SOE had no aircraft at its disposal and the few first 'special duties' flights by the Air Force were reserved strictly for its rival, the Secret Intelligence Service. As late as March 1941 Gubbins thought that all those agents then in training 'may well have to be landed by sea as no other means exist'. What, then, were the seaborne options for crossing the English Channel to France or the Low Countries? They were hardly encouraging. Even the SIS was struggling to find effective ways and means of getting its agents in and out of Hitler's Europe. After the fall of France, Commander F. T. Slocum was appointed by 'C' to do the job for both SIS and Section D, but even he had to beg and borrow craft from the Navy. By October 1940 not a single SOE agent had been successfully landed on the European coastline.

Despite SIS resistance, however, Baker Street did in the end carry out several operations using small boats for ferrying agents in and out of Brittany. These exploits lay firmly in the buccaneering tradition of the Scarlet Pimpernel, the fictional English secret agent who rescued French aristocrats from the guillotine during the French Revolution – a tale of derring-do that in turn was based firmly on real historical fact. On one occasion an SOE agent actually discovered that he was using a secluded beach in Brittany used for the same clandestine purposes in the 1790s.

The story began with a man named Gerry Holdsworth, a quiet but forceful character who might have been chosen by Hollywood central casting for the part. Like many SOE operatives, he'd come to Baker Street via Section D after a chequered career: first, as a rubber planter in Borneo, then several years making advertising films for various companies, including Phillips in Holland. He was also an expert small-boat sailor. One of those who worked with him described him as 'good looking, well-educated, a wonderful man, brave, brave as they came'. Section D first recruited him for work in Norway and gave him a short course in demolition techniques at the St Ermin's Hotel. After the collapse of France, and when it became clear that SOE could not depend on Slocum, he was sent instead to set up a new service for transporting agents across the Channel.

After careful reconnaissance he chose his base on the Helford River near Falmouth in Cornwall, a sheltered and secluded estuary chosen by the novelist Daphne du Maurier as the setting for her famous novel, *Frenchman's Creek*. He also selected a house, 'Ridifarne', for accommodating both crew and agents. He could hardly have picked anywhere more appropriate. It was the summer retreat of the family whose firm had developed the Bickford fuse, a device originally made for the Cornish mining industry and adopted by SOE as a component of its demolition charges. To run the house he chose his wife Mary. Said by those who knew her to be a pretty and fragile-looking blonde, she too was a Section D recruit. 'She was a very kind-hearted lady…[but] not to be bossed about by a bunch of idiots,' remembered one crew member. An accomplished commercial artist, she had even made detailed drawings on such arcane subjects as how to construct a home-made mine for Section D's handbook for saboteurs. Both impressed the team they collected; the Holdsworth style was informal, as one of its number, Tom Long, recalled: 'No bullshit or anything at all, he didn't want you to salute him, he wanted you to call him Gerry. He was the finest officer going. If there was any trouble he was very brave, but on top of that if anyone upset him, he was like a tiger.'

For transport, Holdsworth acquired a variety of small craft. The most memorable was a sixty-foot French yawl named the *Mutin* ('The Rebel'), a former French Navy training ship which resembled a typical Bay of Biscay tunnyman. She was much appreciated by her crew, as Long remembered: 'She was brought over at Dunkirk by the Green Howards…She was very wide on the beam and she drew nine foot six of water. She was designed and built for the Bay of Biscay, for the heavy seas…She'd sail very close to the wind and you could nearly talk to her. She was the most wonderful, sea-going ship I've ever been on.'

The *Mutin*, however, needed a refit and, among other things, a powerful diesel engine. Crew member Len Macey witnessed the conversion:

Holdsworth found an old boat that had come over in the 1940 exodus from France and it was owned by the racing driver Bugatti, I think his name was, and there were two engines in this boat. Gerry Holdsworth confiscated them and got them sent down to us and put one aboard… it was a Mans diesel engine, a beautiful engine, and …that was the start of the *Mutin* as such being prepared for sea; but we didn't know what we were going to do. We knew we had a boat and we went off sailing from Dartmouth now and again and that was fun.

While the *Mutin* and another small French boat were being refitted, Holdsworth used a seaplane tender, known simply by its number 360, which he managed to obtain from the RAF. She was really too small and slow for SOE's needs, but Holdsworth had little choice.

Crews were recruited largely by word of mouth. They included a tough Channel Islander named 'Bunny' Newton, 'a physically diminutive but streetwise larger-than-life Guernsey fisherman'[1] He was recommended by none other than Ian Fleming, who'd interviewed him at Naval Intelligence after his escape in advance of the German occupation of his island. Also on board was a Breton fisherman called Pierre Guillet, and several Cornishmen. As second-in-command, Holdsworth selected Francis Brooks-Richards, a young naval lieutenant who had been injured on board a minesweeper when it struck an acoustic mine in the approach channel to Falmouth Harbour. Len Macey had been a signalman on a trawler when he was injured in a bombing attack on a convoy. Recruited in March 1941, he had little idea of what he'd let himself in for when he was collected at Dartmouth and driven to Helford.

When I joined Gerry Holdsworth I had no idea what we were going to do. I plainly thought it was Special Forces of some kind, but I'd never heard of SOE or any of these other names, so I really didn't know. It was all quite a shock but it was fun…When we got down there it was a beautiful river…at that time of course there was nothing in it really…there was the lovely Ferry Boat Inn on one side and the other pub, the Shipwrights Arms, on the other side.

Holdsworth quickly put him to work fitting both the *Mutin* and 360 with W/T sets. These were to be used only in emergencies, for mayday appeals in case of German attack. But as a security precaution these were to be RAF sets using Air Force frequencies – an enemy would be looking for a plane, not a boat. Macey remembered this: 'The idea was, of course, at the time our planes were going over bombing, coming back, bombing, coming back, so if I was to use the W/T set I used all the things that they had in their planes, and therefore my operating signals would be RAF ones…The Germans would think we were an aircraft, or so Commander Holdsworth told me at that time. That would give us more chance to get away; they wouldn't be looking at the sea, they'd be thinking it's up in the air.' Macey, a trained signalman but not a wireless operator, was sent off to a local RAF station for training. He then returned with a couple of Air Force helpers to install the sets.

I'm tacking all these wires along and eventually we get the sets working and then we have a big problem because they've got a bloody big aerial up there and it works beautifully with this, but when Holdsworth comes aboard he said, 'The French will know it is [an aerial] so you can't have it, you've got to do something else.' So we thought of some way of winding the aerial all round the rigging or we made a special rigging for it just to look like rigging and that worked very well. So everyone was happy and we went to sea, me having been taught all the RAF signs, call signs, and what not and they said, 'Don't worry because you're never going to use it.'

Tom Long was recruited several months after Len Macey. A pre-war merchant navy seaman from King's Lynn, with experience of France and the Low Countries, he was serving as a quartermaster on a destroyer in the Firth of Forth when he received his transfer orders. He was interviewed at Baker Street: 'I was interviewed by Admiral Holbrook [Rear-Admiral Holbrook, head of SOE's Naval Section] and he told me I'd been selected for Special Service. Was I prepared to do it? So I said what have I got to do? He said, "Well, we can't tell you...but if you don't want to do it, we'll put everything in reverse."'

He soon discovered just what he had signed up for: 'The whole job was landing agents, supplying them with stores and picking them up again and all these operations were done with nothing written about them...all top secret.'

The timing of his introduction to the Helford team was unfortunate. The *Mutin* had just returned from a Brittany mission during which she had been machine-gunned by a German bomber and the engineer had been killed.

I saw this beautiful river and it was a lovely day and it really looked wonderful. I thought, God, I'm going to be happy here. We went down to Bar Beach and a young chap called Gerry de la Rue, a Channel Island boy, rowed over and picked me up. So I put an oar in the stern and I sculled. I was there sculling away. He said, 'I've always wanted to do that, will you teach me to scull?' I said, 'No, not now!' We went alongside the *Mutin*, a French yawl, and there were shipwrights digging out shrapnel from all over the vessel and patching it all up and there was a heap of sails there, they had blood and they were all shot up, and I thought, Jesus Christ, what the hell have I let myself in for now?

Like Len Macey, his special skills were quickly put to work on the small SOE flotilla. The next day one of the officers took him out to the 360 which had been refitted with two underwater exhausts which, when in the water, sucked power from the engine. Long was to devise a solution, which he practised first in wood and then in wire: 'I said, "I've got to have new ends that control the pro-pellers." He said, "Just what we want." So he left me to it...

I rigged it up and he came back, then I showed him how it worked and all the rest of it. He was absolutely thrilled. He said, "We're going over the other side tonight, would you like to come?" So, "Yes please!"

However, further training was called for. As Macey recalled, he and Long were sent to Brickendonbury for the unarmed combat course:

> We went to this vast house in the country and first thing in the morning we were told to report to the Army drill shed or some such place. There was a sergeant standing on a great big mattress there and he said, 'I want you to run at me and knock me over,' and we thought this a bit funny. He said, 'Come on. Don't hang about.' So I ran at him and the next minute I was flying over his head…It was that kind of thing that happened at Brickendonbury and then they taught us how to use the yellow plastic explosive. Tom and I had to crawl around Hertfordshire…putting it on train lines and pretending that we were blowing up the trains. We never blew them up, of course, but I still don't know whether the stuff was fake or not.

The two new recruits to the Helford Flotilla also met the legendary 'Shanghai Buster', William Fairbairn. He left a strong impression on Macey.

> We had a fellow come down and they said, 'He's an unarmed combat expert and he will show you a few things.' This guy came aboard and said, 'Get a chair, please,' so I went and got a chair…and he sat someone in it and the next moment he's got his arm around his neck and he's got a knife in. He said, 'Do you know I'm just showing you how easy it is to kill a person.' So a couple of days he showed us all kinds of things – how to kill people with two fingers or hit them in certain places…He didn't look like a killer at all or a policeman, but he was a great expert.

Over the winter of 1940–1 the *Mutin* and her companions made several night-time landings on the Brittany coast, a treacherous place with its jagged, indented shore and numerous islands, inlets and reefs through which tides as high as thirteen metres can rip at frightening speed. In war, with the constant danger of German patrol boats, and sailing on moonless nights – the only safe ones to operate on – it was even more hazardous. With the 'main' boat staying offshore, landings and pickups took place with small rubber boats that could easily capsize in the hands of the unskilled. These were extremely high risk operations, which took place without the help of buoys or other navigational aids and with only the occasional muffled torchlight flashing from the shore. Here the Breton's seafaring skills came fully into play, for Pierre Guillet had the local fisherman's knack of knowing where he was by little more than feel and smell. Tom Long, who steered under Guillet's directions, relied totally on the Breton:

> He'd been a fishing boat owner and been at sea all his life. He was a very fine sailor and he had a wonderful knowledge of the French coast…When we got over there, put down the under-water exhausts, Pierre would go to the bow and he'd be waving this way, that way and…I'd steer under his directions. There was great rocks looming up and I used to think, Jesus Christ, a bloody fish couldn't swim through there without scratching its bloody tail!…When we got there and anchored, Pierre used to cry like a baby because he was on French soil.

Len Macey also recalled the Frenchman with affection and gratitude – 'Old Pierre was a magnificent guy and couldn't speak a word of English but he never seemed frightened, so no one else was.'

Operations took place in almost total darkness. Long recalled that they 'worked in the new moon period and there wasn't a light to be seen anywhere. You put your hand up in front of your face and you couldn't see it…we became like owls for seeing things in the dark.' He also recalled that landing crews were specially kitted out for these sea and land operations:

> When we rowed ashore, we had a special khaki uniform which had been treated so that the water ran off. We had very high boots, high ankle boots, non-slip. We started off with ones with rope soles [but] when you're scrabbling over rock in the dark

and all the rest of it, it's easy to fall down and we used these for three times and when we came to use them for the fourth time, we found all the rope had shrunk and they was only a quarter of the size and all twisted. So then they made us special boots made of hardened felt...When we'd land on a beach, we didn't know whether that was mined, we didn't know whether there was a party there of Germans waiting to welcome us and we didn't know, unless there was resistance there, how to dispose of the stores we got.

Once safely ashore, the men set about delivering the so-called 'Helford containers' – full of useful things for the resistance, including incendiary devices such as the phosphorous wafers that looked like, and were opened like, giant sardine tins. More unorthodox were the ingenious products of The Frythe. Long was impressed: 'They had rats that had been doctored up, containing explosives...the rats look a bit mangy... and the idea was someone would get a shovel and throw it on the furnace and that would burst the boiler and close the factory down.'

Equally dubious were the exploding crustaceans, as Long also recalled.

They used lobsters, crayfish and crabs. I remember one day there was a special delivery that we was going to take over the other side. Well, when I got up there, Commander Holdsworth said I better see everything's all right. I've never seen anyone in such a temper as he was in, because now lobster that's in the sea, that's a bluey colour, but when that's boiled, that's red...Now whether he'd ordered blue or red I don't know but they'd sent the wrong colour and so that operation had to be cancelled but oh, he was jumping mad over it, because they'd made him the wrong colour.

For emergencies, the landing crews had what they called the 'operational box'. Tom Long's included rubber truncheons, a tommy-gun, a Smith and Wesson automatic, fighting knives and a knuckleduster. His personal weapon was a machete – 'I was told if I got near a German and gave a swipe, that'd take his head clean off. I carried that several times, hoping to meet a German, but never saw one!'

Long also admired how signalling between the mother ship and the landing party called for ingenious devices: 'These luminous balls were just smaller than a golf ball and they were the most wonderful things we had, because when you were coming back, you held up your luminous ball so the mother craft could see it. They always anchored on a grass rope so that in an emergency they could cut it and go…You didn't want a chain rattling in the middle of the night, so that was quiet and they could heave up the anchor and come to pick you up. That system worked all right.'

Attacks by patrolling German aircraft or E-boats in the Channel added to the hazards. When the long winter nights gave way to the lengthening days of the spring and summer of 1941, Holdsworth decided the Brittany beaches were too dangerous for picking up or dropping agents. Instead, the *Mutin* was re-converted back to looking like a tunnyman and given a new base in the Scilly Islands. She rendezvoused instead with sympathetic skippers in the genuine French fishing fleet in the Bay of Biscay. Tom Long described her task this way: 'The purpose of the mission was to catch tunny fish for the back room boys so they could make replicas of them which were filled full of explosives…So they could be taken well inland to be used when the invasion started.'

'In this capacity,' wrote one source, 'she delivered sizeable quantities of plastic explosive disguised cunningly as fish.'[2]

Delivering and picking up agents was sometimes equally surreal, as Len Macey recounted: 'Suddenly we were in a pool, a great big pool, and there were six or seven chaps and the memory I have of them was of them all with Homburgs on, old Homburg hats, with suits on, overcoats, sitting in a big rubber dinghy. We just picked them up and took them away…You think about the chaps you've brought, where they've gone, they've vanished, they came ashore, and they were dispensed with, it seemed. We on board never knew where on earth they went.'

The Helford Flotilla ferried several of SOE's early agents across the Channel. This was two-way traffic. Getting agents out of France after they had completed their missions was as important as getting them in. But some never made it back. One of the more unusual drops was that of a female Soviet agent, infiltrated into France as part of a deal struck between SOE and the NKVD after Moscow's entry into the war. Her name was Anna Uspenskaya. Landed on the Brittany coast in February 1942 she lasted only until July, when she was captured and shot by the Germans.

By this time the Helford Flotilla itself was under a death sentence. In order to protect some highly sensitive SIS operations, Slocum placed a ban on all SOE sea operations to western Brittany. Holdsworth, fed up, left with most of his team for the Mediterranean and took the *Mutin* with him. After the liberation of North Africa they set up a highly successful naval operation ferrying agents in and out of southern France.

The Helford Flotilla never carried the agents or supplies to the French resistance that Holdsworth and his team had hoped and Gubbins expected. Inevitably too, as SOE air operations gradually developed, its efforts became less important. But during Baker Street's difficult teething period it delivered useful results, the bravery of its crews was exemplary, and it gave them invaluable experience for their successful Mediterranean operations. Above all, it instilled a sense of achievement which the crew, such as Tom Long, felt deeply: 'It was lovely, because…I thought of women and folks at home, that they was getting bombed and we were doing something against the Germans and we really felt good about it…We were delighted every time there was an operation, but very disappointed when something went wrong and had to be cancelled.'

While the *Mutin* and its crew braved the treacherous Brittany coast, another clandestine sea operation was building a link across the North Sea. Based at Lunna Voe near Lerwick in the Shetland Islands, the nearest British territory to Norway, it used fishing boats provided by their Norwegian crews who had fled the Nazis and became known as 'The Shetland Bus'. It worked for both SOE and SIS, and Baker Street's part in its operations were controlled by David Howarth, who wrote a book about it.[3] Unable to operate during the long summer nights which offered no protection against patrolling German planes, and often plagued by appalling seas during winter, its efforts were heroic and far from negligible. In its first three years it carried almost a hundred agents and over 150 tons of supplies to western Norway. Then, after obtaining three fast American submarine chasers, it infiltrated another 153 agents in its last two seasons. Because of the perils of air operations to Norway, it remained a prime clandestine route throughout the war.

But however resourceful and brave, by their very nature Holdsworth's and Howarth's seaborne operations could never satisfy SOE's needs for transporting its agents to set Europe ablaze. Throughout the first half of 1941 Baker Street worked hard to increase the resources it could draw on. In July – exactly a year after his midnight assignation with Churchill that placed him in charge – Dalton told the Prime Minister that by late 1942, if SOE were so directed, it could set in motion 'large-scale and long-term schemes for revolution in Europe'. But the key to this lay in the air. SOE would need 1200 aircraft sorties to supply resistance on the scale he envisaged. Unsurprisingly, the plans encountered stiff resistance, not least from those determined to concentrate the RAF's effort on the bombing campaign. 'Your work is a gamble,' Air Marshal Sir Charles Portal complained to Baker Street, 'which may give us a valuable dividend or may produce nothing. It is anybody's guess. My bombing offensive is not a gamble. Its dividend is certain; it is a gilt-edged investment.'[4]

Despite this, SOE won a small victory. That summer the RAF special duties flight of three aircraft was increased to a full squadron. It was still woefully inadequate. But it meant that Baker Street could finally begin to infiltrate agents behind enemy lines on a scale that could make a difference. In the meantime it worked hard to catch the eye of Churchill and convince its critics it could produce results. Early in 1942 came the first of several successes that year which helped prove its case.

NOTES
1 Brooks Richards, *Secret Flotillas*, p. 101.
2 Patrick Howarth, *Undercover*, p. 182.
3 David Howarth, *The Shetland Bus*.
4 M.R.D. Foot, *SOE in France*, p. 13.

CHAPTER 5

A BURGLAR'S OPERATION

It was a hot afternoon in August 1941 when the *Maid Honor* slipped quietly out of Poole Harbour in Dorset. For weeks a small crew had been sailing the two-masted Brixham trawler from its hiding place on an isolated creek inside the harbour on training exercises along the English coast. Its russet red sails had become a familiar sight in such places as Weymouth and Portland. Now the training was over and it was embarking on its first mission.

Lunch that day was a boisterous affair. It was held at the Antelope Hotel, an old, redbrick coaching inn on the High Street which had rapidly become the crew's favourite watering hole. 'Pop', the genial proprietor, had prepared a magnificent meal and even brought out some of his best champagne. Presiding over the popping corks was Colin Gubbins, SOE's Director of Operations. Despite its innocent appearance, the *Maid Honor* was one of the more unlikely weapons in Baker Street's armoury.

Its crew had been carefully selected. Apart from the skipper, who came with her, the leader was 'Gus' March-Phillips, a tough character with a terrible stammer, a broken nose and an unpredictable temper who'd resigned his commission in the Army ten years before to earn his living as a sports writer and novelist. A romantic by heart, he idealized the buccaneering spirit of Elizabethan England; Sir Francis Drake was his hero. Gubbins had recruited him from the commandos. Now in his early thirties, his quixotic leadership inspired devotion among his men. His second-in-command, a Yorkshireman named Geoffrey Appleyard, was some ten years younger. He had met March-Phillips on the Dunkirk beaches and followed him into the commandos. Appleyard's family owned the largest car dealership in Leeds and he combined a first-class engineering degree at Cambridge with captaincy of the university ski team. He'd even won the coveted 'Roberts of Kandahar', the oldest British downhill ski race held every year at Mürren, in Switzerland. He was already a holder of the Military Cross for bravery in bringing back secret agents by sea from France.

Another crew member was Anders Lassen, a Dane. At over six feet tall with blue eyes and fair hair, he was predictably known as 'the Viking'. A seaman by trade, he'd led a mutiny to ensure his ship sailed to England when the Nazis invaded Denmark. Since then he'd passed through the rigours of SOE training at Arisaig with flying colours. Called by some the 'Robin Hood' commando, he was a crack shot with a bow and arrow and would challenge anyone with a pistol against a target 25 yards distant. Other members included an old boyhood friend of Appleyard who had been around the world on a Finnish sailing ship, a Frenchman who had joined de Gaulle against Vichy and spoke no English, and Dennis Tottenham, one of the first to join the crew.

The lunch finished and the last of the champagne drained, Gubbins walked down with the crew to the waiting boat and pinned a sprig of white heather to its foremast for good luck. Such sentimental Scots superstition paid its dividend. Five months later, and half-way across the globe, the crew of the *Maid Honor* was to spearhead one of the most spectacular operations in SOE's then short history.

SOE badly needed a triumph. So far, 1941 had been a difficult year. Baker Street had been under continuous sniping from its Whitehall critics and had little to show for months of effort to mount operations behind enemy lines. That spring, briefly, it had enjoyed a moment of glory when rebel air force officers in Belgrade overthrew the government of Prince Paul, the Yugoslav Regent, after he signed a pact with Hitler. SOE had secretly subsidized some of the plotters and funded anti-government propaganda. A buoyant Churchill declared that Yugoslavia had 'found its soul' and sent his congratulations to Dalton. He even overcame his visceral dislike of SOE's minister to invite him to Chequers for lunch.

But then the shadows had again descended. Hitler, infuriated by the *coup*, invaded Yugoslavia and also attacked Greece. By June he had conquered the Balkans and driven British forces from Crete. The last remaining SOE networks in Europe were destroyed. The creation of new ones was agonizingly slow. It has been said that

God created France for SOE – but even here, the closest and most likely terrain, scarcely twenty agents had been infiltrated during the year since Churchill's order to set Europe ablaze.

At home, in the treacherous corridors of Whitehall, things were even worse. That summer, as the *Maid Honor* crew were busily learning their sailing, Dalton had lost his battle to keep control of subversive propaganda. Instead, it had been wrested from him and given to a separate agency, the Political Warfare Executive. With it went Dalton's dream of a comprehensive programme of subversion and revolution in Europe. Worse, even as Gubbins presided over the farewell lunch at the Antelope Hotel, the Chiefs of Staff in London rejected Dalton's ambitious plan for vastly expanded resources. The Baker Street mandarins could see the writing on the wall. Unless results were quickly delivered they, and SOE, would be out of a job.

All this unfolded against the grim backdrop of the war itself. In June Hitler launched Operation Barbarossa, his *blitzkrieg* against the Soviet Union, and by mid-August his panzer forces had sliced through Stalin's defences and were within thirty miles of Leningrad. In North Africa, Australian troops besieged in Tobruk for four months evacuated the city. In the Atlantic Doenitz's U-boat commanders were wreaking havoc on Allied convoys.

Churchill, as intrepid as ever, defied the risks and sailed to Newfoundland to meet secretly with President Roosevelt at Placentia Bay the week before the *Maid Honor* sailed from Poole Harbour. Out of this first wartime summit came the Atlantic Charter, a heart-warming declaration about freedom and democracy. Yet the brutal fact remained that when Churchill returned home America had still not declared war. With the Nazi armies triumphant in Russia, would Britain even survive, never mind win, the war? The Bletchley Park codebreakers had barely begun to crack the U-boat codes that would, eventually, turn the tide of war in the Atlantic. In the meantime Britain's lifeline to North America hung by a thread.

It was the U-boat menace that lay behind the departure of the *Maid Honor*. Seventy feet long, she had been built in the 1920s and was named after the daughter of her owner. After fishing commercially for a decade she'd been converted to a yacht just four years before SOE requisitioned her to shuttle agents across the Channel. March-Phillips convinced Gubbins that her appearance provided first-rate camouflage and her wooden hull foolproof protection against magnetic mines. At this early stage of SOE's life Gubbins had virtually no access to aircraft and believed that boats would transport most of his agents to the field.

But here he ran into Menzies' Secret Intelligence Service. SIS firmly vetoed Gubbins's plan. It wanted to keep tight control of cross-Channel operations by sea for its own agents, and was worried that sabotage operations along the coast of France would attract unwelcome German attention and disrupt its own carefully laid plans to establish intelligence networks there. So Baker Street, anxious to prove its usefulness to the war, decided to send the *Maid Honor* off to search for U-boats rumoured to be hiding out in the swampy creeks of French West Africa. Here, it was feared, they were secretly refuelling and revictualling in between attacks on Allied convoys in the Atlantic.

In preparation for its mission the *Maid Honor* was extensively modified. Armour plating was added. A false deckhouse was built that could only be entered from below and was instantly collapsible by pulling a lever; inside it housed a Vickers Mark 8 two-pounder gun. Aloft, crows' nests fitted with bren-guns were added to the masts. In the stern, a number of depth charges were concealed under apparently innocent fishing nets. When Appleyard questioned their value, March-Phillips grinned – if they couldn't knock out a U-boat with the gun then they'd heave the depth charges overboard. 'The sub will then proceed to perdition,' he said cheerily, 'closely followed by ourselves.'

March-Phillips and four others sailed the *Maid Honor*, under a neutral Swedish flag, to West Africa. Other members of the mission, including Appleyard, travelled out on a faster troop carrier. By September the team had established its base off the steamy port of Freetown, Sierra Leone. Housed on a magnificent sandy beach, Geoffrey Appleyard found it all entrancing, as he wrote to his family: 'We are now living here in very pleasant surroundings in tents right on the edge of the sea in a beautiful tropical bay, with a clump of palm and banana and coconut trees fifty yards away. A lovely site – we all spend three or four hours a day in the sea swimming, diving, and swimming underwater wearing goggles and armed with fish spears etc.'[1]

This Club Med existence was broken with exploratory forays along the coast in search of U-boats. There were plenty of adventures. Once, going ashore in a dinghy to scout for signs of U-boats, they were stopped by a Vichy French patrol. They brazened it out with the gold-laced official claiming that fresh fruit was needed for a sick man aboard the *Maid Honor*. They also gave false names for the crew. The Frenchman insisted on visiting the trawler in person; Appleyard deliberately fumbled the dinghy's approach. As he slowly made a second attempt, his companion leaped on to the *Maid Honor* and rapidly briefed March-Phillips. By the time the unwelcome visitor had boarded and downed his welcoming glass of rum, one of the crew had taken to bed with his face whitened by flour and the rest had memorized their false aliases.

More derring-do punctuated the idyllic boredom. On another expedition March-Phillips and Appleyard left the *Maid Honor* and took off in a rubber canoe to explore the mouth of the Pongo River. Lying low by day in the mangrove swamps fending off mosquitoes, they played chess on boards sketched out on the mudbanks and with twigs for chessmen. At night they paddled up the maze of tributaries in search of U-boats. Finally, convinced there were none, they decided to return to sea and their waiting companions. But the going was difficult and the canoe seemed heavy. Inching his way forward, Appleyard peered through the gloom to find a huge crocodile draped over the bow, its row of shining teeth less than two feet from his face. With a quick push of his paddle he knocked it off into the water.

Back in Baker Street there was disappointment at the lack of news. If there were no U-boats, what was the *Maid Honor* to do? More important, how was SOE to make its mark? It was Louis Franck who came up with the answer. Franck was one of the office heavyweights, a wealthy Belgian banker in charge of West African affairs who had endeared himself to colleagues through constant repetition of his favourite epigram: 'Truth,' he was fond of saying, 'is far too precious a commodity to be used lightly.' Why not use the *Maid Honor* to launch sabotage attacks on Axis shipping known to be sheltering in the harbours of French or Spanish West Africa?

It took him weeks to persuade Foreign Office mandarins this could be done without Britain's role being revealed. But in November they finally capitulated. Franck soon identified two potential targets at anchor in the port of Santa Isabel on the island of Fernando Po in Spanish Guinea: a 200-ton German tanker named the *Likomba*, and a 7600-ton Italian merchant ship, the *Duchessa d'Aosta*. Instead of crippling the ships, however, it was decided to capture them. The Italian ship in particular would be a valuable prize. Quite apart from her tonnage, the cargo of wood, copra, coffee and copper was worth some £200,000.

Caught by the outbreak of war, both ships had been lying idle for a year and a half in the steamy equatorial climate. Santa Isabel, which lay some sixty miles north-west of the Nigerian coast, nestled in the crater of a long-extinct volcano breached by the sea. It had been briefly in British hands, as an anti-slavery base, before coming under Spanish control in the middle of the nineteenth century. Since then, little had happened to disturb the daily torpor of its 10,000 inhabitants.

The plan was hatched between Baker Street and Leonard Guise, SOE's man in Lagos, who arranged for a couple of photo-reconnaissance flights over Fernando Po. As this involved breaching neutral Spanish air space, the aircrew were briefed to plead navigational error if challenged. But the flights passed without incident and produced several first-rate, useful photographs of the Axis ships at their moorings. In Santa Isabel itself, oarsmen in sculls – to all the world just enjoying their sport – carefully measured the anchor chains of the two targets.

The *Maid Honor* itself was ruled out for the cut-and-run raid, which by now had been given the codename 'Postmaster'. Instead, a tug, the *Vulcan*, and a fast launch, the *Nuneaton*, were provided by the British colonial authorities in Nigeria. March-Phillips's team was enlarged by members of the SOE mission in Lagos and local volunteers. 'Would anyone like to come to a party?' he asked. The two boats would enter Santa Isabel under cover of darkness, seize control of the two Axis ships, free them from their moorings, and tow them out into the open sea. There, the Royal Navy would escort them to safety and British control.

Vulcan and *Nuneaton* set sail from Lagos at dawn on 11 January

1942. Two days out there was a near disaster when the *Nuneaton* developed engine trouble and was taken under tow. In the heavy swell she began to sheer alarmingly and her keel rose out of the water. In a desperate effort to right her the crew threw most of their provisions overboard and clambered on to one side. But it was only when one of the boarding party seized an axe and severed the hawser attaching her to the *Vulcan* that the situation was saved and she righted herself. The crew then swam around retrieving their possessions from the shark-ridden waters. Once the engine was repaired they resumed their voyage and arrived off Santa Isabel the next night.

The plan, carefully rehearsed on the voyage, was to quietly slip into the Spanish port soon after the lights of the town had been extinguished. Zero hour was midnight. But arriving to find the town still lit up, they were forced to wait. Impatience mounted. The *Nuneaton*, as agreed, slowly began to edge forward when suddenly March-Phillips's well-known impetuosity almost brought disaster. Through the darkness the *Nuneaton* crew heard his unmistakable voice bellow: 'Will you get a b-b-bloody move on or g-g-get out, I'm going in.' This infuriated the *Nuneaton*'s captain who could still see the lights of Santa Isabel across the water, and he forced the *Vulcan* to stop dead by sharply steering across her bows. A furious volley of insults followed before March-Phillips, recognizing defeat, moved off into the darkness and the raiding party resumed its wait.

'Gus himself struck me as completely intrepid, almost to the point of overdoing it,' Guise later said, 'because this was not really a military operation. It was a burglar's operation and burglars don't go in shooting.'[2] Thieves should, however, get their timing right. The British planners had assumed that clocks in Fernando Po would be on the same time as those in Lagos. They reckoned without Spanish pride. Distant Madrid kept it firmly on mother country time – one hour behind the Nigerian capital. Hence the hour's wait offshore and March-Phillips's outburst. On such elementary errors can operations fail.

While this mini-drama was unfolding at sea, on shore the second part of SOE's planning was swinging into action. Santa Isabel housed an office of John Holt, the Liverpool shipping firm.

This provided excellent cover for SOE's man in Fernando Po, Richard Lippett, who posed as one of its staff and whose secret reports on the local scene proved vital. The crew of the *Duchessa*, London learned, were 'debilitated and demoralized [and] appeared to be incapable of sustained activities outside their own pleasures'. The captain had returned to Italy, leaving the chief engineer in charge. Crew morale was low and many were suffering from venereal disease. Apart from a couple of incidents when bottles were thrown at the British Consulate, none of them seemed intensely anti-British.

The local British chaplain also played his part. After duping one of the crew into believing he was Spanish, he was invited on board the *Duchessa* for a party. All went well until his identity was unmasked and he was forced to make a hurried departure; but he had time to confirm that morale was low – and that the crew had removed and sold some of the ship's brass fittings.

Lippett (codenamed W.25 in the SOE files) also had an active role to play in the drama about to unfold. He employed a sub-agent in the port, a Spaniard with no love for the dictator General Franco. Lippett had him arrange an on-shore dinner party the night of the attack for crew members of the two Axis ships. This would both reduce the numbers of men March-Phillips's team had to deal with on the ships and – with plenty of wine and beer around – ensure that their partying compatriots were out of action.

At midnight, Madrid time, the lights in the tiny port went out. From the *Nuneaton* two small rubber canoes were lowered into the water, its blackened-faced crews paddling swiftly towards the German tanker. They climbed aboard, startling the night-watchman who promptly jumped overboard when he saw the knives between their teeth. They then attached lines to the *Nuneaton* and laid charges on the mooring lines and detonated them. As the *Likomba* sprang from her moorings, the *Nuneaton* took up the slack and began slowly to tow her out to the open sea.

While this had been going on March-Phillips and his party from the *Vulcan* boarded the *Duchessa*. Appleyard led the way, athletically jumping a gap of six feet to be first on board, followed closely by Lassen, who expertly looped a connecting rope to the *Vulcan* around a bollard on the Italian ship's deck. Desmond

Longe, another of the team, suffered an unexpected encounter: 'We ran up the little ladder from the well-deck on the promenade…By this time we had a knife in one hand and a pistol in the other. The first thing I knew was something between my legs…and I thought it was a panicking Italian or something or other. In actual fact it was a pig…'³

As expected, the demoralized crew offered no resistance. There was, however, a breathtaking hitch. Appleyard laid his first charge on the anchor chain, took shelter and lit the fuse. To his dismay, in the explosion that followed, the anchor chain remained intact and the ship stood fast. The charge had failed to do its work. Shouting out he would try again, he laid another charge, again pushed the detonator, and this time it worked. To his relief he felt the Italian ship begin to move. 'My God, she's free,' came a shout from the bridge. The *Vulcan* took up the strain and, its propellers thrashing, began to tow its prize towards the harbour entry. Down below in the engine room of the *Duchessa* the Italian stokers, encouraged by a raider brandishing a tommy-gun and lavish promises of money, frantically worked to bring her to full steam. '*Vulcan*'s performance was almost miraculous,' recorded March-Phillips. 'She gave the *Duchessa* two slews, one to starboard, one to port, like drawing a cork out of a bottle, and then without the slightest hesitation, and at a speed of at least three knots, went straight between the flashing buoys to the open sea, passing *Nuneaton* and *Likomba* a few cable lengths from the entrance. This operation, the most difficult in my view, was performed with amazing power and precision.'⁴

The whole operation took only thirty-five minutes. Not a shot was fired, not a person killed. The only casualty was the pig, slaughtered and roasted soon after the *Duchessa* cleared the harbour. It was the perfect burglary.

Back on shore pandemonium had broken out. Amid cries of '*Alerta!*' bugles sounded out. The explosions brought down a glass candelabra in one of the residences and in the darkness, assuming the noise meant an air raid, local anti-aircraft batteries began to fire wildly into the night sky. The party for the *Duchessa*'s crew came to an abrupt halt. The German captain of the *Likomba*, a man named Specht who had been drinking heavily, decided it was time to make for the safety of his bunk. When he arrived at the quayside he found his ship had gone. Drunk or not, he quickly guessed what had happened and turned up at the British Vice-Consulate in a feisty mood.

Here, the Acting Vice-Consul and those of his staff secretly on the SOE payroll had spent the evening on tenterhooks waiting for the raid to begin. Specht, who by now had worked himself into a fury, took a lunge at one of them. Whereupon 'W.51' – as the SOE files call him – leaped to the defence and, in the words of Lippett, 'put some heavy North of Scotland stuff on him, and literally knocked the s—-t out of him. When he saw W.51's revolver he collapsed in a heap, split his pants and emptied his bowell's [sic] on the floor. The police then came up and took him away but he was up and doing the next day.'[5]

The next morning Lippett had arranged to play badminton. When he turned up soldiers surrounded the court and stopped him from playing. He denied any knowledge of the affair: 'The English would never do a thing like that in a Spanish port,' he swore. Then he was summoned before the police and the head of the Colonial Guard, who grilled him closely. His passport was confiscated, and he was put under virtual open arrest. 'Very Gestapo-like,' he complained. Two months later he escaped in a rubber canoe after knocking out two of the policemen watching him.

The *Nuneaton* and *Vulcan*, their prizes in tow, eventually met up offshore with a Royal Navy corvette. There was a brief moment of farce when a sub-lieutenant boarding the *Duchessa* believed he had made a genuine catch with an Italian crew in charge. Refusing to believe March-Phillips's story, he signalled back to the corvette, 'Italian captain speaks good English.' The confusion sorted out, they were escorted back in triumph to Lagos. Here a tremendous reception awaited them. Local colonial officials who'd snubbed them just a week before claimed them as their own. The Cabinet and the Foreign Office wired congratulations. But when the euphoria died down, as one crewman remembered, the jitters set in. What had they been thinking of, dirty tricks in a neutral harbour? As quickly as possible they were removed from Lagos and dispersed around the globe.

Louis Franck had secured reluctant Foreign Office approval

only with a promise to cover up any trace of the British role. To throw the Spaniards off the scent March-Phillips's men scattered sailor caps with Free French insignia on the water before leaving Santa Isabel. The subterfuge worked, up to a point. The next day an official German news agency in Madrid pinned the raid on a Free French destroyer. The story was repeated by the German-controlled Radio Paris. An official Admiralty communiqué in London admitted that Royal Navy ships had intercepted the Axis ships on the open sea but claimed that they had merely been acting on 'information received' and that no Allied forces had been involved in the raid.

But the Spaniards were not fooled by the Free French story and a furious row broke out between London and Madrid. Foreign Secretary Anthony Eden insisted he had nothing to apologize for and after several months the affair died down. The *Duchessa d'Aosta* eventually sailed to Britain, was sold to Canadian Pacific, and assumed a new identity as the *Empire Yukon*.

In Baker Street there was jubilation. Franck and Gubbins were over the moon. When March-Phillips at last turned up at Baker Street to report on his mission wearing his African bush hat, breeches and riding boots, Gubbins threw yet another party. Thus exotically garbed, March-Phillips got into a lift and struck up conversation with the lift girl. Two months later they were married.

Dalton, too, was exultant. Only the month before, SOE's disconsolate minister had written dismally in his diary that 'our last reports have been almost bare, only tales of what has not been done, with most of the blame put on the weather. We are living on the past…just now I am particularly anxious for a successful operation or two.'[6] At last he could report a spectacular *coup*, and he promptly sat down to write a lengthy account of the affair for Churchill. SOE had demonstrated with panache that it could wage ungentlemanly war. The news could hardly have reached the beleaguered Prime Minister at a more opportune time. During the *Maid Honor*'s mission the Japanese had attacked Pearl Harbor and then swept through East Asia driving all before them. One after another British possessions including Hong Kong and Malaya had fallen. Even as Dalton wrote, Singapore was under heavy Japanese bomber attack. Three weeks later it surrendered.

In North Africa Rommel had launched a new offensive and the Eighth Army was in full retreat. SOE's little 'burglary' was a much-needed tonic for Churchill's soul. For months afterwards Baker Street would draw down from its capital.

Churchill admired bravery and ensured that medals were handed out. Looking back, 'Postmaster' might resemble a *Boys' Own* adventure story, but March-Phillips was not amused when his relieved crew had hoisted a Jolly Roger flag over the captured Italian liner. He ordered the skull and crossbones taken down. 'You are British Forces, not pirates or brigands,' he told them. As fate was to prove, such adventures could be deadly. A year later March-Phillips himself was killed on a commando raid in the Channel Islands; Anders Lassen won a posthumous VC on another mission; and Geoffrey Appleyard disappeared soon afterwards while on a mission in the skies over Sicily.

NOTES
1 'J. E. A.', *Geoffrey: Major John Geoffrey Appleyard*, p. 84.
2 Ian Dear, *Sabotage and Subversion: The SOE and OSS at War*, p. 65.
3 Charles Messenger, *The Commandos 1940–46*, p. 54.
4 Dear, op. cit., p. 66.
5 Ibid., p. 66.
6 *The Second World War Diary of Hugh Dalton 1940–45*, ed. Ben Pimlott, p. 329.

CHAPTER 6

KEEP THE FLAG OF FREEDOM FLYING

If equatorial Fernando Po seemed unlikely territory for SOE dirty tricks, neutral Istanbul offered a natural breeding ground for hush-hush intrigue. Here, perched on the literal edge of Europe, exiles and refugees from Hitler's Fortress Europe plotted how to liberate their homelands from the grip of Mussolini and the Führer. The city had a long tradition of intrigue and provided rich fodder for both Allied and Axis intelligence services alike. Bickham Sweet-Escott arrived here from Baker Street in the autumn of 1941. 'The big nightclubs and restaurants like Taxim's and Abdullah's,' he recalled, 'throve on the secret votes of our allies and our adversaries.'[1] He also noted that Istanbul was about the only SOE base throughout the Middle East where anything seemed to be happening.

Housed in the old servants' quarters of what had been the British Embassy in the days when Constantinople – as Istanbul was then called – had been the capital of the old Ottoman Empire, the mission hatched plots to sabotage Axis stores and equipment in Turkey, such as the Italian tankers exporting Rumanian oil to Greece that occasionally docked along the teeming Bosphorus waterfront. But the vigilant Turkish secret police were invariably too sharp for them.

Baker Street's operatives also worked strenuously to re-establish contact with groups inside the occupied Balkans who could get resistance moving. Their chief, Gardyne de Chastelain, had been in the oil business in Rumania before Nazi influence forced him out. Secretly, he had also helped run Section D's operations there. Other former Section D men were also at work in Istanbul. One of them was Basil Davidson. His exploits during the first two years of the war are typical of much of SOE's work.

As a journalist, Davidson had witnessed Hitler's triumphant march into Vienna; events in Austria were to determine his future.

I was a volunteer from the word go and that goes back, if you like, to my own judgement of what the Nazi war meant because in 1938, just before the war, I had been in Austria at the time of the Anschluss, the joining of Austria into the German Reich. I had seen what was being done there. They were rounding up all the left-wing people they could find, the Austrian Socialist party…putting them into camps. What would happen to them there we didn't know, we had no concept of the holocaust at that point…They rounded up all the people who could be described as Jews and they began an anti-Jewish persecution of the most horrible sort. You would see these poor Jewish ladies dragged out of buildings and forced to scrub pavements. And there you were with your hands in your pockets and you couldn't help at all, dreadful. I think that was the start of it as far as I was concerned.

He had also travelled around the Balkans and Italy, and reported from Paris after the outbreak of war. In December 1939 he was diplomatic correspondent of a London evening newspaper, the *Star*. But he was aged twenty-five and wanted a more active part in the war than merely reporting on it: 'In '39, as the army wasn't yet recruiting, they said you go away and we'll let you know. I'm hanging around and my editor called me in. He said, "The War Office wants to see you." I thought he was joking. He said, "You've got to go to lunch with a man at Simpsons in the Strand." I said, "But at Simpsons in the Strand, there are at least 400 people waiting for me there, that's *the* place you go to lunch."'

Swallowing his reservations, Davidson went and there, in the first-floor lobby, perched on a solitary chair, was 'a man of saturnine allure, and with the right newspaper. I recognized him at once as a character out of Eric Ambler.'[2] Over the soup they chatted about journalism. Over the beef the Eric Ambler figure asked Davidson if he knew anything of explosives. By good fortune he once edited the specialist journal, *Quarry and Roadmaking*, so could honestly answer yes. What about the Balkans? pursued his host. Davidson told him what he knew and dropped the names of the best hotels in Belgrade, Bucharest and Sofia.

Davidson passed the test. Just before Christmas 1940 he officially became a member of Section D. It was only then that he learned of his mission.

The first idea was to send me to Belgrade because they had opened a news agency called the Britanova. Then the next idea was to invent one in Hungary next door. That's where I came in. I didn't know anything about Hungary, but I had been there and ignorance of those countries in this country then was practically total. Poland has already gone; Czechoslovakia is going; Hungary we can't be sure of. We therefore should build up a network of contacts, of people who will be our friends.

It was decided that he would begin in Hungary. Late in January 1940 he found himself leasing a spacious office overlooking the Danube in Budapest and hiring staff. Outwardly the news agency, called in Hungarian 'Foreign News', carried out a straightforward job: 'That was an interesting thing to do, taking Ministry of Information telegrams, public information for distribution, nothing secret, nothing invented.'

But there was a clandestine side to this propaganda work. Section D instructed Davidson to wage subversive propaganda war as well.

I was beginning to produce illegal leaflets, anti-Nazi propaganda in Hungarian. I did that through a series of contacts which I made or created. I had a very brilliant journalist called Paloczi-Horvath. He was eager to help; he was anti-Nazi; he wanted to be active. He used to write and translate them into Hungarian from my rough drafts – 'Hungarians, you are being fooled. You are being taken for a ride'. The printing press I found was a state printing press, which could be used at night, not often but occasionally. We were not producing thousands of leaflets every morning – a bundle once a week. We enjoyed the fact the very leaflets were illegal but it was done in a state printing house.

In June 1940, after the fall of France and western Europe,

Davidson found that many more Hungarians were willing to help. Hungary itself was a dictatorship with a powerful fascist movement. While technically neutral, it was under heavy German pressure to co-operate with Berlin. It had also become a refuge for Jews from all over Europe: 'I had an office in Budapest, along the Danube bank and this became known to patriotic Hungarians, especially Jewish Hungarians. It was very obvious indeed that the first people who were going to suffer would be those who could be identified as Jews. There was plenty of evidence of that since we had seen what happened when Austria was sucked into the German orbit. All those Austrians who were against it were eliminated.'

As Nazi pressure increased on the Balkan states and Hungary in 1941, the climate worsened for those supporting the British cause. In the British Legation in Budapest the diplomats became increasingly nervous. The Foreign Office had been suspicious of SOE from the start, fearing its dirty tricks in neutral states could cause problems for its cautious diplomacy. But Baker Street took a far more robust view than the diplomats of what might be achieved through 'subversion'. In practice this usually meant bribery, as Davidson found out after a package arrived from London within a week of his arrival in the Hungarian capital. He also noted that the diplomats, while eager for results, were anxious to wash their hands of the whole business: 'The first message I got, practically speaking, through the embassy channels was a packet of five-pound notes, Bank of England five-pound notes, big white things. They sent me a quantity of these, something like a hundred – to be used to bribe your contacts and to win over friends. I'd practically never seen a five-pound note before.'

But Davidson had a lot to learn about SOE. Instead of taking the money and then finding out how to spend it, 'I sent them all back, of course, because I said I don't know any people, yet. I'd only been in Hungary for about a week. They sent it back to me with a rocket saying you do what you're told, don't ask questions. What happened to the money, dear friend, I'm not in a position to say. I've no doubt it was very useful!'

He soon got another insight into SOE's undercover plans. What would happen if Hungary, despite all his efforts, did join the Nazi camp? Some of the blue diplomatic bags carried across Europe by King's Messenger under diplomatic immunity contained more than letters and despatches and on arrival were promptly assigned to the Legation's cellars.

It was clear that we should build up a reserve of plastic high explosive. This is very handy stuff, very malleable, and a small quantity of that would be useful if we could find people who would use it in a limpet-like fashion. I was in the process of looking for people who would use it and that was very difficult. On the whole I totally failed and built up a reserve of plastic which came in through the Foreign Office bag, which shouldn't have been used for these purposes but were used – unknown to the ambassador, of course.

When 'the local balloon went up', Davidson soon learned, he was to distribute this explosive to volunteers who would use it against enemy shipping on the Danube. Thanks to the SOE boffins at The Frythe, some of the explosive had already been carefully packed inside small containers known as limpets and magnetized for easy fixture to the hulls of ships. He duly found a few helpers prepared to do the work.

Then, one day, he was summoned by the furious British minister. As a security measure he'd asked his military attaché to search the Legation, and the plastic explosive was uncovered. 'He called me in to say, "Are you responsible for this?" I refused to answer. So all our stuff went straight into the Danube. That was a very bitter time, nothing to be done, of course.'

But if SOE still had to face that kind of internal opposition, the national enemy was becoming daily more dangerous. By March 1941 it was clear that Hitler was poised to take action in the Balkans, and Hungary was coming under even greater pressure from Berlin to halt pro-British activity. Davidson thought it time to get out: 'I'm sitting in Budapest, having lunch with the Hungarian Foreign Office man who was my protector, looking across the Danube and seeing troops coming down. I said to him, "Those are Germans." "No," he said, "they can't be." Of course, it was the Wehrmacht on its way to invade Yugoslavia. I said it's time. So I called in my Hungarian friends who were running the agency.

It was clear to them; and we wound up everything like that.'

On 3 April he and some of his team left by train for Belgrade. Three days later Hitler's Luftwaffe subjected the Yugoslav capital to heavy bombing and, along with fellow SOE operatives in Belgrade, Davidson joined the British Legation staff and set off for the coast, where they hoped to be evacuated by submarine. With him was a motley group of people he was determined to get out of Hitler's rapidly expanding Europe. Davidson had nothing but praise for the Ambassador: 'He turned out to be a man of great strength of character and courage called Campbell. He said, "Well, you'd all better be press attachés." So he had fifteen press attachés or whatever it was. Nobody believed that story, of course.'

Davidson eventually ended up in a seaside resort in Montenegro. Here, finally, he was overtaken by Italian troops who had entered the country as part of an occupation deal with the Germans. He and his fellow SOE refugees had reason to be worried. He was not a regular diplomat and, unlike the rest of the Legation staff with whom he was travelling, enjoyed no diplomatic immunity. And the chances were that the Gestapo had a file on him and knew exactly what he'd been up to: 'We were all rounded up and made prisoners of war, fortunately by the Italians, by the fascists and not by the Germans. The Germans knew perfectly who we were and what we'd been up to, the Italians didn't.'

The Italians transferred him, first to Albania, then across the Adriatic back to central Italy.

We were held in a rather comfortable hotel in Tuscany...in a situation which the fascists had organized, it's called *confino*, [which] meant no arrest, imprisonment, but you were put in a place in a village and you could move 100 yards in that direction or 100 yards in the other direction but you were not actually a held prisoner. To escape was easy enough if you walked out of the front door and vanished. But where would we go? Where would you find your friends? There was no army left except in Gibraltar which was 1200 miles away. So it was hard to know what to do.

But salvation was unexpectedly at hand. British forces in East

Africa routed the Italians in Ethiopia and captured their commander, the Duke of Aosta, the cousin of Italy's king. Anxious to get him back, the Italians agreed to an exchange with the British group from Belgrade who were put into a train and eventually reached Lisbon. Davidson and the rest of the SOE contingent were flown to Gibraltar to wait for a plane to London. Here he heard over the radio news of Hitler's attack on the Soviet Union. Soon after he reported back to Baker Street. But if he expected a long and joyful reunion, he was mistaken. Londoners were still under attack from German bombers and Baker Street was preoccupied with its own problems – it still had little to show for its efforts. Davidson described his welcome this way.

> They said, 'Okay, that's fine. You've arrived,' making some silly joke like saying, 'You took rather long getting here, didn't you?' Baker Street at this point was desperately trying to know what they should do next. They were treading water. So we ended up in Istanbul, being the furthest you could get in neutral territory or non-combatant territory and we waited there for…instruction, until it was clear how the Balkan situation was going to unfold.

So, in the autumn of 1941, Basil Davidson found himself in Istanbul. Hitler's troops had entered Kiev, encircled Leningrad, and were racing towards Moscow and Stalingrad. It even seemed possible they might burst through into the Middle East. Churchill, back from his first meeting with Roosevelt off Newfoundland, was still hoping for American entry into the war. And, making its slow and solitary way along the African coast, the *Maid Honor* was heading south for Operation Postmaster.

For Davidson, Istanbul was a paradise, its exotic beauty etching itself indelibly on his memory. Standing on the Asia shore of the Bosphorus, he wrote later:

> There was the unforgettable beckoning of Stamboul on the other shore and the minarets of Aya Sofia and her companion mosques, slim fingers to the sky above the rig and ruck of ships on the Golden Horn, and, along from these, moving east, the

bridge of Pera choked with distant ferries and again, further along, the rising hill of Pera and the cliffs of old Byzantium all barely visible through mist and evening sunlight where they housed, white shadows in the dusk, the fretworked palaces of forgotten lords and pashas.[3]

He was put in charge of re-establishing what contacts he could inside Hungary. With a passport under someone else's name and some minimal disguise, he lived in a small flat near the Pera Palace Hotel, the legendary terminal for passengers detraining from the Orient Express. Here he struggled to do his best with minimal tools. It was a difficult and unrewarding task, a time of mounting misery and frustration that slowly built up into a sense of guilt and pointlessness. After several months he was eager to leave.

But if Hungary seemed barren, other lands occupied by Hitler's and Mussolini's forces held out more promise. One of Davidson's colleagues in Istanbul was David Pawson, on the Greek desk, who had worked in Athens for Section D. Before quitting the Greek capital when the Germans arrived, Pawson had managed to hand over one of SOE's rare W/T sets to a republican Greek colonel who took the codename 'Prometheus'. He in turn passed the set on to a captain in the Greek navy, who took the codename 'Prometheus II'. Late in 1941 he managed to make short-wave contact with SOE in Istanbul using an agreed code. It was based on a Turkish paperback book, one copy of which Pawson sent to Prometheus II while keeping the other himself. He sent the book by courier, using caiques, the small fishing boats crossing the Aegean between Greece and Smyrna. The Turkish secret police turned a blind eye. In this way SOE slowly built up a picture of what was happening in Greece and the possibilities of resistance. All its future operations there were to flow from this small but crucial contact.

Another Balkan state where things were beginning to stir was Yugoslavia. Quickly overwhelmed by the Wehrmacht, King Peter and his government had fled to the Middle East. Meanwhile, their country was dismembered. Croatia (including Bosnia-Herzegovina) became an independent fascist state, while Italy seized western Slovenia and occupied the Adriatic coast and

Montenegro. Germany annexed eastern Slovenia and along with Bulgaria occupied most of Serbia, while Hungary annexed the Vojvodina. Attacks on the occupying forces began almost immediately and by the summer German troops could travel safely only in convoys. The puppet government in Serbia under General Nedic, a former war minister, introduced summary execution for 'anarchist' activities and the Germans began to shoot a hundred Serbs for every German killed.

Only slowly did reports began to filter through to the outside press of armed groups of men operating in the mountains. Escaping Yugoslavs added to the story. Then, in September, a British ship in the Mediterranean picked up signals being transmitted from Serbia by units of the Royal Yugoslav Army that had continued the fight in the hills under the command of a Colonel Draza Mihailovich. A forty-eight-year-old Serb who had fallen out with Nedic before the war, he was now leading a resistance force known as the Chetniks. Soon after, an emissary from Mihailovich arrived in Istanbul with orders to establish links with the outside world. SOE Cairo decided to dispatch an exploratory mission into the country.

They sent Captain Bill Hudson, a South African mining engineer who before the war had managed one of Europe's largest mineral mines, at Trepca in Serbia, and had carried out some useful anti-German sabotage for Section D. A tall, well-built, former amateur boxer, he spoke fluent Serbo-Croat and knew the country well. In September 1941 the British submarine, the *Triumph*, landed him and two officers from the Royal Yugoslav government-in-exile on the Montenegro coast. Within weeks he was sending encouraging intelligence back to Cairo about Yugoslav resistance. In Istanbul, Davidson watched progress with rising hopes.

When I and others in SOE got back to the job at the end of '41 and beginning of '42, we had got a situation in which it was clear that there was a potential resistance – armed resistance in Greece, a potential armed resistance in Yugoslavia, nothing in Bulgaria, nothing in Hungary, but still something to work on. If we could manage to put that together and at the same time build up a means of delivering arms supplies, then it may be possible to form a fighting front which can be provisioned, which can be reinforced, which can be held. It wasn't at all clear whether we could do that, but this is what we set out to do and in fact this is what we did. If you were to ask what could be said for SOE, this organization which had nothing but disasters to report, you could say, well, from these disasters they picked themselves up, dusted themselves down in some way or other and began to form a front of resistance. In a small but decisive way SOE had became a valuable fighting front organization, a means of action. Bill Hudson, with great gallantry and determination, opened up the Yugoslav situation for us.

In London the Yugoslav news came as manna from heaven to Dalton and the Baker Street high command. Here, at last, was promising territory that held out hope of positive action.

Throughout the summer of 1941 Dalton eagerly kept Churchill informed of progress in stirring up trouble in the Balkans. This included news about radio contacts made by SOE Istanbul, sabotage attacks on Axis supplies, and bribes paid out to local officials to obstruct the occupiers. The Prime Minister kept his comments brief – 'good' was the pithy comment he usually scribbled on Dalton's reports, much as a busy schoolteacher might tick the work of a satisfactory student.

But in September he visibly sat up when Dalton passed on details of Mihailovich's guerrillas in the hills of Serbia and of Hudson's landing in Montenegro. 'Thank you very much for this most valuable and interesting report,' he told the SOE minister. 'I have read it with close attention.' As the picture grew more precise, Churchill's enthusiasm grew by leaps and bounds. Here, at last, Europe was beginning to blaze with the flames of resistance he had visualized so graphically the year before in creating SOE.

Early in November he summoned Dalton to see him. In typical Churchillian style it was late at night. The eager SOE minister arrived at the Cabinet War Room at quarter to eleven but was then kept waiting for an hour. When he was finally admitted, a jovial Churchill ordered him to do everything possible to help the guerrillas.[4]

By now, prompted by Whitehall, the BBC was portraying

Mihailovich as an inspirational hero and leader of Balkan resistance. Here was one bright spark of hope inside Fortress Europe. Everything in human power should be done to help Mihailovich, insisted Churchill.

Dalton seized the opportunity to press home demands for greater support from the regular forces. Not even the Japanese attack on Pearl Harbor and its onslaught on the British Empire in the Far East deterred him from pestering the Prime Minister. As Hitler declared war on the United States and Churchill hurriedly prepared to cross the Atlantic to see Roosevelt in the White House, Dalton urged him to give his 'personal attention' to Yugoslavia and keep the revolt going. What was urgently needed, he insisted, was a special air squadron for SOE's exclusive use in dropping agents by parachute. In addition, the Treasury would have to loosen the purse strings. Baker Street estimated that 50,000 gold sovereigns a month would be essential to keep the revolt alive by enabling the guerrillas to buy supplies – and to buy arms from the occupying Italians. Yugoslavia was not a sideshow. It was the first instance of open rebellion. It had to be kept going both for its own sake and as an example for the rest of Europe, especially Greece.

Although Churchill was heavily preoccupied by his Washington visit, all this sank in. After his summit with Roosevelt at the White House he travelled on to Ottawa for talks with Mackenzie King, the Prime Minister of Canada, which for the two years of American neutrality had been Britain's staunchest ally. Asked at a press conference about Yugoslavia, he replied that the Yugoslav guerrillas were fighting with 'the greatest vigour and on a large scale', adding, 'It is all very terrible, guerrilla warfare and the most frightful atrocities by the Germans and Italians, and every kind of torture.' But, he added, 'the people manage to keep the flag of freedom flying'.

These high politics eventually made their impact on Davidson. Steadily during the first six months of 1942 SOE Cairo geared itself up for major operations in the Balkans. In Istanbul, bored and frustrated by lack of progress with operations in Hungary, Davidson requested a transfer. While waiting, he shuttled between Istanbul and the SOE school in Palestine smuggling plastic explosives in diplomatic bags back into Anatolia and on to Smyrna (Izmir), bound by caique for Greece and the emergent guerrilla movement there. Finally, in the summer of 1942, he got his wish. On a regular visit to the SOE office in Jerusalem he learned he was being put in charge of running operations into Yugoslavia. Soon afterwards he found himself proudly inspecting a five-room office suite in the Rustum Buildings in Cairo. Balkan resistance was at last a reality. Even as he unpacked his files, the first SOE mission was being parachuted into Greece.

NOTES
1 Bickham Sweet-Escott, *Baker Street Irregular*, p. 82.
2 Basil Davidson, *Special Operations Europe*, p. 52.
3 Ibid., p. 88.
4 *The Second World War Diary of Hugh Dalton 1940–45*, ed. Ben Pimlott, p. 304.

CHAPTER 7

BLOWING UP BRIDGES

SOE's agents and local guerrillas had been struggling on foot through the rocky slopes of the Greek mountains for weeks. They travelled by night, keeping watch for Italian patrols, making cautious contact with friendly villagers who gave them food, and sleeping in caves or in tents roughly fashioned from the silk parachutes that had landed them safely. It was getting colder by the day; they could see the snowline steadily creeping towards them. Having long since learned to live with lice and fleas, they were tired and dirty.

On the night of 25 November 1942 they finally reached their target: a viaduct built on stone and metal pillars high above the rushing waters of the Gorgopotamos River. And across its 300-metre length ran the single-track line that linked Salonika in the north to Athens and the Mediterranean in the south. Plastic explosive was moulded into the girders of the iron pillars, and the fuse was lit. A few seconds later there was a massive explosion. Two of the bridge's spans rose briefly into the air, hung for a second, then crashed spectacularly into the gorge below. By dawn the next day the saboteurs had melted back into the mountains. For the next six weeks the only railway link from south-eastern Europe to Piraeus – the port of Athens – and across the Mediterranean to North Africa was out of action. It had been carrying as many as forty-eight trains a day packed with supplies for Rommel's troops. Operation 'Harling' – for that was its codename – had been a spectacular success.

Its triumph also reverberated throughout Baker Street. For in bringing down the Gorgopotamos Viaduct, SOE, acting at the military's request, demonstrated conclusively that it could hit targets of direct strategic interest. The mission thus marked another victory over critics at home. It was recorded: 'It showed for the first time in occupied Europe that guerrillas, with the support of

Allied officers, could carry out a major tactical operation co-ordi-nated with Allied strategic plans. It stimulated ambitious plans for developing resistance, primarily in Greece, but also elsewhere.'

These words were coined by 'Monty' Woodhouse, one of the SOE team who blew the Gorgopotamos Viaduct.[1] For him, the story had begun several months before, in Cairo.

An Oxford student with a promising academic career in front of him, Woodhouse had instead found himself in Greece in 1941 as an intelligence officer with the British Military Mission. After Hitler's forces drove out the ill-fated British expeditionary force sent to help the Greeks, he was posted to the SOE training school at Haifa where he learned unarmed combat and how to handle explosives. He then spent six months in German-occupied Crete and was back again in Cairo when Rommel's Afrika Corps drove the British Army back to El-Alamein inside the Egyptian frontier and set off panic in Cairo and London. In the purges of his top generals that followed, Churchill gave Alexander and Montgomery the task of defeating Rommel. Soon they were planning an offen-sive to drive him out of North Africa that would coincide with American and British landings, codenamed Operation 'Torch', on the French North African coast. It was Montgomery's campaign that explained the Harling mission, as Woodhouse found out one day in September 1942.

After his adventures in Crete Woodhouse had grown bored. So when a friend asked him if he'd like to join the SAS (Special Air Service), he decided to resign from SOE. Instead, when he got to its headquarters at Rustum Buildings (known to every Cairo taxi driver as 'the spy house'), he was told that someone had been looking for him: 'In the room to which I was directed sat a lieu-tenant-colonel behind a desk at right-angles to the window. In the blinding light through the window I could only see his profile; I never learned his name. He looked up from the papers on his desk simply to say: "Would you be willing to be parachuted into Greece next week?" Again there seemed no reason to say No, so I said Yes.'[2]

Over the next few days, Woodhouse learned a lot more. At twenty-four, he would be second-in-command of a twelve-man team led by Colonel Eddie Myers, a regular soldier in the Royal Engineers whom Woodhouse quickly learned to appreciate as 'a man of great courage and talent and intelligence'. After parachute training, they would be divided into three teams, each with a wireless operator, and flown over Greece in separate planes that would drop them to a waiting reception party. The explosives and weapons, packed in metal containers, would also be dropped separately so that, if necessary, the groups could act independently. They would contact Greek guerrillas to help them and it would be up to Myers to decide which of three viaducts on the line to blow up. Of the twelve, seven were British, two came from New Zealand, one was half Sikh and half Scottish, and one was Rumanian; he, like Myers, was also Jewish. The only Greek, Themistocles Marinos, a friend of Woodhouse from the Haifa training school, made up the party.

It was virtually mission impossible. Montgomery wanted the line cut *before* the launch of his big offensive at El-Alamein in mid-October. Yet here was Woodhouse being told of the plan only four weeks before. And he, like most of the others, still had no idea how to parachute.

Two days after my arrival in Cairo I was driven to the school for parachutists at Kabrit in the Suez Canal Zone...of the next week I recall only the terrors and the macabre humour. Our instructors were paternally protective towards their own class, but brutally cynical towards everyone else. The flight-sergeant in charge of our course gave us great confidence, telling us that we would all make superb parachutists, unlike the neighbouring class...We watched one of them almost kill himself struggling to free a twisted parachute as he fell like a bomb. 'Stupid clot's done a Roman candle!' remarked our instructor contemptuously. It was understood that under his guidance none of us would be guilty of a Roman candle.[3]

It was not until the end of September that they were ready to go and receive their briefing. Woodhouse only learned later, however, that Montgomery told SOE they had three weeks to destroy it: 'It was inconceivable that we should destroy it within the time limit he imposed, because he simply didn't realize that in Greece you don't drive along motor roads, you walk over mountains. It took longer than three weeks for me to walk across Greece and find two teams of guerrillas. We didn't do it in three weeks, we did it very impressively in five weeks.'

At dusk on 28 September Myers's team boarded three American Liberators and headed north. Four hours later they were over central Greece. But they spotted no trace of the waiting signal on the ground and returned to base. Two days later, they tried again. This time they decided to parachute, ground signal or not. Putting on the padded suit he wore over his British battledress, Woodhouse found a ladybird. It became his special talisman: 'I cherished it all the way across in my aeroplane. And I told myself that I knew I would be all right if the ladybird was still there when I arrived in Greece. And thank goodness it was. I opened my harness and there was the little ladybird inside and I kept it as long as I could.'

His parachute training, as well as the ladybird, stood him in good stead. His landing was far better than any he had done in the desert. Although the ground was steep, he found landing 'no harder than stepping off a table'. The wireless set attached to his harness fell neatly behind him. His parachute almost folded itself, as there was no wind to carry it away. At last, he was back in Greece. He lit a red flare to guide the aircraft for its next run, with their stores, and signalled in Morse with his torch, 'Harling OK'.

As he was busy doing this, a group of men scrambled up the hillside out of the darkness towards him.

The first thing we met was a group of young Greek officers who just happened to be there because they were hoping for a drop of explosives to be used in an operation that they were engaged on at the Corinth Canal. Our meeting was a tremendous occasion. They saw four men in parachutes coming down. One of them, rather alarmed, shouted, 'Germans.' Another one stood his ground, and as soon as I touched the ground I called out to him, 'I am a British officer.' To which he replied, 'I am a Greek officer,' and rushed forward and kissed me on both cheeks. I was terribly sorry for him because I couldn't afford to give him any of my explosives. We needed the whole lot.

Woodhouse was less fortunate in guarding his plastic explosive from some other members of the population, however: 'We found some children in the neighbourhood who were very excited by the explosive, which they thought was fudge. They started eating it and making themselves sick. This was disastrous for them, but it was also disastrous for us, because it was reducing our essential explosives. But very characteristically their grandfather said they were silly children and it served them right.'

Two things quickly became clear. As the mix-up with the Greek officers revealed, no one really knew what was going on, neither those on the ground nor the SOE team being dropped to help. And, second, the local population was friendly and the agents needed their help.

Intelligence about what was happening inside Greece, especially in the remote interior, was fragmentary. SOE's principal source was still Prometheus II, who began passing on news about *andartes* (guerrillas) operating in the mountains. When asked by Cairo if one of the railway viaducts would be a feasible target, Prometheus II answered yes – provided the British could provide help to the local *andartes* by way of demolitions experts and explosives. The Athens group also requested an officer equipped with a wireless set who could act as a liaison with a retired republican army colonel known to have organized a guerrilla band in western Greece, a man named Napoleon Zervas. Woodhouse was selected by Cairo as the contact with Zervas. But little was known about him or any other of the partisan groups, and because of a garbled transmission Woodhouse was dropped a considerable distance away from Zervas's headquarters. Neither he nor Myers received any briefing in depth on the guerrillas before leaving Cairo.

After several days spent regrouping, collecting their supplies, finding a secure base in a cave on the slopes of Mount Giona, they sent out messengers on foot to Athens seeking more information about various guerrilla groups. In the meantime, Myers instructed Woodhouse to go and find Colonel Zervas. He set off with one of the villagers, Barba (Uncle) Niko, who gave the SOE agents tremendous help, introduced them to other villagers, and located a safe hideaway for them. A butcher by trade, Barba Niko had lived for a while in the United States and could speak some English.

'He knew people and things,' recalled Woodhouse, 'and would make the impossible possible.'[4]

Barba Niko appeared among us quite suddenly with a kind of saucepan and with his little daughter. They came and sat down by us and just obviously wanted to help us, nothing else. He would go anywhere to make people send what we needed. If he went to a village where the head man wouldn't send us any supplies because it was too dangerous, Barba Niko would reply, 'You, my fellow, are not living, you are wandering about on the surface of the earth without object or purpose.' That was the way he rebuked people. His little daughter brought her needle and thread and stitched up our clothes and we gave her a parachute so that she could make herself a wedding dress. I remember one day Eddie asking Barba Niko, who had been with us for weeks and weeks, why he had devoted himself so completely to helping the British. Barba Niko replied in Greek, 'Because God told me from heaven that the English were coming and I knew it was my duty to service them.'

But the old man was soon defeated by the rough terrain and Woodhouse sent him back to Myers's group in the cave. A week later, walking fifteen miles a day, he himself reached Zervas's headquarters. As he introduced himself, Woodhouse could hear artillery fire from a nearby battle against an Italian patrol. The man who emerged from one of the huts was portly and wearing a well-cut khaki tunic and breeches, and a brown leather cap. He greeted Woodhouse with a kiss on both cheeks. 'Welcome to the Angel of Good Tidings,' he said, with obvious satisfaction. Woodhouse wrote a formal note placing himself at Zervas's disposal as his liaison with GHQ Cairo. Then he explained what he wanted him to do. Zervas immediately agreed. 'From that moment,' wrote Woodhouse, 'I had an unreasoning confidence that the Gorgopotamos bridge was as good as destroyed.'[5]

Unknown at this stage to Woodhouse, Zervas had enjoyed a colourful and disreputable career, having turned professional gambler after being cashiered from the Greek army following his involvement in a *coup d'état*. Now he headed the National

Republican Greek League (known as EDES, its Greek initials), a guerrilla force of several thousand based mainly in north-west Greece, his homeland. Despite Zervas's faults, Woodhouse liked him from the start: 'He was a big man, a jolly man. He enjoyed life; he made mistakes. He was devoted to me. He was an unscrupulous man; he liked sovereigns. He wasn't absolutely, totally honest. He believed in getting things done in the way that suited him. He had very good officers under him, very good officers.'

It was now that Woodhouse found the supply of gold sovereigns given to him by SOE Cairo, securely hidden in his belt, invaluable. There was no doubting Zervas's good will or desire to fight the enemy. But hard evidence of British gratitude was always appreciated and his force, too, required the means to purchase food and supplies. He had with him about sixty or seventy men. It was obvious to Woodhouse at first glance that they were pitifully equipped: 'Few had any military uniform. Even fewer had boots: leather slippers, strips of goatskin tied around their ankles, slices of rubber tyre fastened with wire, in some cases nothing but threadbare socks. Apart from one tommy-gun and a light machine-gun captured from the Italians, they had no weapons but Mannlicher rifles, an Austrian product from before World War I.'[6]

Zervas's EDES was not the only guerrilla force in the mountains of central Greece. There was a rival group, the Communists. Soon after landing, Myers and Woodhouse had learned something about them from local gossip. Their movement was known as ELAS, the National People's Liberation Army, and it was led locally by a man known as Aris Veloukhiotis, a former schoolmaster who claimed to have been trained in Moscow. Woodhouse and Myers realized they would need his co-operation if they were to get the numbers that the attack on the viaduct would require. So Woodhouse had a messenger take him a handwritten note requesting help. By this time Myers had carried out a reconnaissance of all three viaducts and decided that the one over the Gorgopotamos presented the best target. Local Greeks provided him with the back-up intelligence he needed about the Italian garrison guarding it, such as their strength and details of the barbed-wire fencing surrounding the viaduct's piers.

Three days after Woodhouse set off with Zervas to join up with the rest of the SOE party, Aris, bringing a band of his own *andartes*, met up with them. While the three men conferred in a house in the local village, the two partisan groups mingled uneasily in the square. It was the first time Zervas and Aris had met. Each was deeply suspicious of the other. Aris made no secret of his Communist sympathies, nor of his ruthless attitude towards dissent within his movement. Aris's men seemed tougher and more determined than those of Zervas, and were subject to much harsher discipline, as Woodhouse recalled.

> Aris would without hesitation shoot one of his own men who didn't agree with him. He murdered or executed a young air force officer, a Greek who wanted to join Zervas, and Aris regarded that as treason and shot him. I realized I was dealing with a very tough organization under Aris, but we had to have him, otherwise he would fight us. We continued the following day our walk towards the railway line, and Aris's band and Zervas's band went more or less in step together, until they got to a certain village. Aris stopped there and conducted a private meeting with his own fellow Communists at this village. Zervas and I went on because we were in a hurry, we had to get to the river, to the railway line. I didn't know whether Aris was now going to desert us. But he didn't; he followed us a day or two later. Obviously the leading Communists in the area had told him to go ahead and help us and not sabotage our operation – a mercy for us. With Zervas's team alone we would not have had enough.

This alliance of necessity soon provided an early example of Aris's ruthlessness and of the difficult position Woodhouse now found himself in. Woodhouse was also made aware of Aris's hostility to himself as a British officer and the fact that the ELAS leader might defect at any moment. Themi Marinos's group, travelling separately from the other two after being dropped three weeks later, had quickly run into Aris's men. Despite their motley garb, all wore caps with the ELAS insignia. Marinos thought this was a misspelling of ELLAS – Greece. When they explained what it meant, he was almost overcome: 'I became enthusiastic, national pride swelling within me and shivers of patriotism running through my body. My thoughts did not turn to politics as I was not interested in their political beliefs. For me those men were brothers, patriots, fighters against the occupier.'[7]

He assumed they were on the same side, but quickly had to qualify his view when he met Aris face to face. Instead of a warm greeting, the ELAS leader accused them of being German spies, locked them up, and ordered Marinos to be shot. He only relented when he realized the popular enthusiasm that had greeted his visitor in the surrounding villages. 'They are agents of the imperialists and capitalists who have come to work against our people,' was his first response. 'They may knock down some bridge, but they principally came to divide us, make us kill each other so they can put us back in their harness.'[8] Only his calculation that not supporting Operation Harling would damage his local credibility, and a determination to prevent Zervas from gaining all the glory, led him to collaborate with the SOE group.

Two or three days into their joint march towards the bridge, the ELAS group captured a gypsy carrying an Italian identity card with his name on it. Woodhouse recalled the gruesome outcome.

He admitted that he was paid by the Italians to report on the Resistance. Aris insisted that he should be hanged and I had to witness that he was hanged. It was a time when I couldn't offer a denial, while I was still very uncertain about how Aris was going to respond to our operation. And there's no doubt this wretched youth was a spy. He had accepted money from the Italians, and if we let him go, he would go back to the Italians and give us away. This was three or four days before we were due to attack the bridge. Zervas would not have done that; Zervas would have let him off. But you could never induce Aris to be tolerant. You'd just be getting yourself into worse trouble. I can only say I felt very ashamed of this.

Two days later Woodhouse was reunited with Myers in the cave on Mount Giona. They had agreed on a deadline of 17 November for Woodhouse to return. Myers looked at his watch and said, 'You're quarter of an hour late,' then laughed. He could afford the joke.

Now, with both Zervas and Aris on board, the group could finally turn its attention to the bridge they'd come to destroy.

For a couple of days the SOE team put the *andartes* through a concentrated version of Arisaig training on how to use Sten guns and Mills hand grenades. The exercise was marked with great enthusiasm but little experience, which had Woodhouse dreading the casualties that might occur even before they attacked the target. Fortunately there were none. At dawn on 23 November the force of about 150 men and twenty mules loaded with explosives and weaponry moved off to its forward base, a deserted sawmill about a six-hour walk from the viaduct. Travelling through a blizzard in intense cold, they reached the mill that afternoon and made camp. The next day Myers, Woodhouse, Aris and Zervas made a final reconnaissance of the bridge and confirmed that their existing intelligence about the disposition of the Italian garrison was correct.

Although Zervas was in nominal command, Myers drew up the plan of attack. The *andartes* were split into seven groups; two would attack the Italians guarding each end of the viaduct; two would head north and south along the railway line to neutralize any reinforcements the Italians might call up; one was to occupy a small wooden road bridge about four kilometres away to halt any road reinforcements. The sixth was the demolition party, headed by Major Tom Barnes, one of the New Zealanders, which included guerrillas of both forces as well as auxiliary helpers for unloading the explosives from the mules. The seventh group was the command post, with a thirty-man reserve force for any unforeseen circumstances. From here, high up the gorge on its northern side, Myers, Woodhouse, Aris and Zervas directed the action.

At 10.00 pm on the evening of 25 November they left the sawmill, walking in single file down the steep mountainside in heavy drizzle and intense darkness, each man occasionally touching the man in front so as not to get lost. Five hundred metres short of the bridge they parted for their separate tasks. Zero hour for the attack was 11.00 pm, with simultaneous attacks on the pillboxes at the two ends of the bridge. Unexpectedly and unscheduled, a minute before zero hour a train packed with people crossed from the south. After a short delay to let it clear, the attack opened.

According to Woodhouse: 'They began with hand grenades thrown into the pillboxes. Of course a lot of Italians burst out; a lot were killed and a lot came out. But they came out with no morale and mostly they just ran away and were shot by the guerrillas. It was just a sort of shambles of noise.'

While this battle was being fought, down in the gorge Barnes and his group were making their way towards the pillars of the bridge. This meant crossing the river to its south bank, a particularly tricky task with the numbers of mules they had, as Woodhouse explained.

There was only one plank bridge. The explosives were loaded on the mules and they were led across by their favourite mule-teers. It had to be the right muleteer which led each mule, because mules are mules and they wouldn't go with a rival leader. So we lined them up and walked them across the bridge. We had to make absolutely sure that none of them slipped into the water. If a dead mule had floated down the river with explosives on his back even the Italians would have noticed it.

But all went well. It was an hour before Myers signalled to Barnes that the Italians had been overcome and he could safely start laying his charges. Running down the gorge from the command post to a point where he could look straight across the valley, he flashed his torch and shouted at the top of his voice: 'Go in, Tom! The south end of the bridge is in our hands. Go in! I will join you as soon as possible.'⁹ Barnes swiftly moved to the pillars and attached the plastic explosive. This took longer than expected because in his earlier reconnaissance Myers, looking through binoculars, had misjudged the shape of the pillars and thought they were L-shaped. But they were U-shaped, and Barnes's team had to remould the plastic, which they'd carefully shaped before setting off, to fit. The task done, he loudly blew a whistle, lit the fuse, and everyone took cover. There was a flash, a rumble, and two spans of the bridge rose a few feet in the air and then fell into the gorge.

At the command post, Woodhouse joined hands with Aris and Zervas and the three of them danced and sang a Greek ballad, 'Three Lads of Volos'. Myers, who had left them to inspect the damage, then ordered Barnes to use his remaining explosives to wreck the severed piers to make them totally unusable. The whole affair was over by 2.30am, when the guerrilla force headed back to the sawmill. Struggling through thick snow, they reached it well before dawn.

There was only one casualty on the guerrilla side, an *andarte* hurt by a piece of flying shrapnel from the explosion. But if up to this point the story resembled a glorified Boy Scout caper, the grim events that followed foreshadowed a far more brutal future.

At least thirty of the Italian garrison were killed in the attack and, contrary to orders, Zervas's men took a prisoner back to the sawmill. Here, the ruthless Aris took charge of him. The next day the ELAS group left with the hapless man. He had been stripped to his underwear and socks and he cried out in pain as they dragged him through the snow and rocks. When he couldn't move any more, they kicked him, blue and shaking with cold. Finally Aris announced he should be executed. Myers protested, as did Woodhouse, but Aris insisted. Eventually Myers, now fairly exhausted, gave way. The guerrillas pushed forward a sixteen-year-old boy, a shepherd, who had not joined in with the others to taunt and kick the prisoner. 'He'll kill him with a knife,' shouted the partisans, shoving a knife in his hand. 'He hasn't blooded himself yet.' To the terrified boy they laughed: 'Now you'll show what a man you are and if you can cut throats.'[10] Aris stood smiling. Before the slaughter, they removed the last of the Italian's clothing. Afterwards, they threw his body in a ditch.

This murder in turn provoked an even more barbaric response by the Italians, as Woodhouse recorded: 'They took fifteen or sixteen villagers, completely innocent villagers who just happened to be walking round. They took them to the bridge, sat them down at the foot of the bridge, at one of the pillars we had broken down, and shot them. It was a terrible, terrible war.'

This should dispel any notion that the Italians, by contrast with the Germans, were a benevolent occupying force in Greece. The destruction of the Gorgopotamos provoked an immediate German response. The next day General Loehr, commander of the 5th Army Group, reported to the Supreme Command in Berlin that he had ordered repairs on the sabotaged bridge to begin and estimated it would take a week to repair. In the event, it took six. After that, the Germans took over the guarding of the bridge themselves.

There is now a memorial at the bridge listing all the names of the murdered hostages. Woodhouse returned to the scene ten years later.

> We had a ceremony at the scene of the operation, very grand, with Cabinet ministers and generals. Eddie Myers and I were together watching what was going on. Two little old men, whom we'd never met in our lives, came to Eddie and myself and said, 'We must thank you for what you did for us.' These were two Jews. Eddie rather sheepishly said, 'Well, I'm afraid we didn't do anything for you.' One of the two old men said, 'Never mind, you were there, you were there.' That really moved him, and moved me.

The civilian massacre was unknown until later by the guerrillas. After the murder of the Italian prisoner and another day's walk into the mountains, they went their separate ways. While the SOE group and Zervas headed west, towards Epirus and the coast, Aris and his ELAS group stayed in the central highlands. The Gorgopotamos operation was the first and last time they worked together. From now on politics and an increasingly brutalized civil war would mar their relations.

Woodhouse had been told before leaving Cairo that while he would stay in Greece as liaison officer with Zervas, the others would be evacuated by submarine from the west coast. But the success of Harling led GHQ to change its mind. Now they could see SOE carrying out further useful operations. By the time this was signalled by wireless to Woodhouse, the group to be evacuated had been waiting for several days for the submarine. When Woodhouse caught up with them and passed on the news, some of them were furious. Unlike Woodhouse, who loved Greece and the Greeks, not all of them were so enthusiastic. But they had little choice. Over the next few months they formed the nucleus of what became a larger and larger SOE presence among the Greek guerrillas. Within months, this time acting without the help of Aris and his ELAS guerrillas, they destroyed the Asopos viaduct carrying the same railway line which was blocked for four months. Baker Street was again thrilled and quickly let Churchill have the news. A delighted Prime Minister chuckled and pored over photographs of the damage. But as subsequent events were to reveal, the true picture in Greece was to become far more grim for SOE.

NOTES

1 C. M. Woodhouse, *The Struggle for Greece*, p. 26.
2 C. M. Woodhouse, *Something Ventured*, p. 21.
3 Ibid., p. 22.
4 Ibid., p. 34.
5 Ibid., p. 41.
6 Ibid., p. 42.
7 Themistocles Marinos, *Harling Mission 1942*, p. 72.
8 Ibid., p. 73.
9 Quoted in Ian Dear, *Sabotage and Subversion*, p. 58.
10 Marinos, op. cit., p. 134.

CHAPTER 8

'THESE HEROIC MEN'

'Of all our operations,' wrote Hugh Dalton in his memoirs about SOE, 'that against German heavy water supplies in Norway was, in my view, by far the most important.' By delaying progress in German research on the atomic bomb it ensured that the first nuclear weapons to be dropped in history fell on Hiroshima, not London.[1]

Since Dalton wrote, it's become clear that Nazi atomic research was probably on the wrong track. But hindsight shouldn't diminish the extraordinary achievement of the small handful of SOE-trained Norwegians who destroyed the heavy water supply at the Norsk Hydro plant in southern Norway on the night of 27/28 February 1943. Even Gubbins, not known for his loquacity, described it as 'an enthralling story of high adventure'.[2] Hollywood agreed, celebrating the achievement with its swashbuckling version of events starring Kirk Douglas, *The Heroes of Telemark*.

The story began in 1941. Late that year secret intelligence from Nazi-occupied Norway filtered through to the Secret Intelligence Service about a massive increase in heavy water production at the Norsk Hydro plant at Vemork, near Rjukan, in the region of Telemark, about 80 kilometres west of Oslo. British scientists were already well embarked on their own quest for an atomic bomb and immediately recognized the potential significance of this news: heavy water – otherwise known as deuterium – was an essential component in the production of plutonium necessary for construction of a bomb.

So seriously was this viewed that the War Cabinet ordered SOE and SIS as a matter of 'the highest possible priority' to neutralize the threat. Frantic discussions over the summer of 1942 produced a plan. In October SOE would parachute a party of four Norwegians (codenamed 'Grouse') into southern Norway to prepare the way for a direct attack on the Vemork plant the next month by a Combined Operations party of thirty-four commandos. This large group (codenamed 'Freshman') would land near the target from gliders towed by planes from Scotland. The Grouse team would receive them and guide them to the target.

Grouse was made up exclusively of Norwegians, as were all missions (with one exception) sent by SOE to Norway. Norwegian society was small, intimate and closed. Strangers, however good their Norwegian, would immediately be identified, and possibly denounced. Norway, after all, had suffered the misfortune of producing Vidkun Quisling, whose pro-Nazi 'fifth column' movement had welcomed the Germans with open arms and whose name had become (as it remains) a byword for collaborator or traitor. It would take only one Quisling in a small community to bring all SOE's efforts to a halt. Quisling's treachery at home hardened the patriotism of those in exile. The King of Norway and his government had left the country rather than submit to the Germans, and were based in Britain. With them went thousands of seamen from the large Norwegian merchant fleet. They were all determined that liberating their country and redeeming its reputation should be the work of Norwegians.

Then there was the terrain: harsh, mountainous, remote, mostly roadless and for most of the year under a dense cover of snow and intensely cold. Even hardened Norwegians, as events were to prove, found survival tough; few British agents would have made it.

This was why SOE training for their Norwegian agents was especially rigorous, and why they had their own separate school near Aviemore, on the edge of the Cairngorms in Scotland, the harshest mountain terrain in Britain. Knut Haukelid, one of those involved in this story, described his training this way: 'We lived a good, tiring, open-air life…The British soldiers' rations were comparatively slender for the big Norwegian lads, and without extras from the mountains and rivers we would have lived much less well than we did…The object of the life was clear. We were to learn to fend for ourselves, like the men of ancient Sparta.'[3]

After weeks of strenuous exercise (including parachute jumps at Ridgway), four men were picked for the Grouse team. Its leader was Jens Poulsson, a first-rate hunter. His second-in-command was Arne Kjelstrup, a plumber from Oslo wounded during the German invasion who'd reached Britain after a lengthy odyssey via Sweden, Russia, Iran, South Africa and the United States. The party's wireless operator was Knut Hauglund (who later joined the famous *Kon-Tiki* expedition), an agent considered a 'terrific coder' by SOE. The party was completed by Claus Helberg – 'the sort of man', wrote Haukelid, 'who might at any moment have a piece of bad luck and get into fearful difficulties, but he had also a remarkable capacity for getting out of them'.

This was no overstatement. Helberg's exploits even before he joined SOE were notable in their daring. Captured during the German invasion of Norway, he faked illness, escaped from the ambulance taking him to hospital, skied to Sweden and made contact with Malcolm Munthe – nominally the assistant military attaché at the British Legation in Stockholm but in reality running secret operations in Norway. Early in 1941 he was back in his homeland on the first of several clandestine trips providing intelligence about the Germans and reconnoitring possible landing sites on the west coast of Norway for clandestine transports from Britain.

Helberg was driven by an angry determination to liberate his country from the humiliation of 1940 and by his firm conviction that Britain under Churchill would win the war.

> I was extremely angry to be invaded in such a brutal way and disappointed because the Germans didn't meet any resistance along the coast. We were too weak, we were not prepared. In that period I was quite depressed. Three or four weeks after I had escaped from the military prison camp, and after Paris had fallen, I met a friend of mine in the street in Oslo and I said I am depressed because of the situation and he said, no, you should cheer up, now Churchill has taken over as the Prime Minister, so he was quite certain that Britain would win at the end. After that talk with him I was quite certain that Great Britain and Norway would win in the end.

Eventually Helberg was flown to Britain, where he promptly joined the Norwegian forces. But within weeks Malcolm Munthe, who had been expelled by the Swedes as *persona non grata* for his clandestine activities and was now in Baker Street, had recruited him for SOE. It gave Helberg exactly what he wanted – the chance to hit back at the Germans: 'When I got into the SOE I knew that now it was a possibility that I could be sent back to Norway, to do something, to do a job, to do sabotage. I waited for the possibility to get back to Norway and I was very pleased when I understood at the autumn time 1942 that I would be sent back in connection with an action at Vemork.'

Essential to the mission assigned to Helberg and the others was precise and up-to-date intelligence about the Norsk Hydro plant itself: exactly where the heavy water was manufactured and stored, detailed plans of the interior, points of entry and exit, internal plant security, and, of course, where and how it was guarded from outside.

To this end SOE had already stage-managed a particularly skilful *coup*. One of the Norsk Hydro engineers was named Einar Skinnarland. Like Helberg and many other young Norwegians he dreamed of escaping to Britain. In March 1942 he took a month's holiday and with ten other like-minded friends hijacked a small coastal steamer across the North Sea to Aberdeen. SOE at once realized his potential. If they could brief and train him in time he could be parachuted back to Vemork and resume his job at the heavy water plant before anyone knew he'd even been in Britain.

After hasty parachute training, he was dropped back home just eleven days after arriving in Scotland. It was only the second parachute operation to Norway carried out by the RAF. Norway was ill-suited to air operations. Possible dropping grounds were few and far between, the mountains were thickly clustered, and the terrain threw up treacherous air pockets and currents. And weather conditions were rarely the same in Britain and Norway. A night of ideal take-off weather in Britain might be treacherous over Norway, or vice versa. No wonder that most Norwegians went instead by boat, via the Shetland Bus operation from northern Scotland.

After a nervous landing Skinnarland returned to work, his absence unnoticed. He made contact with the chief engineer of the plant who provided extensive details of its working which Skinnarland arranged to be sent back to Baker Street. Of all SOE's operations this was probably the most well-informed, its intelligence on the factory and its site perfect down to the last detail.

In London, SOE's cryptographic genius Leo Marks carefully briefed the Norwegians on their codes. As he entered the Norwegian section's flat in Chiltern Court, just off Baker Street, its head,

Colonel Jack Wilson, greeted him. 'I don't expect them to send much traffic,' he said casually, 'but what they do send could be pretty important. I don't want one indecipherable!' Marks found the group disciplined and impressive, and their coding excellent.[4] On the night of 18 October 1942 – three weeks after 'Monty' Woodhouse's group had parachuted into Greece for Operation Harling – the Grouse team boarded a Halifax bomber of the Special Duties Squadron 138 for the flight to Norway. Piloting the aircraft was Squadron Leader Ron Hockey, an airman credited with many of SOE's most difficult long-distance operations. Four hours later he dropped them successfully into a desolate mountain plateau close to Vemork. It was only then that Helberg learned what the mission was – and realized the importance of one of his earlier missions for Munthe.

> I was hurt by the landing, I hit a stone, it was rather rough terrain, stony, no snow, but I wasn't too badly hurt and Poulsson told us in an hour or two that the mission was to receive British soldiers coming by gliders and our task will be to accompany them down to Vemork and I remember I said to Jens Poulsson, 'Well, at one of the missions I went to Norway from Stockholm I got information about heavy water at Vemork. I was told that the Germans increased the production of heavy water and I brought this information back to [Munthe].'

Helberg and the others also decided that the plan almost amounted to a suicide mission. For even if successful in attacking the plant, how were the commandos to get away afterwards? Helberg remembered: 'We said to each other that this is going to be a suicide mission for the British because we couldn't see how they could get back from Vemork to Britain. Maybe they had their own plans but we knew nothing about that.'

In the meantime they had their own mission to concentrate on. With them were six containers and two packages weighing 250 kilos containing their skis, a W/T set, a Eureka homing device (a portable battery-operated radar kit with a five-foot mast to enable them to guide an aircraft to a drop site), a Sten gun, two accumulators, and food for a month. As each man could only carry 30 kilos, he had to make two trips every day. Fortunately the team quickly acquired a ski toboggan on which all the heavy equipment could be carried. Even then their journey to the base at which they would wait to receive the Freshman party was almost enough to finish them off. The ground was exceptionally rugged, the snow heavy and deep, and milder than usual weather meant it stuck to their skis and made progress slow and exhausting. The ice on lakes and rivers was unreliable and more than once they either had to make long detours or fell through the ice, getting cold and soaked in the process. After a week, Poulsson later reported, 'We were fairly done in.' But eventually, three weeks after their landing, they arrived at the base and Hauglund radioed the news to SOE. Ten days later he received the codeword 'Girl'. It meant that Freshman would land that night.

Back at Skitten airbase outside Wick, in northern Scotland, the Freshman team took off in two gliders, each towed by a Halifax bomber, shortly after 6.00 pm. Six hours later, at five minutes before midnight, the radio operator in the first plane reported that it had released the first glider. All seemed well. On the ground, the Grouse team waited expectantly. Earlier that night they'd placed torches on the landing site and set up the Eureka set. Helberg recalled the sense of excitement as they heard it emit the distinct 'beep' it made on contact with the receiving set on the leading aircraft.

We knew now they are not far away from us and we are very excited of course at this, now they are on the way and they couldn't miss and then we heard an aircraft engine and we knew that in a few minutes they will land, the gliders will land here. Then the sound of the engines disappeared and then the sound of the Eureka, we didn't hear it any more, it disappeared and we understood it had lost contact with us but we didn't understand why and so we went back to base.

Helberg and his friends were not to know that disaster had struck. The first plane had encountered dense fog over southern Norway and both it and the glider began to collect ice. Both rapidly lost altitude and the glider, once released, immediately crashed on the coast north of Stavanger. The Halifax returned safely to Scotland. Its companion, however, almost certainly the one that briefly made contact with the Eureka, failed to show up. At nine minutes before midnight it signalled Wick for directions home. That was the last that was heard from it. This plane, too, had been plagued by icing. Flying low, it and its glider hit a mountainside near Egersund just four minutes after its last signal home.

There were heavy casualties all round. Of the seventeen men in the first glider, only nine survived and four of these were badly wounded. Fourteen commandos survived the second glider crash, but three of them were critically injured. None of the crew of the Halifax tow plane made it out – wreckage of the aircraft and remnants of its crew were found strewn over hundreds of metres of mountainside.

The Germans then inflicted savagery on the survivors. The four seriously injured commandos from the first glider were taken to Stavanger jail and injected by the Gestapo with a mixture of morphine and air. Semi-conscious, one was hanged from a radiator by a leather strap and lifted up and down until he was dead. Another had his head banged on he floor until he too died. The neck of the third was crushed by Nazi boots and the fourth was shot in the back of the head. The corpses of all four were then driven to the quayside in a truck, weighted with stone, and sunk offshore. The other five survivors of the first glider were sent to a concentration camp in Oslo and kept in solitary confinement. Several months later they were shot.

The fourteen who survived the crash of the second glider fared little better. Assuming they would be treated as POWs, since they were in uniform, they gave themselves up to the Germans and were taken to a military hospital that same night. Hours later they were taken out, made to stand by the roadside, and shot in the head, one by one. Their bodies were then buried on a local beach.

The fate of these men was the result of a personal order by Hitler. Worried by the rising tide of resistance across Europe and provoked by a commando raid on the Channel Islands, he had issued a general order just the month before that all those carrying out sabotage operations should be wiped out, whether or not they were wearing uniforms and whether or not they had willingly surrendered. Even those spared for interrogation, declared Hitler, should be shot immediately afterwards. This was the grim backdrop against which all SOE operations now took place.

With the failure of the commando raid, what was to be done about the Norsk Hydro plant?

It was decided to send in a hand-picked SOE team of six Norwegians, codenamed 'Gunnerside'. Its leader was Joachim Ronneberg, a training officer in sabotage and demolition at Aviemore. Summoned to London, he was told about the Freshman disaster and the urgent need to destroy the heavy water at Vemork. He was left in little doubt about the importance of the task and quickly chose his team. He had a clear view of the qualities needed: 'I knew most of the people so it was easy. The difficulty was actually to pick out the five I wanted to take because there were so many that were more or less equally good. [I wanted] people with the right fighting spirit and also people who had quite a bit of good humour so that they could take situations and make them probably able to laugh off difficulties and that sort of thing. That was very important and they had to be very social.'

The five he chose were Knut Haukelid, Fredrik Kayser, Kasper Idland, Hans Storhaug and Birger Stromsheim. Haukelid, who should have dropped with the Grouse party had he not injured himself in training, later published a classic memoir of the mission under the title *Skis Against the Atom*.

Urgency was the order of the day. The Gunnerside team went through a short course in sabotage and were briefed thoroughly on the Rjukan plant by Professor Leif Tronstadt, a Norwegian scientist and exile in Britain who knew the factory inside out. Evidence culled from the ill-fated commando raid had put the Germans on their guard and they had laid a minefield around the Norsk Hydro plant and installed floodlights. 'They will do all they can to catch you,' warned Tronstadt. Grimly, he gave them only a 50 per cent chance of surviving. All were issued with SOE's death pill, cyanide in a rubber cover that once bitten through ensured death in three seconds. Ronneberg never forgot: 'We knew everything, we knew that the people had been taken in uniform and that those who had not been killed in the crash were shot and that those who were severely wounded they were taken to hospital and experimented on until they died and were thrown into the North Sea. It takes some time to get used to the idea that this is probably the last thing you do but we knew what occupation was and we fought against it willingly.'

But winter could also kill. Ronneberg went to considerable pains to equip his men with the best winter kit he could find. Their woollen battledress provided good basic clothing but what would they sleep in? They would travel light, without tents, so special sleeping bags were needed.

I remember I went down to a very expensive bedding firm in London, down in the area around Leicester Square and Piccadilly Circus, and went in there and the man behind the desk sort of looking at me, saying what are you asking for? But I got the name of a production director down at the docks and took a taxi down and talked to him about sleeping bags. I said I was a Norwegian officer and we were training outside in Scotland and we needed a light and warm sleeping bag. He said, 'Well, I've never done it before but if you can tell me how to make it I will make it for you,' and so we sat down at the table with paper and pencil and I told what I wanted and we made sketches and so on, and after about an hour he said, 'Well, you just come back tomorrow afternoon and see what I've done.' And when I came the next day there was a sleeping bag ready on the table. It was just what I wanted.

There was extensive briefing on the target. This was where on-site intelligence sources proved their worth, a point Ronneberg never forgot.

They had all the models because the production director at Vemork had been taken through Sweden to Britain and had brought all the drawings and things so they had built mock-up models in full scale and we could just go in there and train. It was very impressive because you had never been there but you knew it exactly, how the buildings were placed compared to each other and where you could get cover and so on. I remember Professor Tronstadt told me one day – just more or less by fun, I think – 'If you need a room to lock up the Norwegian watchman, the key for the lavatory is on the left-hand side of the door when you leave the high concentration room.' They had contacts in the community and if anything changed, and if there was a new guard posted or anything, they would know it immediately.

The drop was due for December but was postponed because of bad weather. In the meantime they waited in the Norwegian country section house, Gaynes Hall, in St Neots in Cambridgeshire. It left a vivid memory on Haukelid:

> The place was very closely guarded. A number of servicewomen kept the house in order, cooked the meals, and gave the men some social life. They belonged to the special section called 'Fannies' (FANYs). These girls did an uncommonly good job, seeing that everything went as it should and doing their best to prevent the delays from getting on our nerves. And, when the commandant suggested it, they were always willing to come to Cambridge in the evening for a little party…The Fannies had their own cars, and very fine ones. When we drove into Cambridge for an evening it was usually to the best restaurant in the city where we would eat and drink at the expense of the War Office; the main thing being to enjoy ourselves as much as possible before we went the way of the gliders.[5]

Finally, on the night of 23/24 January 1943, the team received their final briefing and boarded their Halifax. But further frustration was to come. The aircraft reached southern Norway but there it encountered fog, couldn't locate the drop zone and was forced to return to Britain. The next flight would have to wait another month until the moon was right.

In the meantime, Ronneberg and his men, at their own request, were accommodated in a small crofter's cottage on an island off the Scottish coast. In mid-February, as the full moon approached, they were taken down south again to be near the airbase.

'At eleven each morning,' recalled Haukelid, 'a notice was put up saying whether an operation for our section might be expected in the evening. "No operation today" was the continual refrain. Sometimes we were told to be ready to start that evening. But in the course of the day, a post supervisor would come and tell us that the order had been cancelled. One day we waited a long time for the supervisor. He did not come…In the evening we went in cars to the airfield.'[6] The date was 16 February 1943. Two weeks before, Field-Marshal von Paulus and his German

6th Army had surrendered at Stalingrad. The tide of war was beginning to turn.

It was raining hard at the airfield when the Gunnerside group arrived already garbed in their white camouflage suits. As happened with every SOE team, they received their final farewell at the old Gibraltar Farm that stood on the edge of the runway next to the waiting Halifax. Tronstadt said a few encouraging words, and they were off. This time all went well. It was a clear night, visibility was good, and shortly before midnight – Ronneberg jumping first – they were gently swinging down to earth. Haukelid remembered the moment vividly.

> While I hung in the air I saw the plane disappearing northwards, returning to England – to rain, to nice hot tea, to a party tomorrow. Beneath me was nothing but snow and ice. Here lay Hardanger Vidda, the largest, loneliest and wildest mountain area in northern Europe. Some 6000 square miles of naked mountains, at a height of about 4000 feet above sea level. Only for a short time in summer does a little grass and moss grow up among the rocks and snow. No human beings live on these desolate expanses, only the creatures of the wild; there are large herds of reindeer, which shun mankind and whose wants are small.[7]

It was an almost perfect landing, the six men and their containers arriving close together except for one that was caught by the wind and whipped across the snow for almost a mile before they recovered it. They found a hut, broke in, and made it their depot. This was none too soon. That night a storm came up, one of the worst that Haukelid, a mountain dweller himself, had ever experienced. Ronneberg tried twice to fix a broken ventilator on top of the chimney but was lifted by the wind and thrown over to the other side of the hut. For three days the storm whirled around them, and when they emerged the landscape had been transformed; they had also eaten all the food they'd brought with them for the trip to Vemork and back. Fortunately, they had found a map in the hut and knew exactly where they were.

As they prepared to move out, a man on skis suddenly approached and made for the hut. They had no choice but to seize and

Above: The destruction of the Gorgopotamos Viaduct in Greece was the first clear proof of SOE's strategic importance.

Top left: 'Monty' Woodhouse, who stayed on with the Greek resistance after helping to destroy the Gorgopotamos Viaduct.

Top right: The 'Maid Honour' crew, whose daring exploits in West African waters gave a much-needed boost to SOE morale in its early days.

Above: The Italian liner Duchessa d'Aosta, prize trophy of Operation 'Postmaster', seen here at anchor in Fernando Po before her capture.

Top: The Norsk Hydro plant at Vemork whose heavy water was crucial to plans for a Nazi atomic bomb.

Above: The Norwegian SOE team that destroyed the heavy water plant at Vemork in 1943. From left to right, standing: Hans Storhaug, Fredrik Kayser, Kasper Idland, Claus Helberg and Birger Strømsheim, and seated: Jens Anton Paulsson, Leif Trondstad and Joachim Rønneberg.

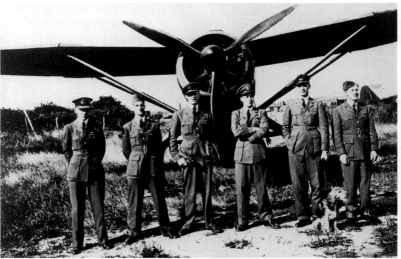

Top left: SOE penetrated occupied Europe by boat as well as air. Here one of its fleet is seen training near Falmouth.

Top right: The Helford River in Cornwall provided a secret base for SOE seaborne operations. Here is one of the apparently innocent fishing boats they used.

Above: Hugh Verity (centre, arms folded) and members of 161 Squadron under the sheltering wings of a Lysander between moonlight missions.

Top: SOE signallers at Grendon take a much-needed break. They provided the first port of call for agents' messages coming in from the field. Picture includes (on back row from second on the left to end) Patricia Simpson, Joan Simpson, Beryl Simpson and Jill Price.

Above left: Veronica Horning, who ran SOE's coding room at Grendon and toiled ceaselessly on agents' codes.

Above right: Peter Wilkinson, military assistant to Gubbins and SOE agent in the field. In later life he became Co-ordinator of Intelligence in the Cabinet Office.

Above: German Abwehr operator with direction-finding device used in tracing SOE wireless operators.

Top: SOE liaison officers and their suitcase radios rest in a Chetnik camp in Serbia. The man on the right may be consulting a code book.

Above: Draza Mihailovich, leader of the Chetniks, (centre, with glasses and beard) with British liaison officers.

Above: Tito, seated, leader of the Yugoslav partisans, who emerged as the post-war communist dictator of his country.

interrogate him. This was an encounter that could undo them. They could not take him with them, but neither could they let him go in case he was a member of the Nasjonal Samlung (NS), Quisling's party. In that case they would have to liquidate him. Ronneberg had to make a quick decision.

> He said he was a quisling and that was probably natural because we were in uniform and this was in the middle of an occupation and uniformed people had to be either Germans or Norwegian police and he probably chanced that saying he was a quisling [we] would treat him well. But in the end we had to tell him he was wrong, we were Norwegian soldiers and we said to him, 'Well, we expect you look forward to the day when the King and government is back established in Norway,' and he said, 'Well, King and government has never done me any good.' Then it became difficult. I remember I decided I couldn't shoot him there, we had to bring him with us.

Tying him to the toboggan, they set off that night in the direction of their prearranged rendezvous with the Grouse group.

The next morning they spotted two heavily bearded skiers in the distance. Haukelid packed a pistol under his camouflage suit and set off to see who they were. If strangers, he was to say he was a reindeer hunter. The precaution was unnecessary. They were Claus Helberg and Arne Kjelstrup from the Grouse mission. Ronneberg remembered: 'We were sort of lying still in cover and watching and we heard a yell of happy crying telling us we had met. It was a great moment actually. I remember they were thin and they had long beards, they had been in the mountains for three months.'

By late afternoon the two SOE groups had been united. The frightened lone hunter was given money, ten days' rations and instructions not to return home for three days, and told to hold his tongue: 'We made a declaration for him which he signed saying that he was a trapper, he was illegally shooting reindeer meat and he was selling on the black market and we said to him, "If anything happens to us we will see to it that the Germans get this declaration but we will add on to it that you were guiding us at the time." It was a difficult decision, but it's a very difficult decision to shoot the man whose only fault is that he is on the wrong spot at the wrong time.'

It was a gamble, but the man did not betray them.

It was hardly surprising that Ronneberg noted the poor physical state of the Grouse team. They had suffered a hard and bitter winter after the catastrophe of the glider groups, hiding out on the Vidda from German search parties and ceaselessly hunting for food. They lived far above the timber line, in a small cottage, occasionally raiding small hunting huts for morsels of food. But there was little to be found because of the general food shortage in wartime Norway. They even wondered if they could survive at all. Helberg remembered how desperate they became: 'Jens Poulsson said if the reindeer could eat and survive by eating reindeer moss we could do it, so we tried that but I'm not quite certain it gave us any nourishment. Another difficult thing was the heavy snows. The temperature wasn't very low so we couldn't get far away from the hut because of the storms.'

Then, just before Christmas, Poulsson managed to shoot a reindeer, their first meat in weeks. It made for happy seasonal festivities: 'We had Christmas Eve, we had music, music from the wireless, the wireless operator arranged some music for us and got news from BBC from London. We had a happy Christmas night in the hut, we had a little wood so we could heat the hut and the wireless operator made some decorations, with his knife he cut angels, I remember we had a little tree. Yes, it was a very happy Christmas Eve.'

One thing Hauglund received on his wireless set apart from Christmas music was the news that for security reasons, and because of the change of plan, their codename had been changed to 'Swallow'.

The first thing Ronneberg did was send Helberg into Rjukan to get the latest intelligence from a contact there about the plant. A good skier, he made the journey with no problem, stayed overnight with his contact, and was back up on the plateau in less than twenty-four hours. The two teams decided to move forward to a jumping-off position as near to Vemork as possible. Leaving the two wireless operators behind in the mountains, they reached this spot two days later. Then, at eight o'clock on the evening of 27 February, the sabotage mission set off for the target.

The Norsk Hydro plant was a huge seven-storey building lying like an eagle's eyrie half-way up a mountainside. Behind, the pipelines steeply funnelling the water from a reservoir into the factory created a massive gash down through the forest. In front, a 600-foot precipice plunged steeply to the floor of a gorge and the Maan river. Access to the plant lay across a heavily guarded 75-foot suspension bridge over the water and then up a steep narrow path. 'The colossus,' wrote Haukelid, 'lay like a medieval castle, built in the most inaccessible place, protected by precipices and rivers.'

There was considerable discussion about how to approach the factory, with a clear disagreement between Ronneberg and the Swallow group. The latter favoured a direct approach across the suspension bridge, mixing with the night shift and taking care of any suspicious German guards by shooting them if necessary. Ronneberg didn't like this idea at all. He wanted to find an alternative route across the gorge. If possible he wanted to avoid any shooting, which in his opinion would only endanger the mission and heighten the likelihood of severe reprisals on the local population: 'I didn't like that idea at all so I told Claus Helberg that he should go down and reconnoitre if it was possible to cross the gorge. I don't think he expected to come home with a positive result so he was a big smile when he came up again saying that that is possible.'

So it was decided to descend to the floor of the ravine, cross the river over an ice bridge, then clamber up the other side until they reached a small narrow-gauge railway line used occasionally to carry machinery to and from the plant. They would then follow this back to the factory and force their entry. They also carefully plotted their retreat. Again, there was much discussion about using the suspension bridge, and again this was dismissed. They would return the way they had come and then disperse into the mountains.

On arrival at the plant they would split into two groups. One, led by Ronneberg, was to carry out the sabotage. The other, commanded by Haukelid, would provide cover and fight off the Germans if necessary. Knowing what had happened to the glider teams, each man agreed that if he was wounded he would take his cyanide pill.

They set off at eight o'clock at night. It was a half moon, but its reflection on the snow was sufficient for them to see in the darkness of the trees as they skied down the mountainside. They then abandoned their skis and most of their equipment – to be collected later on their return – and walked cautiously in single file along a road, then slithered down through the thick wet snow to the river. Crossing it proved easy, as the water was low, and then, after a steep breathless climb, they were on the railway. Remarkably, it was not guarded. They walked along a track by its side until at half past eleven they came to a small building 500 yards from the target. Here they rested and ate some chocolate, waiting for half an hour until the guards changed. Here all their hard training in Scotland began to show its dividend. Ronneberg remembered:

> When we were sitting there waiting it was like a short rest on a training trip in Britain more or less. It was the same atmosphere, the same telling of stories and so on, the noise of the factory was so strong we could talk more openly and we could even laugh. It was a moment when you felt that this will be a success because everyone seemed tremendously calm and you were so concentrated on your job that I don't think you thought of dangers at all.

Then Haukelid and Kjelstrup slowly advanced to the gate across the line and severed the chain with cutters. A few moments later every man was in his place for the attack. They were well-armed; each man had a pistol, knife and hand grenades, and in addition there were five tommy-guns and two sniper rifles.

It was now up to Joachim Ronneberg and his sabotage team to enter the factory itself. It had been agreed with inside contacts that the cellar door would be left open, but the man concerned had fallen sick so it was locked. They made instead for an alternative place they'd learned about from the mock-up training in Scotland – a tunnel where cables entered the factory. While searching for it Ronneberg and Kayser became separated from the two others in the break-in team. It proved remarkably easy to crawl through and soon Ronneberg was laying charges on the components producing the heavy water while Kayser held a gun at the night-watchman. Outside, the covering team were poised ready to hold off any attack. But the Germans in the guardhouse had not yet noticed anything amiss.

Suddenly Ronneberg's work was interrupted by the noise of smashing windows. It was only the other two members of his group who had failed to find the cable tunnel and had decided instead to break in. One of them, Birger Stromsheim, now began to help Ronneberg with the charges and the work speeded up. Stromsheim double-checked the charges. Ronneberg had originally planned a two-minute delay on the fuse. But the work had gone so well he didn't want anyone coming in and spoiling it so he shortened the time to thirty seconds. This was personally highly risky – it gave them hardly any time at all to get out of the building and take shelter.

While he and Stromsheim were tensely discussing all this a small moment of banal humanity briefly leavened the scene, as Ronneberg later recounted. It started when the Norwegian night-watchman asked if he could have his glasses back, because they were so difficult to get in Norway those days.

The natural answer would probably have been 'Damn your glasses, we haven't time for those details,' but instead you dropped what you were doing, searching round in the room for glasses and in the end you found them and said, 'Here you are,' and he said, 'Thank you very much.' And I was down on the floor making up the last of the charges, making ready for blowing, and he says, 'I'm sorry but the glasses are not inside the box,' and I had another search and I found them as a bookmark in his log book. It's amazing what you do in a stress situation.

Outside, Haukelid and the others had remained on the alert for any sign of action by the German guards. The waiting seemed like an eternity, but in reality it was no more than about twenty minutes. Helberg remembered it vividly: 'The only thing I was thinking about was if or when a German guard would come, what should I then do. Should I let him pass, hide myself, should I shoot, that's what I was thinking about. It was dark there so probably he would not see us, or me, so I was thinking I will try to avoid the German guard, try to hide myself so he is not seeing me.'

When the explosion came it was almost an anti-climax, a dull thud, the noise cushioned by the fact that it took place in the basement of a concrete room surrounded by other concrete buildings. As Haukelid wrote, it was 'an astonishingly small, insignificant one. Was this what we had come over a thousand miles to do? Certainly the windows were broken, and a glimmer of light spread out into the night, but it was not particularly impressive.' The only thing that happened was that a single, unarmed, German sentry came out of the hut, looked around, tested a door, found it locked, and then a couple of minutes later reappeared with a torch. This time he made in the direction of Haukelid and Poulsson who were hiding close by. Poulsson put his finger on the trigger of his Sten gun and waited. But after shining his torch perfunctorily on the snow the guard wandered back to the hut. Haukelid assumed he had thought falling snow had triggered a land mine.

After he disappeared, the two groups slipped out of the plant and escaped back along the railway line and across the river. At last they heard the sirens, indicating that the Germans had finally realised what had happened. But by this time the SOE party had collected their skis and equipment and was climbing steadily through the dense forest and up the mountainside. It took them three hours to reach the Hardanger Vidda. Here they walked for about ten kilometres until they stopped for a rest. For Ronneberg it was an unforgettable and lyrical moment.

It was sunrise, it was a lovely morning, excellent, and we were sitting there knowing that the job was done, nobody had been hurt on either side, we hadn't even loaded our guns. And when we were sitting there we were eating chocolate and raisins and biscuits and nobody said anything at all, they were occupied by their own thoughts. When you looked across the valley you saw this 2000-metre-high mountain lit in the morning sun and we had mackerel skies and there was a small bird singing in a tree telling us that it was nearly spring. Now we felt the Germans are down in the valley, we don't think of them because now the fight will be between us and the Norwegian nature and that we knew was a good friend and not an enemy.

Later that day, exhausted, they reached their base camp in a snowstorm. The wind was so strong that the snowflakes tearing past them were mixed with earth and grit and they had to keep their hands over their mouths and the ice-needles tore their faces until their cheeks felt like open wounds. But painful though it was, they knew the Germans would not brave the savage conditions to follow them. They were safe.

Now they broke into two groups. Ronneberg and most of the Gunnerside group headed east and after a 400-kilometre trek on skis, and in uniform, living exclusively off supplies brought with them, crossed the Swedish border in mid-March and eventually returned to Britain; Haukelid stayed behind to organize local resistance groups. Of the Swallow group, all of them also made it back to Britain, although Hauglund stayed behind for a while to train Einar Skinnarland as a wireless operator and Claus Helberg opted to distribute the equipment they had brought to the local resistance. It almost cost him his life.

Three weeks later, returning to the Gunnerside mountain base to pick up the weapons they had hidden there, he was surprised by several German soldiers waiting in ambush and had to flee on skis. After about twenty minutes he had outskied all but one of them. For the next two hours Helberg skied for his life, trying to throw off his pursuer. But to no avail. The man even began to gain on him as they entered a long downhill slope. When he was fifty metres behind Helberg he shouted, 'Hands Up!', so Helberg stopped, turned and fired his pistol, missing with both his shots. The German returned the fire, also missed, and when out of shots fumbled his attempt to reload, turned tail and fled. Helberg briefly gave chase, shot at him again a couple of times, and then continued his escape while cursing himself for his stupidity in walking into the ambush.

There were more close adventures to come. It was now dark and, making haste for shelter Helberg went over a small precipice and broke his arm. In great pain he skied on for more than 60 kilometres to a house he'd heard was safe. To his shock it was full of Germans. Hastily he made up a story that he'd been working as a guide for the Germans on the Hardanger Vidda, had broken his arm, and needed help. They accepted his story, gave him shelter for the night, and then took him to a doctor who arranged for transport to Oslo the next day. In the meantime he checked into a hotel, had a good dinner, went to bed, and immediately ran into his next misfortune. Josef Terboven, the German Reichskommissar for Norway, arrived at the hotel with a group of German soldiers searching the Vidda in the wake of the Vermork attack. Looking for company, he asked a young Norwegian woman to join him for dinner, and when he asked about her parents she replied provocatively that her father was in England and she was proud of it. Terboven, in a fury, had all the guests, Helberg included, arrested. The next morning he was put on a bus with the rest for Oslo. Fortunately it was lightly guarded and he managed to open the door, roll out into the ditch, escape injury from a grenade thrown by the guard, and make his escape. Eventually, after several days in hospital, he made it back to Oslo and then across the border to Sweden.

Meanwhile Ronneberg had succeeded in getting a message back to London. It said simply: 'Attacked 0045 on 28.2.43. High concentration plant totally destroyed. All present. No fighting.'

Its reception in Baker Street was ecstatic. It was not just that the target had been destroyed. The *coup* also handed SOE a badly needed weapon in its ceaseless Whitehall battle for more resources, not to mention survival itself. 'It was the classic proof,' recorded Bickham Sweet-Escott, 'of our contention that one aircraft which drops an intelligent and well-trained party can do more damage than a whole fleet of bombers.'[8]

Churchill was both delighted and impressed. As usual, he made clear his admiration for the bravery of the agents who had carried out the mission, asking, 'What rewards are to be given to these heroic men?' Poulsson and Ronneberg, the leaders of Grouse (Swallow) and Gunnerside respectively, were awarded the DSO; the officers – Hauglund, Idland and Haukelid – received the Military Cross; the other ranks were given the Military Medal. Leif Tronstadt and Jock Wilson each received the OBE. The Prime Minister's faith in SOE was both justified and enhanced. He was to be an important ally in troubles yet to come.

Even the Germans were grudgingly impressed. Josef Terboven turned up in a rage and immediately ordered hostages to be taken. But when General Falkenhorst, the commander of German forces in Norway, made a personal inspection of the plant he declared it had been a purely military operation – 'the best' job of sabotage he had ever seen – and ordered the hostages released. A huge sweep of the mountains by over 10,000 troops followed, with no success.

It was then that Helberg had his adventure in the hotel.

More successful were the Germans' frantic efforts to get the plant working again. By diverting heavy water cells destined for another plant to Vemork they were able to get heavy water manufacturing resumed by April. The news quickly filtered back to London, and by August SOE was under pressure to carry out another attack. But Baker Street decided it was impossible to repeat the performance. German security measures had been rigorously tightened up and SOE estimated that success would be impossible without at least forty well-trained and heavily armed men. Instead, in November, the American Air Force carried out a daylight precision bombing raid with 145 B-17 bombers and put the plant out of action for the rest of the war.

But there still remained a role for SOE. The Germans now decided to move the remaining heavy water stocks and the undamaged apparatus used for making it back to Germany. Sources inside the plant soon relayed the news to Haukelid, who had stayed on the Hardanger Vidda since the February operation. In turn he informed London, and in February 1944 he received orders to destroy the heavy water.

After exploring many options, he decided to do this while the shipment was being transported to Germany. Part of the route involved taking the ferry down Lake Tinnsjo. Two days before the two railway trucks carrying the load from the Norsk Hydro plant were due to board the ferry he posed as an ordinary civilian passenger, casually but carefully reconnoitred the boat's layout, and decided where best to lay the charges. Before dawn on the morning of the actual sailing he smuggled himself and three helpers on board while the crew were playing a poker game. There was an alarming moment when they were interrupted by a Norwegian guard. But he turned out friendly when they convinced him they were on the run from the Gestapo and left them alone. Meanwhile Haukelid laid eight kilos of plastic explosive along the keel and fitted a timer to explode the charge six and a half hours later when the ferry would be at the deepest part of the lake. Before it was light the sabotage team slipped away from the ferry and back into hiding.

The plan was perfect. The ferry sank in more than 300 metres of water well away from the shore. Fourteen Norwegians and four

Germans on the ferry were killed. Apart from four partially filled barrels that floated to the surface, all the heavy water sank. That was the end of any hopes of the Germans using it for an atomic bomb.

It was left to Ronneberg to reflect on SOE's Norwegian operations and the bonds that were forged between Norway and Britain. His sentiments must have been echoed by hundreds of others of many nationalities who fought under Baker Street's wartime flag.

I remember we landed at Leuchars airport outside Edinburgh and then we really felt at home when we sat down in the mess there and got a cup of tea. When I look back on the wartime I think we were so well received by the British people the whole way. If you were out in dancing halls, whatever, people were always friendly. They knew we had a merchant fleet that carried a lot of petrol that the British army used in the fighting and so on so we felt that we were not guests, we were partners, because we paid for ourselves. When we were in Britain we were always talking of home, thinking of Norway. Once down on Norwegian ground we started talking about home and we were thinking of Britain, and so it has been ever since. I am one of the few people with two homelands, one where I was born, one where I lived during the war, where I had lots of friends.

NOTES
1 Hugh Dalton, *The Fateful Years: Memoirs 1931–1945*, p. 376.
2 Gubbins, introduction to Knut Haukelid, *Skis Against the Atom*, p. 1.
3 Haukelid, ibid., pp. 45–8.
4 Leo Marks, *Between Silk and Cyanide*, p. 61.
5 Haukelid, op. cit., pp. 76–7.
6 Ibid., p. 79.
7 Ibid., p. 82.
8 Bickham Sweet-Escott, *Baker Street Irregular*, p. 114.

CHAPTER 9

LANDING BY MOONLIGHT

Hand in hand with these operational successes, Baker Street consolidated its beachhead at home. The first six months of 1942 saw a significant improvement in its fortunes. The regular military had been suspicious of SOE's irregular warriors from the start. But Sir Alan Brooke, the new Chairman of the Chiefs of Staff, was far more receptive. Early in the New Year he and Dalton discussed SOE and its plans over dinner. Brooke agreed that there still remained a lot to be done. 'I don't feel we are doing anything like enough,' he said. Three days later Dalton had a similarly upbeat meeting with Admiral Mountbatten, the newly appointed Chief of Combined Operations and a fellow enthusiast for irregular warfare. One of SOE's strongest supporters was Admiral John Godfrey, the head of Naval Intelligence. Despite frequent petty clashes with Baker Street over cross-Channel transport, he thought their sabotage work good and professional. He was also scathing about the footdragging of the Royal Air Force in helping with parachute operations. 'We should do all that we can to assist them in their task,' he insisted.[1]

But Dalton himself was not to reap the benefits of this warmer climate. Disasters in the Far East after Pearl Harbor – Singapore surrendered to the Japanese on 15 February 1942 – precipitated a major government reshuffle and he was moved by Churchill to the Board of Trade. Lord Selborne took over in his place. A Tory grandee and grandson of Lord Salisbury, he'd supported Churchill in his fight against mainstream Conservative policy over India in the 1930s.

Outwardly Selborne seemed an implausible figure to set Europe ablaze. A small, quiet and stooping figure, he had authored a book on Post Office reform and was a former director of cement at the Ministry of Works. Yet, in marked contrast to Dalton, he was a friend of Churchill – who often addressed him by his nickname 'Top' – and was as tough as the cement of the pillboxes whose construction he'd overseen during the invasion scare of 1940 and whose remnants still litter the British countryside. He made some rapid and ruthless changes in Baker Street.

One of the first to go was Sir Frank Nelson, SOE's first executive director (known as 'CD'), who'd valiantly burned himself out during its first eighteen months of existence. He was replaced by Sir Charles Hambro, a merchant banker and Chairman of the Great Western Railway who'd been controller of Baker Street's Scandinavian division for the previous two years.

Tall and athletic, with broad shoulders and a wide smile, Hambro gave one SOE agent he briefed the distinct impression that he regarded the war as a cricket match. He had, in fact, captained Eton at cricket. Cynics claimed he won his way by bluff and charm. But he and Selborne began to make serious headway in Whitehall. The minister enjoyed Churchill's full support and Hambro was a quick and energetic fixer. For eighteen months they oversaw SOE's expansion into an impressive global empire of secret war. But eventually they clashed over personality and policy differences and Hambro learned painfully who was boss. Once, he emerged from Selborne's office, leaned against the door, and said to the secretary, 'Don't ever let anybody tell you that he's a weak man.' He added that he'd never received such a dressing-down in his life. In September 1943, after one too many rows, Selborne clinically despatched him. 'Charles, you'll have to go,' he said.[2]

His replacement was Colin Gubbins, who now ran SOE's affairs until the end of the war. A natural and inspiring leader, he emanated energy and inspired undying loyalty among those who worked for him. He fought tenaciously for SOE and didn't mind if his views made him unpopular in Whitehall. His firm belief that SOE had to serve Allied strategic plans, rather than act as some independent wild card, suited Selborne's views and fitted the needs of the day. Gladwyn Jebb, one of Dalton's right-hand men, said of Gubbins that, 'I have seldom met a man more vigorous and a more inspiring soldier, or incidentally one possessing more "political sense". There is no doubt that he is the linchpin of the existing machine.'[3]

Prior to becoming 'CD', Gubbins had been in overall charge of SOE's western European operations, a familiar figure to those in the training schools and country sections. To them he often showed a human face he hid in Whitehall. Ernest van Maurik remembered:

> He really did inspire you and he was down to earth. When I was in the Air Liaison Section he was always popping in and sort of saying how are things going...the sort of chap instinctively one would have followed. He'd got a good sense of humour and didn't mind letting his hair down. He was a wonderful party man and had a party trick which he would perform on special occasions. He'd take his jacket off, stand on his hands and call for a half pint of beer and then slowly let himself down until he could get the glass of beer in his teeth and he would proceed to drink it still standing on his head. How, I don't know.

Selborne's arrival at the helm did not, however, mean that SOE was out of choppy waters just yet. Indeed, the first six months of the year were extremely fraught. The Foreign Office remained at best wary and at worst hostile, particularly where SOE subversion in neutral countries was involved. On both sides feelings became acrimonious and Sir Alexander Cadogan, the permanent under-secretary at the Foreign Office, even muttered darkly about having 'to crash [sic] SOE altogether'.[4]

Neither could SOE count on the automatic support from Allied governments or leaders in exile in London. General Charles de Gaulle, leader of the Free French, had been suspicious of special operations into France from the start and in December 1941 told Foreign Secretary Anthony Eden that so far as he was concerned SOE could be dispensed with. The leader of the Poles, General Sikorski, was also dissatisfied; enthusiastic hopes of support for the Polish secret army during SOE's first months had foundered on the rock of scarce or non-existent resources and the almost insuperable difficulties in mounting air operations to such a distant target. But Sikorski blamed Baker Street and in April 1942 he asked Churchill to set up a general staff of all the occupied countries to plan future insurrections. Effectively this was a massive vote of no confidence in the very agency Churchill had created.

Added to all this was the continuous and chronic sniping from the Secret Intelligence Service. This broadened out into a vicious whispering campaign in Whitehall hinting at a catalogue of incompetence and mismanagement at Baker Street that climaxed soon after Selborne took over. Such bureaucratic guerrilla attacks even prompted the Joint Intelligence Committee to consider returning SOE to SIS control.

Two things prevented this from happening. First, Selborne strenuously fought back and briskly commissioned an independent report by a senior Treasury official, W. E. Playfair, and a Bank of England Director, John Hanbury-Williams, to investigate the charges of waste and mismanagement. Their report – released publicly in the summer of 2000, some fifty-eight years later – delivered a strong vote of confidence in Baker Street. They concluded that while it had certainly suffered teething problems it had achieved a remarkable amount in a small time, was far from wasteful, and had an important future before it. Referring to the allegations against SOE, they pointed an accusing finger at SIS: 'Those who have most to do with SOE have least to say against it…with one notable exception. SOE's relations with SIS, which are more at arm's length than should ever be the case between two organizations which must be so closely connected…We have seen enough to assure ourselves that the fault is not all on one side. We hope that in future a friendlier climate will prevail.'

Most important in the long run, however, was their recommendation that SOE should now gear up for the future by some internal reorganization.

> In considering the future of SOE it must be remembered that it will constantly have to work more closely with the Services, and in particular the Army. When it first started it had a programme of its own…largely independent of day-to-day strategical developments. In a not very distant future, it may be destined to provide an integral part of the military machine of invasion. It is thus most important that SOE's machine should not only run smoothly, but should be capable of being easily geared in to the military machine.[5]

Selborne found the report 'immensely satisfactory', circulated it to all the right places in Whitehall, and ensured that Churchill was fully on board behind its conclusions. Assured of support, he then embarked on his housecleaning operations to prepare SOE for its principal task in assisting invasion. Nelson's departure came not just because he was exhausted but because he lacked the temperament, experience and vision to transform SOE into a paramilitary machine.

The all-too-practical and immediate task of getting on with the real war in Europe and planning invasion was now visibly driving the agenda. The Soviet Union had survived Hitler's onslaught and Stalin was calling for a Second Front. Roosevelt was giving heavy backing to Churchill and joint Anglo-American strategic planning was under way. Even before Hanbury-Williams and Playfair delivered their report, the Chiefs of Staff, now talking openly about the possibility of an invasion of Europe the next year, issued a general directive to SOE. Dated 12 May 1942, they instructed Baker Street to develop all its future plans in close collaboration with them: 'SOE is required to conform with the general plan by organizing action by patriots in the occupied countries at all stages. Particular care is to be taken to avoid premature large-scale risings of patriots...SOE should endeavour to build up and equip paramilitary organizations in the area of the projected operations [western Europe].'

Preventing enemy reinforcements reaching the beachhead by road, rail and air, the disruption of enemy signals communications in and behind the battle area, attacks on enemy air personnel and aircraft, the disorganization of enemy rear services by the spreading of rumours and counter-sabotage, would all be tasks for SOE at the time of liberation.[6]

The directive was a vote of confidence in SOE that defined its priorities for the year ahead and signalled support from the top. It was now firmly on the map. Gone was any talk of abolishing it, or of giving it back to SIS, or of superseding it with a general staff such as proposed by Sikorski. Even the Foreign Office was happier after it signed an agreement with Baker Street that same month that laid down ground rules for subversive operations. This affirmed the general principle that whenever foreign policy issues came up the Foreign Office had a rightful interest. Specifically, from now on the Foreign Secretary would decide whether or not SOE should launch 'dirty tricks' in neutral countries and local ambassadors would have a right of veto over particular operations; SOE would operate in Vichy France only with general Foreign Office consent; and any peace feelers would be immediately referred to the Foreign Office.[7]

To top it all, SOE was at last acquiring the practical tools to run operations on the scale it wanted. By the summer of 1942 it was finally getting access to sufficient aircraft to carry out significant drops of agents behind enemy lines. In the long run, too, it benefited from an agreement of June 1942 with its American counterpart, the Special Operations division of the Office of Strategic Services (OSS). From now on the two allies shared a commitment to special operations that climaxed in joint planning and an integrated headquarters for D-Day operations into France. In the meantime SOE began to benefit from technical and logistical resources of the vast American arsenal.

A milestone in SOE's life was passed in March 1942 outside the unlikely village of Tempsford, in Bedfordshire. Here, on flat swampy ground just east of the Great North Road (A1) and three miles north of Sandy on the main London–Edinburgh railway line, a wartime bomber airfield had been built the previous summer. It now became the permanent base of two special duties squadrons, 138 and 161. The airfield had the reputation of being the foggiest and boggiest airfield in Bomber Command.

Cynics joked that 'Bomber' Harris, the head of Bomber Command whose dislike of SOE was notorious, must have chuckled at the choice. But they would have been shocked to learn that even as Tempsford's SOE life began, Harris was scheming to get back control of the two squadrons and roundly denounced their operations as 'sidelines and comic departments'.[8] Fortunately for Baker Street and its growing clandestine networks his frantic pleas fell on deaf ears.

Ron Hockey, one of 138's leading pilots, recalled that when he arrived at Tempsford only the runways were showing through the water. 'When I inspected the aircrew accommodation,' he added, 'most of it was under water as well, Nissen huts and so forth. So the first job I had to do even before we unbogged one of the aircraft was to billet all the aircrew, eighty of them anyway, in the local village that same night.'[9] Conditions were not much better by the end of the year, when Lewis Hodges arrived as a pilot after flying bombers for two years: 'It was extremely primitive. We lived in Nissen huts. It was pretty rough and ready, not a very congenial place, but it served the purpose. The main thing was it had good airfield approaches and good runways.'

Up till then SOE had shared a handful of two-engined Whitley bombers with SIS which operated from a series of temporary and unsatisfactory bases in East Anglia. 138 Squadron was formed in August 1941 and given three Halifax four-engined bombers to add to the slow and outdated Whitleys. By the end of 1942 there were fifteen Halifaxes in the squadron and, by the spring of 1943, twenty. A couple of Wellington bombers and a Lockheed Hudson added to the complement. Flights were still shared with SIS but now there was a much greater capacity for landing agents and equipment all round and much less conflict than before.

Besides, 138 Squadron was not the only special duties group at Tempsford. There was also 161 Squadron. In addition to some Whitleys, used for standard parachute-dropping operations, it specialized in 'pick-up' operations by landing small aircraft behind enemy lines. This squadron, too, serviced both SOE and SIS. The plane usually used was the Lysander.

This legendary aircraft of the resistance was a high-winged monoplane originally designed for reconnaissance and front-line support for the army. It could seat two – or at a squeeze three – passengers in addition to the pilot, who acted as his own navigator. One of its great advantages was its fixed and sturdy undercarriage suitable for landing on rough ground. It had a standard range of about 600 miles extended to 900 with the addition of reserve tanks mounted outside the fuselage. It took off and landed at about 80 mph and had a cruising speed of 165 mph. An advanced base for the Lysanders was established at the RAF fighter base at Tangmere, on the Channel coast near Chichester.

The modifications to the Lysander helped solve a security problem at Tempsford highlighted by Lewis Hodges – the fact that the London–Edinburgh mainline railway ran right alongside the western boundary of the airfield and so lay in full view of the passengers (the sharp-eyed passenger can still, today, catch a glimpse of what is left of the airfield). Hodges remembered: 'The Lysanders that we had at Tempsford had special long-range fuel tanks mounted between the undercarriage legs. They were long tubular tanks and the story goes that people passing up and down the railway lines saw these long-range tanks underneath and said these must be torpedo bombers. So perhaps that helped the security problem.'

SOE flights were regulated by the cycle of the moon. Only on nights immediately before and after the full moon was night visibility good enough for the pilots to find their way. Even then the weather could interfere and there were only a few nights each month when flights could operate. During this moon period the Lysanders would move from Tempsford to the Tangmere base ready for action.

Hugh Verity ran the Lysander operations for about a year during the peak period of SOE operations into France. Like many of those who volunteered for wartime special operations, he fell into the work almost by accident.

In 1942 I had had a very unsuccessful year trying to be a night fighter pilot and they'd taken me off and put me in charge of the Operations Room in Fighter Command which controlled long-range night fighters operating over Luftwaffe bases on the Continent. One night I saw a plot of a single aircraft leaving England and then later coming back from the French coast. I didn't know what these specials were but somebody came in and explained to me that they were Lysanders going to put people down and pick people up for the French Resistance and Intelligence networks. Well, I talked a bit of French and had done quite a lot of night flying, so I thought I'd like to get in on the act and asked if I could join the squadron that was doing these jobs and luckily for me the squadron leader who was running the Lysander flight was just about to become tour-expired and so they gave me the flight to run...I hadn't succeeded in shooting anything down and was really feeling rather anxious to get a more active role. That's how it happened.

His introduction to 161 Squadron provided him with the range of experience he could expect as a regular Lysander pilot.

My first flight over France was not an operational flight at all, it was a training flight and I was given a pinpoint to go to and come back. When I got there I found it had a rectangular perimeter brilliantly floodlit and I reported this when I got back and they said, 'Ah good, you made it.' This was actually some sort of a concentration camp mainly for gypsies. New pilots had to find it for themselves and then the flight would know they had actually got there. But the first actual operation I did was a failure because the whole area of the target was covered in fog.

The Lysander operation was still a small-scale affair using about five pilots. The previous twelve months had seen several casualties and on arrival Verity found an atmosphere of 'cinematic stunt-riding about the whole operation'.[10] He quickly determined to transform it into a serious and well-thought-out operation that would eliminate as many risks as possible.

Its main base was at Tempsford, but the advance jumping-off point at Tangmere aerodrome became its real wartime home. Here the special duties crews had their own private accommodation, Tangmere Cottage, just opposite the main gate of the base.

It was a fairly primitive sort of holiday house. We had two rooms on the ground floor, one for an operations room and a green scrambler telephone and big maps, and across the hall there was the dining room which had actually been a Roman Catholic chapel for RAF Tangmere before. Upstairs we had a few bedrooms in which as many beds as possible were squeezed on to the floor space rather like a cheap Turkish hotel. The kitchen was really like a guard room. We had two excellent service police, NCOs, looking after our security and fetching night-flying suppers for us from the officers' mess just across the road. We were well away from all the administrative controls of a proper RAF station. We were free to have a little party with our airmen who'd come in and have a beer with us every time we had a new decoration to celebrate.

If this all sounds very jolly, like a Biggles book, it was a deadly serious business where security and operational accuracy was a life-and-death matter, as Verity recognized.

It was really our agents who had to be anonymous and unrec-ognized. They could come in through the back door and nobody could see them get out of their station wagons. We'd have a drink with them and take them and show them the aero-plane if they didn't know it already and we'd be quite friendly with them before we took them off. It was a very friendly, relaxed unit, but my goodness we were jolly keen to get all our operational details right.

On operational nights Verity received an air transport form from the Air Liaison Section at Baker Street which gave the exact loca-tion of the pick-up field in France and the Morse signal due to be flashed from the ground that the pilot should look for. Then he and his team would study aerial photographs of France provided by the RAF Photographic Reconnaissance Unit which showed in intricate detail such features as cart tracks, shrubs or anything that could be a dangerous or fatal obstacle on landing – they even showed the height of trees surrounding the landing place.

He would then plan a route across the English Channel that would take the Lysander to a point on the Normandy coast. If the pilot found himself slightly off route this would give him an indi-cation of wind speed and he would adjust his route for the next leg of the journey. This often took him down, flying well below the cloud, across the Loire River.

We had a favourite crossing place which you couldn't miss near Blois. You could always tell the difference between water and land where the coastline or a river gives you a fix and you know where you are, so you go from one leg to another, each about maybe an hour's flying, and get a fix at the end of each leg and then the last little leg would be quite short, just two or three minutes from some recognizable village, railway junction, or whatever and then you'd see your friend on the ground flashing the Morse letter that you were expecting, so it was marvellous.

Even then the pilot could not relax – far from it. The Morse signal gave him a direction but the actual landing path had to be clearly marked as well so as to bring the Lysander in safely.

The flare path was L-shaped and you landed by the first light and turned around between the other two lights 150 yards further on. The passenger with the agent in charge of the field would be on the left of those lights and there would be nobody on the right. You landed, turned round, came back to the first light, turned round again, pointing in the direction of take-off, kept the engine running and you'd probably be on the ground only for about three minutes if everything went smoothly and there'd be no mud on the field or anything to hold you up.

Waiting on the ground was tense because there was always the possibility the Germans had found about the landing and would pounce during the operation – or even that they'd deliberately set up a drop that was a trap from the very beginning. That never happened to Verity. The only serious dangers he ever personally faced was when he almost flew into a wireless mast after peering at the map in his cockpit for a little too long near Lyon to get his bearings, and then when he crash-landed in heavy fog at Tangmere after returning from a successful mission.

He did, however, encounter a problem with one landing field in France that highlighted some of the dangers.

On one occasion I landed on a field where since the agent in charge had last visited it had been ploughed up and there was just this narrow band of grass left to land on. It worked out all right but there was also a haystack rather near the flare path. The main problem we had with fields, though, was mud. You think the field is all right when you walk over it during the day and it's frozen hard by frost and then there's a sudden thaw and by the time the aeroplane arrives in the middle of the night the hard surface has become mud. We had two occasions when Hudsons got stuck in the mud and it took several hours to extract them, and there were several Lysanders that couldn't be extracted at all and had to be set fire to and the pilot would go and hide up with the resistance until he could be picked up possibly in the next moon period.

Lewis Hodges faced another problem on one of his Lysander runs that was often faced by the Tempsford pilots. He had made a successful landing in France to pick up some passengers returning to Britain when the agent in charge of the operation told him that that they had not yet arrived at the airfield so he should switch off his engine and wait: 'I said no, I'm not going to switch off the engines because there was a grave danger that if one switched off the engines one wouldn't get them started again. One relied on a battery in the aeroplane and it could easily discharge it in trying to start. So we kept the engines running, and they were running for about twenty minutes altogether before the people arrived, but they did eventually and all was well and we got off.'

It was a tense twenty minutes behind enemy lines, eased only slightly by the assurance that members of the Maquis were guarding the field looking out for any approaching Germans.

Procedures for the Whitley and Halifax parachute flights varied only slightly. Lewis Hodges flew Whitleys for his first few months at Tempsford.

We had to drop the agents and containers containing weapons from a height of about six to eight hundred feet. When we crossed the Channel we came to a low altitude over the sea to avoid detection. Arriving at the coastline we climbed to about 1500 feet to be able to get a clear indication on the coast as to our exact position. Then we would descend down to low level again, perhaps 800 or 1000 feet depending on the terrain and weather, all the way to the dropping zone.

Agents were known as 'Joes'. They were trained endlessly on the procedure that began as soon as the pilot arrived close to the dropping zone. There were two lights over the dropping hole in the rear of the fuselage, one red, one green. When the pilot spotted the drop zone he would switch on the red one to alert the despatcher, who would then fasten the agent's parachute to the static line inside the aircraft that made it open automatically. The agent then sat with his or her feet on the edge of the hole, ready to jump. When the navigator indicated that the plane was in the correct position over the 'DZ' (dropping zone) the pilot would switch on the green light, and the agent would jump. Usually, as Hodges recalled, he made two circuits of the drop zone: 'One would do one run over the dropping zone and drop the agents. The containers would usually be dropped on a separate run. One would make a turn, do a circuit run, and make another run over the dropping zone and drop the containers separately.'

Flying these moonlight operations demanded intense concentration. Pilots had little time to reflect on the dangers. These, at least in the air, were relatively slight. Unlike the bomber crews with their nightly packages of death for heavily guarded German cities, the Lysander pilots found France relatively lightly defended except for ports and airfields. Danger arose only if bad weather took them off track and by ill luck they stumbled across some Luftwaffe base, in which case they could expect to be shot at and in some cases shot down. Good navigation was crucial, as Verity stressed.

One had to do all the navigation as well as the flying and try to work out what's happening to the weather and if you had a spell of flying over fog you'd stick to your compass and heading and speed and hope that when you could see the ground again it would be more or less where you were planning to be. But if it wasn't you had quite a job to find yourself on the map so you didn't have time to get really alarmed by what was really after all quite a dangerous form of operation.

Lewis Hodges found the transition from flying with large bomber crews to the single-crewed Lysander difficult. It was not just a lonely job, it meant he had to do everything himself. With navigation so crucial, it caused problems: 'One had a map on one's knee and a torch and you just had to try and relate the map to the features you saw on the ground. Most of the operations we did were in the area of the Loire Valley so that was a good landmark but on occasion it happened that as you were flying along looking at the map one's torch fell on the floor of the cockpit and it was quite difficult to retrieve it sometimes. It made life quite tricky.'

In such conditions the pilot would become oblivious of the agent sitting behind him. Indeed, it was basic security procedure that pilots knew as little of the agents as possible and certainly nothing about their identity or their mission. Each agent would arrive at Tangmere or Tempsford from a nearby holding centre – usually a requisitioned country house – accompanied by an escorting officer from either SOE or SIS depending on the mission. They were brought to the airfield about an hour before take-off, where they would be fitted with their parachute and had their clothing searched for tell-tale evidence such as bus tickets, underground railway tickets, photographs, and so on. To the aircrews the agent would remain anonymous, except for a codename, and even that would be different from the codename to be used in the field. 'It was pretty impenetrable,' recalled Verity.

Even on board, anonymity ruled. On parachute drops the only crew member who had any contact with the agents was the despatcher, and on Lysander flights there might be a brief handshake or nod of the head before the agent clambered into the seat behind the pilot. So rigorously were agents and air crews kept apart, indeed, that on one occasion an aircrew flying a parachute operation from Tempsford reported that they had dropped the four men safely over the target – not even realizing that one of them was a woman. The only exception to this generally tight procedure was when an agent would return from a mission and be bursting to talk – in which case it could be like taking a cork out of a bottle and the agent would release the tension in a frenzied burst of words.

After an agent had left, and if he was not actually piloting a flight himself, Verity would often sit around with the escorting officer waiting for an incoming flight bringing an agent, or 'Joe', who required an escort back to their SOE or SIS holding base. This was a time for relaxation: 'We were very friendly and relaxed with representatives of both SOE and SIS. We'd sit around in comfortable chairs in the Ops Room smoking like chimneys with cigarettes provided by the Secret Service and chatting. In fact we did more pick-ups for SIS than we did for SOE. SOE operations are much more written about and publicized and SIS kept all their operational details pretty close to the chest.'

Left: Arisaig House, headquarters of SOE's paramilitary schools in Scotland.

Centre: SOE headquarters in London – its denizens were known as 'Baker Street irregulars'.

Bottom left: 'Dr Dynamo' – Hugh Dalton, SOE's ebullient first Minister, 1940-42, instructed by Churchill to 'set Europe ablaze'.

Below: Sir Frank Nelson, SOE's first Executive Director, 1940-42, who burned himself out establishing its credibility.

EUROPE UNDER THE NAZIS 1942

△ concentration or labour camp
O site of SOE activity

0   300 km

NORWAY
SWED

Shetland
Islands

Bergen O
Oslo O
Vemork O

O Wick

O Aviemore

Arisaig O

North
Sea

DENMARK

• Edinburgh

• Belfast

Copenhagen •

UNITED
KINGDOM

Hamburg •
Ravensbrü

REP. OF
IRELAND
• Dublin

O Manchester

Belsen △
Berlin •

Tempsford O

Amsterdam •

GERMAN

London •
NETHERLANDS

Dora △ △

Beaulieu O O

Falmouth O
Tangmere

Brussels •

Buchenwald △
Pragu

BELGIUM

Frankfurt •

ATLANTIC
OCEAN

Brittany

Paris •
Seine

Rhine

Dachau
△   △

Danu

Nantes •
Loire

Valençay •

△
Natzweiler

Munic

FRANCE

Vichy •

SWITZERLAND

Geneva •

Vichy
France

Lyons •

Rhône

Venice •

ITALY

ANDORRA

Corsica

Rome •

PORTUGAL

Madrid •

• Lisbon
SPAIN

Sardinia

Sicily

Tangier •
• Gibraltar

Algiers •

Tunis •

Spanish
Morocco

Casablanca •

Algeria

Tunisia

Morocco

FINLAND

Helsinki

Leningrad

Tallinn

Stockholm

Estonia

Latvia

Riga

Dvina

Lithuania
Reichskommissariat
of Ostland

Moscow

Memel

Königsberg

Vilnius

UNION OF SOVIET
SOCIALIST REPUBLICS

Danzig

East
Prussia

Vistula

Brest-Litovsk

Stalingrad

Volga

Warsaw

Kiev

Don

Oder

General
Government
of Poland

Reichskommissariat
of Ukraine

Dnieper

Auschwitz

Cracow

Lvov

SLOVAKIA

Transnistria

UNION OF SOVIET
SOCIALIST REPUBLICS

Vienna

Bessarabia

Budapest

Odessa

HUNGARY

ROMANIA

Crimea

Sevastopol

Zagreb

Bucharest

Black Sea

CROATIA

Belgrade

Danube

SERBIA

Sofia

BULGARIA

Istanbul

Tiranë

Ankara

Tigris

ALBANIA

TURKEY

GREECE

Izmir

Euphrates

Gorgopotamos

Athens

SYRIA

CYPRUS

LEBANON

Damascus

Crete

Haifa

Mediterranean Sea

Jerusalem

Palestine

Trans-
Jordan

Alexandria

EGYPT

Libya

Cairo

ATLANTIC
OCEAN

Nigeria

Cameroons

Fernando Po

Right: Banker Sir Charles Hambro on the firing range – SOE's Executive Director 1942-43.

Centre left: Sir Colin Gubbins, the mainspring of SOE throughout the war and its Executive Director 1943-45. A professional soldier with unorthodox views, he proved an inspiring leader.

Centre right: Vera Atkins, 'F' Section's intelligence officer, whose concern for missing SOE agents took her on a sombre mission to postwar Germany.

Below: A fake passport produced by SOE's skilled forgers.

Left: The House in the Woods – the officers' Mess at Beaulieu, SOE's 'finishing school'.

Centre: SOE agents in training learn 'instinctive firing'.

Bottom: SOE behind-the-scenes technicians at work on props in a secret workshop.

PLASTER LOGS.

A range of plaster logs designed for shipping arms and ammunition. The arms are packed in cardboard containers and sealed to protect from damp. They are then built into dummy logs made of plaster, which are modelled on actual types of trees common to the countries to which the shipments are being made. The plaster is then painted and garnished with moss, green lichen, or other tree fungi.

Wooden logs with a hollow cavity in the centre are also used for concealment of stores and ammunition. See illustration below.

Above and right: Secret wireless transmitters were concealed in imitation logs and bundles of sticks like these to enable the agent to send messages home from abroad without detection.

CAMOUFLAGE OF WIRELESS SETS

The size and shape of wireless receiving and transmitting sets used in the field, and the fact that they are mostly required to be assembled ready for use, presents a difficult concealment problem but, as the following list shows, a large number of articles have been successfully used to conceal wireless sets:—

Artist's paint box.	Portable gramophone.
Blocks of granite.	Geyser.
Bundles of faggots.	Munro adding machine.
Bathroom scales.	Paint and oil drums.
Car batteries.	Rocks, rubber, tin, papier mache.
Concrete posts used in fencing.	Rubber armchairs.
Cement sacks.	Vacuum cleaners.
Driftwood.	Vibro massage sets.
Domestic wireless sets, continental type.	Workman's tool boxes.
Electrical testing meter.	

Each item is either "manufactured," e.g., made with Papier Mache, Plaster, etc., or, in the case of bathroom scales and other mechanical objects, the machinery is replaced by the wireless set, and the outside appearance remains as the original innocent domestic appliance.

The following examples and illustrations are typical of wireless concealment devices.

BUNDLES OF FAGGOTS.

A tarred wooden road block of normal size is made with a hollow interior which is filled with P.E., into which is set a 1 oz. Field Primer. Initiation is by means of a short length of safety fuse with a No. 27 Detonator crimped on one end and a Copper Tube Igniter crimped on the other end. A length of dowelling keeps the passage to the Primer clear until the insertion of the initiation unit. The whole is tarred and aged to resemble a worn road block which may be found in any pile or dump of wood.

RATS, EXPLOSIVE.

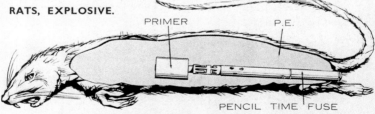

A rat is skinned, the skin being sewn up and filled with P.E. to assume the shape of a dead rat. A Standard No. 6 Primer is set in the P.E. Initiation is by means of a short length of safety fuse with a No. 27 detonator crimped on one end, and a copper tube igniter on the other end, or, as in the case of the illustration above, a P.T.F. with a No. 27 detonator attached. The rat is then left amongst the coal beside a boiler and the flames initiate the safety fuze when the rat is thrown on to the fire, or as in the case of the P.T.F. a Time Delay is used.

Above: This SOE manual shows one of the ingenious ways that explosive devices were camouflaged to enable agents to carry them undetected in enemy territory.

Left: Barely visible amidst the mountains – bonfires guiding an SOE flight to its target.

Above: Supplies for the resistance being dropped from an SOE flight somewhere in occupied Europe.

Above: Arms drops like this demonstrated SOE's commitment to the maquis and their importance to London.

Right: An SOE saboteur laying charges on a French railway line. Such tactics disrupted German troop movements on and around D-Day.

Bottom right: Derailing trains using plastic explosive was one of SOE's favourite tricks in France.

Above: Noreen Riols, one of the young secretaries at Beaulieu, who shadowed agents in training and tested their tolerance for drink.

Below: Francis Cammaerts (codename 'Roger'), one of SOE's most secure and effective agents in France.

By the end of 1943 Verity had completed thirteen moon periods with 161 Squadron and was due for a rest. He was reassigned to Baker Street working inside its Air Liaison Section. SOE was now working close to peak capacity and at this time, given the right moonlit night and weather conditions, there might be about a dozen or more different parachute operations of an evening and perhaps half a dozen Lysander operations.

The task of the Air Liaison Section was to link agents' travel plans and country section missions with the special duties flights, and to negotiate priorities for flights with the SIS through a monthly meeting at the Air Ministry. Ernest van Maurik arrived there late in 1941 when there was only a handful of staff. By the time he left two years later it had grown into a major operation. His tasks were varied: 'One of my jobs was to go and meet the chap who was going to be parachuted. I would get the maps out, tell them where they were going to be parachuted, what the country was like around it. I would then tell them about the pills they might take with them, the Benzedrine that would keep them awake for another three hours after they felt they were absolutely done in, and the 'L' tablet, which was cyanide in a little rubber coating which it was left up to them to take or not.'

Another task was carefully checking map co-ordinates. It was all too easy for a country section to pass on information coming in from the field about the location of some projected drop to contain a small but potentially disastrous error, as van Maurik recalled: 'It was a very good safeguard because on more than one occasion we found that the country section had made a mistake and on one occasion we were asked to parachute somebody in the middle of the Bay of Biscay – but we put that right!'

Eventually they built up a huge data base of dropping zones and their co-ordinates. In the pre-computer age it was all rather primitive. But it worked, as van Maurik explained.

We called it the 'Knitting Needle' card index and it was really very ingenious. It was a card with a whole lot of holes along the front, and we numbered them and against the numbers we put co-ordinates of dropping areas: is it suitable for parachute and/or Lysander or Hudson landing. Anything that wasn't applicable you cut out so that when you pushed what was the equivalent of a knitting needle through the hole and lifted it up only those that had not had their holes cut away came up on the end of the needle and you found out what you wanted to find out. It was really very ingenious and it worked well.

Sometimes van Maurik would accompany agents to Tempsford to see them off, but, as he soon learned, this could be a frustrating time. He vividly remembered, for example, that there was a board in the Air Liaison Section with cards listing the priorities of operations and that the Gunnerside card for the Norsk Hydro sabotage attack stayed up for weeks while they waited for favourable weather. Once a flight had left, the air liaison officer at the airfield would then ring up van Maurik or someone else in the section with the results of the operation which would then be passed back to the relevant country section.

By early 1944 the soaring demands of D-Day began to make their presence felt. Churchill twisted arms and insisted on more aircraft being made available for weapons drops to resistance forces in France such as the Maquis, those bands of young men hiding in the countryside and ready for action. The Americans released bombers flying from US Air Force bases such as Alconbury to help with the task. By this time, too, many OSS officers were now working in tandem with SOE, as Hugh Verity recalled.

My job was to make sure that the RAF got the right information in correct detail about each operation that they were asked to do for SOE in Western Europe, Scandinavia, and down to Italy. The section consisted of a big operations room which, in order to confuse anybody who needed to be confused, was called the conference room. One wall was covered with a huge display board of all the operations and highlighting those that were due to fly that night and giving all the details. My office was just next to the conference room and later on I had to share my office with an American major who was my deputy for the OSS flights and SOE operations flown by American squadrons, who were known as 'Carpetbaggers'. They had Liberators and Dakotas so it was a joint show between the Americans and us.

Several nights in the spring of 1944 I could go into the Ops Room and see that that night there would be over a hundred four-engine aircraft carrying loads to flare paths or secret dropping zones in France and Norway and the Low Countries.

Next door to the operations room (run by a WRAF squadron officer) was the plotting room. Here half a dozen people converted map references from some local Michelin guides, provided by SOE country sections, into British co-ordinates used for briefing the pilots. This was a demanding task that had to be done properly. The grids on French maps used Paris, not Greenwich, as their basic reference point, so had to be carefully converted if the landing point was to be correctly identified. There were other challenges, especially when it came to using French Army maps, valuable sources of topographical detail, as explained by Verity: 'They were awfully difficult to read, they were very old-fashioned and black and white and very heavy hatcheting on the hills, but they were better than nothing as a sort of detailed local map. But our flying maps were very much easier to use in the air. We had half a million maps and for the target area we'd perhaps have a quarter of a million. We had a huge chest of these wonderful maps.'

The exact place and time for D-Day was one of the best-kept secrets of the war and only those who had to know it were briefed. Sensitive D-Day documents carried the security classification 'Bigot', and those cleared to read them were thus known as 'Bigots'. This included Verity because SOE had its own special part to play on the day that could make, or break, the Allies. Like others who were in on the secret, Verity was 'Bigoted': 'You'd make sure that the person you were talking to or dealing with was on a list and had one of these Bigot cards before you could mention anything to do with that.'

One of SOE's secrets for D-Day was their part in the deception plan designed to fool the Germans about the exact location of the landings. These, in reality, were to take place in Normandy. But the deception plan depended on indicating they would take place further north in the Pas-de-Calais. Several tricks were used to fool the Germans, including the use of double agents. SOE's part was to suggest that networks in the Pas-de-Calais were being readied for the day. Verity thought it remarkable: 'I remember the Air Commodore in SOE saying to me one day, "Hugh, it's the first time I've heard of a secret organization being used as part of a deception plan." But in the weeks running up to D-Day we had to make sure that there were twice as many sorties going into France north of Le Havre and rather than west of it, so the operational plans of the squadrons had to be moved over as part of the deception plan.'

But it was not just the British who used deception. The Germans ran their own highly successful deception campaign against SOE for several months. They called it the *Englandspiel*, or 'English game'.

Lewis Hodges got a whiff of it during 1943. Operations to Holland followed the route of the huge Bomber Command raids flying towards the Ruhr and the industrial heartland of western Germany. So the route was heavily defended by German night fighters and heavier losses than those on flights to France were expected. But something still didn't seem right, as Hodges remembered: 'I did some operations in 1943 into Holland and we did have a lot of trouble in the losses and this was rather difficult to understand. As the losses began to grow more and more queries were being raised, and particularly by SOE themselves.'

Hugh Verity also learned of it in the Baker Street operations room late in 1943 when he heard that the Dutch section of SOE had had to suspend its operations. Why, was unclear. But the higher reaches of Baker Street knew all too well. For most of that year and much of the previous one SOE's Dutch networks had been thoroughly penetrated. Every agent parachuted into Holland had dropped directly into German hands, to a total of 53. Nearly all were killed. It was the worst ever disaster experienced by Baker Street and it handed a ready weapon to its enemies in Whitehall. Over the winter of 1943–4 SOE came closer to being abolished than ever before in its brief but glorious life.

What lay behind this catastrophe?

One of the several steps forward taken by SOE in 1942 was to break free of its dependence on SIS for its secret communications. After months of negotiations it finally won the right in June that year to run its own, independent, radio networks and its own home stations for communicating with agents overseas. These were at Grendon Underwood and Poundon, on the Oxfordshire–Buckinghamshire border. It also won the right to develop its own codes and ciphers. Up till then, it had been completely dependent on Broadway.

Control of its own communications was a great step forward, a token of the growing army of agents behind enemy lines dependent on the lifeline of radio to keep in touch with home base. But this lifeline could itself bring danger. Radio turns over every message to the enemy. Codes and ciphers are vital bodyguards for an agent's instructions or reports. But if the armour fails, disaster can follow. In 1943, it did.

NOTES

 1 David Stafford, *Britain and European Resistance*, p. 76; Admiral John Godfrey, 'Special Operations Executive – a Review,' 27 December 1941, in ADM 223/481, Public Record Office.
 2 Patrick Howarth, *Undercover*, p. 227; M.R.D. Foot, *SOE*, p. 32.
 3 Peter Wilkinson and Joan Bright Astley, *Gubbins and SOE*, p. 102.
 4 Stafford, op. cit., p. 77.
 5 John Hanbury-Williams and W. E. Playfair to Lord Selborne, 18 June 1942, in SOE file HQ 60. Advance copy prior to public release kindly provided by Duncan Stuart, CMG, SOE Adviser to the Foreign and Commonwealth Office.
 6 'SOE Collaboration in Operations on the Continent', Chiefs of Staff Directive of 12 May 1942, in Stafford, op. cit., pp. 246–7.
 7 'Relations between SOE and the Foreign Office', Annex 1 to Hanbury-Wiliams/Playfair report, op. cit.
 8 Harris to Portal, 28 March 1942, in AIR 20/2901, quoted in David Nicolson, *Aristide*, pp. 72, 185–6.
 9 Quoted in Freddie Clark, *Agents by Moonlight*, p. 48.
10 Hugh Verity, *We Landed by Moonlight*, p. 63.

CHAPTER 10

THE RADIO WAR

Barely three weeks after Selborne took command in London the Germans arrested an SOE operator in Holland. On 6 March 1942 Herbert Lauwers, a Dutchman, was poised to make a transmission to England from his wireless transmitter concealed in a small downtown flat in The Hague, when the owner reported that four black cars had drawn up outside. Lauwers immediately asked the owner's wife to dispose of his set out of the window, left the flat, and strolled away from it as casually as he could. It was too late. One of the black cars drew up beside him, two men jumped out, and he was arrested. On him were found the ciphered texts of the messages he had been about to send. Stuck in a washing line beneath the window of the flat, the Germans found his wireless set.

This was all bad enough. But to Lauwers's dismay the Germans deciphered one of his messages under his very nose. A Dutchman helping Thys Taconis, the organizer of Lauwers's circuit, turned out to be a German informer reporting to Hans Giskes of the Abwehr. At Giskes' request the Dutchman had fed Taconis and Lauwers with false information about the German warship, the *Prinz Eugen*. This they had incorporated into their message to London and it gave Giskes enough clues to figure out which code Lauwers was using. The SOE wireless operator was then given a choice. Either radio back to London as though nothing had happened, or be turned over to the Gestapo. Lauwers made a show of reluctance before agreeing. He was confident that London would notice when they read his message.

There was an agreed procedure for such situations. Every SOE wireless operator included a secret security check in a message. If it was missing or changed, it meant he or she was operating under duress. Lauwers did just that, confident SOE would notice. But to his dismay London soon sent him another message announcing the arrival of a new agent. When this one duly parachuted in he was immediately arrested. The same happened again; and again; and again. In fact, this went on for almost eighteen months and, by the end of the *Englandspiel*, the 'English game', the Germans knew virtually everything about SOE networks in Holland and had captured all its agents as well as large amounts of supplies and weaponry dropped for the Dutch resistance. Nearly all the captured agents were killed.

Lauwers, meanwhile, had never ceased using his security check to alert London to the danger. Something, somewhere, had gone terribly wrong. In France in 1943 the Germans ran four such 'radio games' with captured SOE transmitters. Here the damage was smaller, although it, too, cost lives. It touched only a small minority of circuits in France and when Baker Street realized what was happening it turned the game back against the Germans in a deception ploy of its own. But both episodes highlighted the dangers and vulnerabilities to SOE of waging war by radio.

Until June 1942 SOE depended entirely on its rival, SIS, for passing messages to and from its agents overseas. This included codes and ciphers, the bodyguards that protected messages from being read. Some in Baker Street considered the main enemy to be SIS itself and even suspected it of reading the messages in order to hamper its rival. Maybe it did, maybe it didn't, and SIS is far too canny even today to let anyone into its archives. But by 1942 it was being overwhelmed with its own agent traffic and had far too much to do to be bothered with SOE. It was probably relieved, therefore, to grant Baker Street its independence in signals and codes as preparations for D-Day began seriously to expand its operations.

SOE's two main wireless stations were at Poundon and Grendon Underwood. The latter, then known as Station 53a, is now an open prison. But fifty years ago it consisted of a big old house, Grendon Hall, built in spacious grounds near Aylesbury where Nissen huts sprang up overnight like mushrooms. Inside worked some 400 signallers and coders, mostly young women in their late teens and early twenties enrolled in the FANYs. Their social life and work regime, if not quite that of a prison, was certainly spartan. Most of them were housed in the Nissen huts, eight to ten to a hut, where they shared cubicles built for two. Others were billeted out in houses nearby and some were lucky enough to be housed in

Grendon Hall itself. Barbara O'Connell, one of the coders, arrived there after a brief course in Morse at Fawley Court, SOE's school near Henley, in Oxfordshire. She found herself housed in an attic: 'It was pretty basic. We used to have an electric fire we used to cook on, but when there was an inspection it had to be put in the cupboard rapidly and that's how I burned my greatcoat.'

Worse was the food, remembered for the rest of their lives as truly awful, as Barbara O'Connell also recalled: 'The sad thing was that nobody told me that I had to bring my own knife and fork and spoon and so for the first fortnight, until I got leave, someone very kindly lent me a teaspoon. Well, actually, you could get all you needed to eat on a teaspoon because the food was so awful, so that was not a worry. All I remember is wanting to get something to eat.'

But this was wartime, they were young, and hardships were easily endured. Social life was minimal. Grendon was deep in the country, there were no taxis, no visitors, and after daytime or night-time shifts most of these young women were simply thankful to grab a bite to eat and then tumble into bed and sleep. Patricia Jones arrived as a coder in 1942, and remembered that 'most of the time it was pretty humdrum. I really don't remember what we did in the evenings, no idea, unless we were working. I don't remember any play time and God knows what we did in the summer.'

Barbara O'Connell likened it to boarding school or university, but with a difference: 'I found a lot of people I could be friends with. It was very exciting to be among so many people of your own age and outlook [although] it's not like university in that you were sitting up all night talking and discussing things because as soon as you were off duty you either went out or went to bed, but it was a very good time. Ask any FANY and they're still in contact or still look back on their FANY days with nostalgia.'

Coders and signallers lived and worked in different buildings and on different shifts and so rarely, if ever, mixed. Not surprisingly friendships were forged between those who worked most closely together. Jill Price, who began the war as a dance teacher in Stratford-on-Avon before being recruited through a family friend for SOE, was a signaller. After strenuous training, including an interlude at SOE's wireless sub-station in a requisitioned school at

Dunbar, in Scotland, she arrived at Grendon in 1943: 'We never seemed to meet any of the coders or had anything to do with them. In fact you really only knew the people on your own shift, because even the other wireless operators were either asleep or out or on duty. I made some very good friends and one of them I'm still friendly with.'

For Barbara O'Connell it was the same: 'When I arrived we were all very frightened because it was all so new to us, but people quickly became friends and I can't say that all the time I was here I ever met anyone that I actually disliked and I'm still in contact with a lot of the people. I could say with my hand on my heart I'm still in touch with my best friend that I met here.'

Such friendship and security at home only emphasized the isolation and danger of the agents whose traffic they were servicing.

Of all SOE agents behind enemy lines, none were more vulnerable than the radio operators. Taught in radio by experts from the Royal Corps of Signals at Thame Park near Oxford, initially they received security training at STS (Special Training School) 52, which was also at Grendon. But this soon proved inadequate. Their 30lb radio sets were impossible to disguise. Spending several hours a day transmitting back to Britain, they were often quickly caught by the efficient German radio-detection service. Many of SOE's early networks were destroyed this way. So in 1942 Baker Street decided to send them for far more vigorous training at Beaulieu. Here they were housed mainly in The Vineyards, spending two weeks practising their technical skills and having it drilled into them to move base frequently, never transmit twice from the same place, and vary the time and frequency of their transmissions. Even then, they remained the most vulnerable of all agents in the field and suffered especially high casualties. Their average survival time was three months.

Hubertus Freyer trained as a Wehrmacht radio specialist and became head of its radio detection service for western Europe. His task was to transform the service from military tasks into working the Abwehr to hunt down SOE agents. He thus joined the shadow world himself. Here, too, as for the agents he pursued, there was much to learn. One of his first jobs was to disguise his work.

For direction-finding vehicles we used bakers' vans. Those were fitted with a wooden construction which didn't interfere with the direction finders and we fitted them with removable signs on the outside. So they had 'launderette' or 'bakery' written on them and the number plates of the respective countries in their respective colours. The next task was to give the soldiers civil clothes. The ones sent us by the Wehrmacht were so horrific that we said, 'Everyone can see from a mile off that that's a German,' so instead we bought clothes in the country and gave them proper haircuts – to the dismay of the military police who kept sending me reports such as, they appeared in an unmilitary fashion and looked unmilitary. That's how we started.

Finding an agent was a long, slow, patient hunt. Agents didn't usually transmit more than ten minutes at a time, and usually from a different location, so that pinpointing a transmitter took endless exercises in direction finding. Some raids took up to fourteen days, others lasted for months. But once a van had located an agent's transmission and got close, one of the search crew, looking suitably local, would get out and walk round the neighbourhood to pinpoint a precise address. For this, Freyer's men ingeniously constructed their own special gadget: 'We built our own, very simple receiver that was permanently tuned to the [agent's] transmitter. And then we had a very light wooden frame, which was strung with wire to serve as an antenna. And then the man, he had a wire through his sleeve, to his ear, with a beret on his head, at an angle, so that nothing was visible, and then he strolled through the area, while he kept turning around until he got to the transmitter.'

At this point the detection finder would be hearing only a hissing sound in his ear, not the normal 'beep-beep-beep'. Then he knew he was very close to the unwitting radio operator and would look to see if he could spot the outdoor aerial being used. 'If it was a single aerial, then it was quite simple; all you had to do was look where it led, and that was it. And if there were several aerials, and you couldn't determine where the electricity came from, then you went up and down the house testing the fuse boxes outside the apartments. If the transmission stopped, then you knew, "This is it!"'

Of course, it wasn't always so simple, and then a longer waiting game had to be played: 'Then we waited in that part of town – which we closed off – and then when the guys came out and were carrying a little suitcase, a little brown suitcase, and there was a catch on the locks not typical in France. And when we saw the catches, we knew – that's where the transmitter is. And then we told the gentleman to open it and *voilà!* Then the transmitter appeared.'

Capturing a radio operator was like discovering the key to a door – it opened the way to an entire circuit, as Freyer quickly realized: 'The transmitter of a group of agents is always the "mailbox" where everything goes in and out. And connected to the mailbox there is always the leadership of this organization. And so, if we had the transmitter, then either the boss himself operated it, or it was his right-hand man, and via him we got further and further into the organization.'

This explained why the Germans invested so much effort into radio direction finding and why, also, some radio operators were totally overwhelmed when they were discovered: 'The arrested men reacted in very different ways. Some were sort of composed, some knew their future and had come to terms with it, and in one case we once arrested a man and when we came upstairs and he came to the door, there was a big bang and he had soiled himself. We could smell it.'

Fear and loneliness were the daily lot of the radio operator behind enemy lines. It made the radio link to home all that more important. The Grendon signallers, or wireless operators, were the first port of call for agents' messages coming in from the field. Before leaving on their missions radio operators would be given schedules, or 'skeds' (using the American pronunciation) which detailed the frequencies and times they should come on the air to transmit back home. These skeds, along with the agents' codenames (for security reasons, however, these were different from those they used in the field), were posted on big boards in the transmitting room at Grendon, and told the signallers when they had to appear on duty. Jill Price inhabited this radio front line. This is how she remembered the procedure.

When you were working on a sked, you were always worried that you wouldn't find the operator, then once you found it you worried that it wouldn't be a good signal and you wouldn't be able to hear it properly. Everything started with a cue. There were three letters and each meant something different; you had to ask how they were receiving you and you asked how they were and said how you were receiving them. There was another one at the end for please repeat group and another one, have you any more messages for me? It could be very bad reception or it could be quite good so it was quite concentrated and the skeds didn't last that long. When you were taking down the Morse you weren't sure, for instance, if it was 'B' or 'D'. 'B' was da-de-de-de and 'D' was da-de-de, so you would ask yourself, shall I go back and ask him to repeat that? Or there might be some interference and the group was completely obliterated and then you'd just write the next group.

We were always very much conscious of the danger they were in the whole time they were on the air, from the very first minute. You had to be as quick as possible. It could be very difficult if they were obviously agitated and then sometimes the whole signal would break off and you didn't know if the Germans had actually captured them or whether they just saw them coming and had to move on. I think the problem was deciding how many repeats to ask for because you weren't sure if you'd got it right. Was it better to leave it or was it better to get him to repeat the groups and maybe put himself in more danger? If it was going to be all wrong, the poor coders were going to have a nasty job. It was quite stressful in many ways.

When the signallers had finished their work the jumble of letters they had written down would be passed on from the Signal Office to the coders working in pairs and sitting at long pinewood tables in a building next door.

In 1942 Patricia Jones joined the FANYs, where a cousin, Veronica, was already working. Veronica, it turned out, ran the coding room at Grendon.

I thought we were all going to drive generals about, or drive trucks, so I was slightly surprised when I was made to learn Morse and various other things. My whole life at Grendon revolved around Veronica. We sat side by side decoding. She was extremely good at it and I wasn't half as bright as she was, so I did the easy ones. Anything difficult was passed on to Veronica, who was absolutely obsessive to help the agents and because she liked any form of puzzle, so she worked virtually round the clock. So I was there when I wasn't doing a bit of decoding to give her cups of cocoa and to put a hot-water bottle in her bed and to make her take her pills…

No more than Patricia Jones did Barbara O'Connell realize what she was getting herself into when she came to Grendon. It was obviously coding and decoding, but for whom and what about began as a mystery. This quickly changed.

Nobody told us who we were getting the messages from or whom we were sending them to, but after a bit we gradually got the idea who we were working for, agents in the field. We gathered from the messages that came in that they were in sabotage of some kind and it was extremely dangerous work and therefore the quicker we got on with the message the better it would be for them. We didn't need anything to make us work harder, it was just there, we were all very pleased to do it.

Learning about the work involved, and the agents risking their lives behind enemy lines in the darkness of occupied Europe, could be disquieting, as Patricia Jones realized when she began work at Grendon: 'I remember the first month I was there I couldn't sleep because when it got dark I thought of people being hurtled out of planes into the unknown. We knew roughly when they were going over the other side, not exactly, but we knew when they popped up that they must have arrived and we knew what sort of conditions they were going to. One put oneself in their position and one couldn't have done in a hundred years what they were doing.'

The coder's first step on receiving a message from the Signals Office was to identify the agent's codename and then consult his or her file kept in a filing cabinet close by. This would give the coder the agent's personal code and from that the message could be unscrambled into English and then sent on to Baker Street and the country section concerned.

Coders soon established relationships with agents, as Barbara O'Connell described. The country sections ensured that agents were sent important family news from time to time, but the Grendon coders added their own personal touch.

> Many of the messages that came in gave us great satisfaction because we could see that they were doing wonderful jobs. It was equally upsetting when we heard that someone had been caught. Although they were all given codenames somehow we usually knew who they were because a sort of relationship built up between people and they used to send love to so and so and we'd often say love from somebody or other. It was very silly really to do it because they didn't obviously want to spend longer decoding the message than they had to, but we just added something to make it feel that there was somebody on the end taking an interest in them. If they said love to everybody we were thrilled. It was much more interesting than hearing they'd blown up a train of Germans.

So far, so simple – or so it would appear. But as both the signallers and coders were well aware, agents' messages often arrived badly garbled. This could be the result of atmospheric (or deliberate German) interference that obscured or distorted the Morse signal, or it could originate with the agent in the field: a mistake with the code, a shaky hand, a hurried and perhaps frightened transmission, any one of a number of causes could lead to garbled messages arriving at Grendon. The signallers dealt with this as best as they could before the results ended up on the coders' tables. These garbled messages were known as 'indecipherables'. They created a severe problem for SOE as well as the agents.

Leo Marks was in charge of agents' codes at Baker Street. To him, indecipherables became a major challenge that had to be solved as quickly as possible. He was under heavy pressure from the country sections to know what their agents were trying to tell

them: 'Country section heads were adamant that if they had messages that were indecipherable they had to be broken by the time
of their next sked. Sometimes that next sked was only forty-eight
hours away so we would have a sleepless forty-eight hours, literally
sleepless, because there is no greater failure in the code room than
to know that an agent has risked his or her life coming on the air
to send a message and we can't read it and he'd got to come on the
air again.'

Coming on to the air any more than necessary meant the more
likely an agent was to be detected by the Germans. The pressure
was on to eliminate indecipherables.

Marks was the precocious twenty-two-year-old son of a London
antiquarian bookseller and wondered if he'd been recruited to
SOE by mistake: 'The person who interviewed me did so in the
mistaken belief that I was the son of Sir Simon Marks of Marks and
Spencer whose premises we occupied, so I was given a very gra-
cious interview indeed because they wanted the extra canteen facilities from Sir Simon and I did not disillusion them. And when I
eventually got the job within forty-eight hours Sir Simon granted
the extra canteen facilities and I lived off the credit for the rest of
the war.'

But he'd already demonstrated his flair for codes and threw his
youthful energy and single-minded determination into the task of
making SOE agent codes as safe as possible. A first step was to ask
for all indecipherables to be sent to London so that he could
examine them against the agent's training messages which might
reveal a certain pattern of foibles or errors. The agent might be a
poor speller, for a start. Or might frequently display a certain and
predictable error in transposing their message into code. Having
decided what might work, Marks would then tell the coders at
Grendon or Poundon and they would get back to work on the
message.

When I joined SOE, agents' codes were all dealt with by girls
who were also occupied on mainline traffic, that's traffic around
the world with embassies, traffic that is completely safe, whereas
agents were in the field surrounded by the enemy. They would
make mistakes. They'd have no squared paper, there'd be no

electric light, the Germans would be all round them while they were transmitting and if they made a mistake in their coding and London couldn't read it London would say 'Re-encode that message, that's your next schedule', and he could get caught doing it. So I made a rule, 'There shall be no such thing as an indecipherable message' and got a team of girls to help me and we would work around the clock to break an agent's indecipherable message.

There were no short cuts, however. At Grendon the coders would usually send an indecipherable first to Veronica, their in-house expert, and only if she couldn't break it did it go up to Leo Marks in London. Even equipped with an agent's personal profile and training record, the coders faced formidable problems. Breaking an indecipherable often meant hours of trying out every conceivable trick of the trade, as Barbara O'Connell remembered:

There were many ways that we'd try to get an indecipherable out. You'd try to remember all the ways they could have misremembered their [code], you could also sometimes see the way their radio operator would tap out 'F' instead of 'S' or something like that. There were lots of ways and sometimes like a crossword you'd get a few words out and you made a note of the sort of things that they'd done so it would be easier another time. It was like finishing a crossword puzzle but it was very exciting.

And if they wavered or stumbled there was always Marks to keep them on their toes. Patricia Jones recalled that 'We worked enormously hard when we couldn't decipher them…it had to be deciphered with old Leo Marks's help on the end of the telephone. It had to be done. It could be a couple or forty-eight hours and Veronica might hop into bed for a couple of hours and back she'd go until I presume Leo Marks came to the conclusion that it wasn't decipherable.'

For many of the Grendon coders, indecipherables posed challenges akin to crossword puzzles and sheer determination to solve it was sufficient motivation in itself. This was the case for Barbara O'Connell: 'I quickly became interested in coding because it's rather like doing a crossword and when you start it you want to finish. That's why I became interested in indecipherables, too. If you've got half a crossword you want to fill the whole lot up and get a prize. We got no prizes but it was quite nice to finish.'

To further motivate them, Marks began visiting Grendon to give pep talks about the life-and-death nature of what they were doing: 'I went down regularly and talked to them about the exploits of the agents they never met, the importance of SOE's traffic around the world. I wrote messages on the blackboard and helped them break these messages as if they were the enemy. It was essential to keep those girls interested...an agent had to be real to those girls though they didn't ever meet one, so the lectures were once a fortnight.'

He also made a firm point of meeting the agents himself, an innovation in procedure he felt also helped security.

It was absolutely essential to belong to that agent for a while, to watch his or her coding habits, to photograph them, to remember his speed, it was vital to be present at a final coding briefing. Some of them were very moving because one picked up a special kind of anxiety, not fear, but fear of failing colleagues. The first one I ever briefed wanted to know what would happen if he made a mistake in coding. So I lied, or anticipated a bit, and said, you're going to have a girl who will specialize in your messages and will know your coding style and if you make mistakes, don't worry, she will break it, and there will be others with her. I determined that one day that would be true.

But indecipherables were only one of Marks's worries. Far worse was the problem of the codes themselves.

SOE inherited its codes from SIS. These were known as 'poem codes' because they required agents to base their messages on poems (or famous quotations) they learned by heart and carried in their heads. It all sounded waterproof, not to mention terribly romantic and very English, too. A Shakespeare sonnet, a Keats ode, a Kipling verse memorized and off the agent went behind enemy lines like some latter-day Scarlet Pimpernel. The problem was, as Marks quickly realized, the whole system was horribly insecure. The Germans knew their English literature, too. A few words deciphered could tell them the whole poem, and once they cracked the code they could read every message of an agent, as the poem formed the code for all of his or her messages. Marks decided what needed to be done: 'The first step was to try and substitute original compositions so that if the enemy broke one message at least they wouldn't automatically know the rest of the words, and we'd buy a bit of time for the agent.'

Marks set to work composing poems of his own and others joined in to help. His most famous poem, composed originally for a girl friend who was later killed, was eventually given to Violet Szabo, one of the agents sent to France, who eventually perished in a concentration camp and whose story was told in a postwar film, *Carve Her Name with Pride*.

> The life that I have
> is all that I have
> And the life that I have
> is yours
>
> The love that I have
> Of the life that I have
> Is yours and yours
> and yours
>
> A sleep I shall have
> A rest I shall have
> Yet death will be but a pause
>
> For the peace of my years
> In the long green grass
> Will be yours and yours
> and yours.

But even original compositions were no more than a stopgap solution. What was needed was a whole new system. It took Marks almost a year to convince SOE to adopt it but he eventually won the argument. The agent was provided with unique code charts printed on silk. Here, all the keys had been worked out in advance, with one key for each message. After the message was sent, the agent burned that section of the silk, thus destroying any evidence that the Germans could use to decipher the message. These became known as 'worked out keys', or WOKs, and to Marks they provided the almost perfect answer. The agent 'had no numbering to do and when he'd finished a message he would cut it away from the silk and burn it and he couldn't remember that key, so there was no point in torturing him for it. It changed the face of agents' coding, but if he lost his silk he still had to fall back on a poem in emergency and preferably an original composition which would buy a little more time for him.'

If Marks felt happier, however, agents remained to be convinced. One thing they disliked was carrying anything on them, like these printed silk tables that could incriminate them if they were picked up by the Germans. So camouflaging was introduced. Marks went to talk to Colonel Elder Wills and his camouflage section at The Thatched Barn.

> He was very preoccupied with other matters and when I arrived it was a terrifying experience because he showed me some manure that exploded and he wasn't particularly interested in codes. So I had to work on him by asking the impossible, because I wanted some of the codes to be invisibly printed on handkerchiefs and then erased by a special pencil of some kind so they could not be read again if the handkerchiefs were captured by the enemy. This began to interest him and within a matter of hours he was determined to find a way of doing invisible printing that could be read only with a special kind of torch and then erased with a special kind of pencil. He ultimately perfected it.

After the WOKs, Marks later introduced an even more foolproof system, the one-time pad, which has been described as the 'pinnacle of development in the field of cryptography'.[1] Briefly put, the agent was given a table printed on silk and several microfilmed pages of keys. As soon as ciphering was complete the key was destroyed. The supreme advantage was that there was nothing for the agent to memorize and hence torture by the Germans would be a waste of time.

Meanwhile, as the Signals division expanded to become the largest directorate in SOE, Marks continued to ponder indecipherables. They had been reduced in number but still continued to cause problems. He had also developed an uneasy feeling about the messages coming in from the SOE agents in Holland, but couldn't place his finger on the reason. Agent messages didn't contain the right security checks, but the Dutch country section believed that this was due either to Morse mutilation or to bad training.

This relaxed attitude about security checks was not confined to the Dutch section. The coders at Grendon were obligated to draw to the attention of country sections whenever security checks were missing or faulty, but they knew that the explanation could sometimes be innocent. Barbara O'Connell remembered: 'Very often we had messages with no security checks. Some agents we knew who had gone to France and come out again never bothered with their security checks. Nobody would take a hundred per cent notice of it if it were missing. They were under great stress and it was very easy for them to forget it.'

Whenever Marks queried the Dutch section about their agents he was assured that they were all right because the section had ways of checking up on them. His confidence in their competence wasn't increased when he learned that a member of the section had actually reprimanded one of the agents over the air for not using his security check and then reminded him, by radio, what it was – a grotesque security breach in itself.

The security check, of course, was a point of attack by the Germans. They were well aware that SOE agents had them, as Hubertus Freyer recalled. He also, wrongly, assumed perfect attention to the absence of security checks in London.

When we arrested an agent the first priority was to find his code – either to find it or make him give it to us. Usually it was the case that they didn't want to, and then we started to search the room, and we already knew roughly what it was, usually a book. Or he gave it to us, and then we had to make sure that the security check in the transmission, we got that, because if we sent a transmission in the hand of the old radio operator and it arrived there without this security check, with normally encoded text, then the other side knew, 'Aha, he's in German hands.'

In London one day Marks was explaining himself to the Head of SOE Finance who'd hauled him over the coals about employing some extra women without his permission, when he had a blinding revelation.

I was getting hell and suddenly I started talking to him about indecipherable messages which were so dangerous for agents if we couldn't break them, and he said well, it's dangerous for you if you don't come in future to get permission if you want to employ someone. And suddenly I realized what had been worrying me about the Dutch traffic and I shook his hand and rushed away from the office to see if I were right, and what I discovered was that we had never received an indecipherable message from Holland due to mistakes in coding. Why not?

This moment of revelation sparked several months' quest by Marks, first to prove that the Dutch networks were penetrated by the Germans and then to ensure that agent drops to Holland were halted. Blunt denial by the Dutch section was followed by growing concern in the Signals section. Its head, Brigadier Nicholls, asked Marks to provide convincing proof of his suspicions. He did so by sending an indecipherable message to Holland – one that could only be broken by a trained codebreaker. A genuine agent would have asked for a repeat, but this didn't happen: 'The fact that they didn't say, repeat that message immediately, which is what they would do if they ever got an indecipherable from London, which was very rare, told me beyond any conceivable doubt that the Dutch agents were captured. There was no other conceivable explanation for not telling us they'd received a message they couldn't read.'

One other piece of proof helped seal his case.

There was a very bright radio operator signal master who was also a little uneasy about the Dutch traffic, he had his own reasons and I was deeply grateful that he was also suspicious. He was worried about an agent's touch on the keyboard, he thought it possible this agent was caught and he tried a trick. At the end of a transmission to Holland he sent HH meaning Heil Hitler, which is how German agents signed off, and back came the instantaneous response HH and he knew that the other end was enemy-operated. Nicholls, a Signals man at heart, heard the actual recording HH and was then himself convinced.

But convincing the upper hierarchy proved quite another thing. Caution was their first, and natural, response. SOE plans in Holland were crucial to D-Day, to Baker Street's relations with the Chiefs of Staff, and to its credibility in Whitehall. The Chiefs of Staff were poised to issue their 1943 Directive to SOE laying out their needs for D-Day. To admit, or even to hint at, such large-scale disaster in Holland could be fatal. Marks persisted, however, and his suspicions eventually ended up on Gubbins's desk. In March 1943, long after midnight, he was summoned to see this redoubtable figure.

'Colin Gubbins was a closely packed man,' wrote Marks in his scintillating account of his Baker Street career,[2] 'short enough to make me feel average with a moustache which was as clipped as his delivery and eyes which didn't mirror his soul or any other such trivia.' He failed to convince Gubbins he was right. But he said enough to convince him to set up an internal enquiry. The head of the Dutch country section had already been replaced and, as suspicions deepened, in July that year it was decided to drop no more agents into Holland, although supply drops continued.

But Gubbins was still loath to admit the unthinkable. Whatever private doubts he harboured, the issue was explosive. By now SIS, who were on the trail of the *Englandspiel*, had reported that eight SOE agents in Holland had been arrested. Here was a weapon with which Broadway could finally kill off SOE. So Gubbins played a deliberately slow and calculating game, as Marks reluctantly acknowledged.

> Gubbins's prime concern was the continuation of SOE's mandate on D-Day. He cared about every country section in SOE but he cared about SOE as a whole. He had a very very difficult decision to make as to whether to prejudice SOE's relationship with the Allied High Command or not. He always supported new codes, new concepts, was enthralled by the silks, delighted with the demands for them, although we could hardly afford to supply them. He always supported anything that would increase

an agent's security, but he had decisions to make far beyond the spheres in which I operated.

In November 1943 the Dutch disaster could no longer be denied. That month two of the captured Dutch agents managed to escape from prison to Switzerland, where they reported to the Dutch military attaché in Bern that the Germans had been waiting for them when they had landed in Holland. They also told of all the other Dutch agents they had met in prison. The information was immediately passed on to 'C''s man in Bern, who sent it to London. The cat was now properly out of the bag. On 1 December the RAF announced it was thinking of suspending all SOE flights to Europe in case all their networks were penetrated.

Churchill was in Teheran for his Big Three conference with Stalin and Roosevelt, and it was left for Clement Attlee, the Labour Party leader and Deputy Prime Minister, to deal with the crisis. The day after the RAF's bombshell announcement he summoned Selborne to a special meeting where it was decided to ask the Joint Intelligence Committee for a full enquiry into Holland as well as Denmark and Poland, where the RAF also harboured suspicions. Flights for SOE to all three countries were immediately suspended, although the broader ban for European flights in general never materialized. Gubbins, who was in the Middle East sorting out Balkan problems, was summoned urgently back to Baker Street to deal with the crisis.

The JIC enquiry into German penetration of SOE was sent to the Defence Committee of the Cabinet in the middle of January 1944. It was damning. SOE's enemies in Whitehall coalesced to produce a report going far beyond the issue at hand – the Dutch networks – to a general indictment of SOE that called for radical change at the top, the separate direction of paramilitary activities, and the unification of intelligence and subversion. The hand of SIS was all too apparent. Desmond Morton, Churchill's personal intelligence adviser, and himself a former SIS man, also wielded the knife. Passing the report to Churchill, who by now was in Marrakesh recovering from a severe bout of pneumonia, he told the Prime Minister: 'I have always held the view that on technical as opposed to political grounds at least part of the work for which

SOE is now responsible should always have been carried out by "C".[3] The Chiefs of Staff also demanded greater control by SIS and suggested the problem might be solved if both secret agencies were put under the control of the Foreign Office. But Anthony Eden, the Foreign Secretary, recoiled from this idea.

Churchill sensibly deferred any decision until he got back to England. By this time Selborne had put in a robust defence of SOE. He couldn't deny the facts of the *Englandspiel*, which was SOE's worst single disaster in the field throughout the entire war, but he vigorously argued that elsewhere SOE's success was outstanding, its failure rate no worse than expected given the precarious nature of its work, and its continued existence essential for the needs of D-Day. Finally, Selborne said, SOE should be given its due and its chance. It was a service that had had

> to learn and devise the techniques of subversion, sabotage and secret warfare without any nucleus of experienced professionals to guide them, as in other Services and Government Departments. This Service is accordingly continually growing in efficiency, and daily developing the art of warfare in a new sphere. Notable special operations already stand to its credit, and all that it asks is that it should be given the confidence which it deserves and be freed from the feeling that any setback which the fortunes of war may bring is going to be made the occasion by other Departments for immediately demanding its dismemberment.[4]

Churchill agreed with Selborne. He had a keen ear for the grinding of bureaucratic axes and had learned to live with the war between SIS and SOE. It was, he admitted, 'a lamentable but inevitable' fact of life. In any case, it was far too late now to mess around with the higher direction of SOE when it was on the very eve of delivering dividends on the massive investment in preparing it for its biggest challenge of all – D-Day.

There was a curious epitaph to the *Englandspiel* story. On 1 April 1944, April Fool's Day, Giskes sent an uncoded message direct to SOE. By now he had realized that his game had finally been rumbled by Baker Street and that it had not fallen for his further effort at deception – his plan to convince London that the two escaped Dutch agents were 'plants' by the Gestapo. Hubertus Freyer, who knew Giskes well, regarded him as a highly talented man: 'he was really skilled in his profession, and he managed this whole game with England in a very skilled way. He conducted that like an orchestra.'

And, like all the best orchestras, he finished the score in style with a magnificent flourish. His message to Baker Street read as follows:

TO MESSRS BLUNT, BINGHAM, AND SUCCESSORS LTD STOP
YOU ARE TRYING TO MAKE BUSINESS IN THE NETHER-
LANDS WITHOUT OUR ASSISTANCE STOP WE THINK THIS
RATHER UNFAIR IN VIEW OF OUR LONG AND SUCCESSFUL
COOPERATION AS YOUR SOLE AGENT STOP BUT NEVER
MIND WHENEVER YOU WILL COME TO PAY A VISIT TO THE
CONTINENT YOU MAY BE ASSURED THAT YOU WILL BE
RECEIVED WITH THE SAME CARE AND RESULT AS ALL
THOSE YOU SENT BEFORE STOP SO LONG.

But the joke, in the end, was on Giskes and his masters. In the spring of 1944 SOE parachuted twenty-five sabotage parties into the Netherlands without the Germans finding out, as well as arms for some 20,000 men. More important, however, Britain was about to make its long-awaited visit to the Continent. Barely nine weeks after Giskes' message to Baker Street, SOE unleashed its agents for D-Day.

NOTES
1 Pierre Lorain, *Clandestine Operations*, p. 74.
2 Leo Marks, *Between Silk and Cyanide*, p. 222.
3 David Stafford, *Churchill and Secret Service*, p. 276.
4 DO (44)2, in CAB 69/6, Public Record Office; quoted in Stafford, *Britain and European Resistance*, p. 141.

CHAPTER 11

LIVING ON AIR

Henri Diacono was a young wireless operator in France. He parachuted into Touraine on the night of 5/6 February 1944 with René Dumont-Guillemet (codenamed 'Armand') to set up the 'Spiritualist' circuit. His recruitment, and experiences behind enemy lines, were typical of many SOE wireless operators, for whom a single mistake could make the difference between life and death. Other people may describe how these agents lived and worked, but a first-person account conveys their authentic feelings and thoughts. This is Henri Diacono's story, in his own words.

My father having been posted to Algiers as manager for Barclays Bank, my brother and I were brought up as French boys. We went, of course, to French schools and spoke French much better than English.

In November 1942, when the Anglo-American troops landed in North Africa, I decided to join the Army and was sent to Britain for training. On the ship that took me from Algiers to Greenock I met three other young fellows, also of British nationality and French culture, and we quickly became very good friends. We joined the Army together in Glasgow and were sent for our primary training course at Victoria Barracks at Beverley in Yorkshire. While we were there, three staff officers called one day and each of us had an interview with them. They did not disclose the real object of their visit, but talked much of France. A few weeks later (in the meantime I had been posted to the Royal Fusiliers), I received an order to proceed to London and I had my first contact with SOE, in the person of the very charming Vera Atkins.

As soon as I had given my agreement, somebody asked for my battledress jacket and came back a few minutes later with a shirt, a tie and my jacket now with one pip on each shoulder. That is how I was promoted to Second Lieutenant. A corporal who had seen me entering the building (Orchard Court) as a private was still there when I came out and stared at me queerly before saluting.

The first training school was Wanborough Manor. There we were trained to all sorts of things: toughening physical training, shooting, unarmed combat, handling explosives, wireless-transmission, camouflage and more. All of it was quite new to most of us (we were seventeen in our course, of which four were women) and everybody enjoyed it very much.

One day we were told to sit by the side of a road and we were informed that three men were going to cross the road about ten yards from us and we would not see them. Of course, we thought that was practically impossible, but suddenly there was a violent explosion behind us and we all turned back to see what was happening. When we turned our heads back again the three men had crossed the road.

It was also important to be very clever on fast shooting. We had to walk in a deserted forest and suddenly targets representing a man would come up and we had to see them and shoot as quickly as possible. We were also taught how to lie one yard away from an exploding grenade without being hit, and how to make an explosive charge using the smallest possible quantity of plastic (the item might be scarce in the field) and how and where to fix it on any specific target. Our personalities were also very attentively examined and one day one of the staff officers took a few of us to a party in town and managed to get us well drunk. On the way back, by train, he was able to judge if in such circumstances we could keep our mouths shut.

At the end of the training course at Wanborough Manor each one of us had an interview with the Commanding Officer in order to decide together what would be our speciality in the field, the main ones being: circuit commander, his assistant, wireless operator, weapon instructor or courier.

The rumour used to say that the wireless operator was the most dangerous. It was quite true in the early days when only one out of four managed to survive, but at my time (end of 1943), thanks to their experience and to their sacrifice, one reckoned that three out of four might survive, with a bit of luck. Knowing that the organisation was very short of such specialised agents, I accepted to be wireless operator.

I was then sent to Thame Park, which was a very big and lovely estate, somewhere in England and started that rather awkward training that lasted about three months. We had to learn everything about wireless transmission, including Morse, coding and decoding messages, security measures and repairing our sets in case of breakdown. All this was very stressing and straining and in the end I could not listen to a bird without trying to understand what Morse letter it was singing!

At the end of the training our capacities were tested through a scheme: I was sent to Scotland, to a family who I think were not aware of what I was doing and there, in an unknown town, in an unknown house, I had to make contact with the home station and exchange a few coded messages. I presume all that went nicely.

Then it was decided that we were fit to do our job in France and we went to parachute school. In five days we jumped four times in daylight and once by night. The first jump was something very queer because of course it's against natural things to jump from something so high and you were scared, but when your parachute was open, then you were very proud of yourself. 'I am a paratrooper, I did it so I'm very courageous' – and you feel very nice. Suddenly the ground comes up and then you realize that the most difficult part of it is the landing.

After the parachute school I was ready for action 'stand by' - meaning I had to be available at first notice. Before that, however, I had to learn my cover story. With the help of Vera Atkins I had to invent the complete story of my false life, all about my false father and false mother, where I was supposed to have lived up to now, and where I had served my military time in France with the name of my supposed Colonel; in short, everything to square with the identity papers I was going to be issued with. I was also issued with a complete civilian outfit to make me look like an ordinary Frenchman. When I arrived in France, some of my friends thought I looked like an English lord!

About my false identity, René Dumont, my circuit commander (with whom I had been parachuted) was not satisfied, thinking it did not correspond to my personality and had a new one made for me. In the space of a day, I had to change from a commercial representative to a student in English Literature.

René Dumont-Guillemet had worked in France already with Sidney Jones who had sent him to England by Lysander in order that he be trained. He was very eager to go back quickly. We were 'standing by' in November 1943. We left for our mission, but the plane didn't find the reception committee so we came back. After that we didn't have any news from the people who were supposed to receive us in France in November, December, January, and poor René found the time very long.

In the meantime Sidney Jones had been arrested [betrayed by an Abwehr double agent, Jones did not survive]. So we spent these three months in London. We were very fit when we left the training schools and after three months in London we weren't as fit as we were at the beginning.

René asked me if I agreed to be dropped 'blind', that is to say without anybody expecting us in France. Of course I agreed and we arranged with the pilot to drop us at a certain spot in France between Chartres and Dreux, not far from a farm run by one of René's relatives.

We left London for a place not far from the airfield. It was a sort of hotel where a few 'tourists' like us were awaiting their private planes for different destinations. On the blackboard, in the lounge, were mentioned, every day, the names of the clients leaving. When our names appeared, a very busy day started – meetings with Colonel Buckmaster and a few other staff officers, search of our clothes in order to find if we had not kept some Players in our pockets or the photo of our preferred ATS, issue of our weapons and ammunition and of some French money. A very excellent farewell meal was also offered to us. In the end we left for the airfield where we were introduced to the crew of our plane and slipped into our parachutes. Just before we boarded the plane, Colonel Buckmaster presented each of us with a gift, for me a pair of cufflinks in solid gold, which was also something we could sell in case of necessity.

So we went into the plane. It was a Halifax, very uncomfortable because there were no seats in it. The despatcher offered us a few cups of tea during the voyage and suddenly he said we are getting near to the target. I jumped first and behind me, René. I could see two or three other parachutes with our wireless sets and our suitcases.

We landed, we drew our revolvers and waited to see if anybody was coming. It took us about ten minutes to find each other because it's rather difficult at night. After that we found all the parachutes. We hid the parcels in a small wood. I think when we jumped it was not far from the morning so we didn't have much time and we didn't bury the parachutes. We just put them along one of those furrows, where the plough has passed, and brought back the earth on top of the parachutes.

We then walked in any direction until we found a road sign. We looked on the map and found out that we were about twenty-five kilometres from the spot where we should have been dropped. We left the road, of course, and we walked across fields just with the compass. Eventually I said we can't carry on like this, because we had on our London hats, a nice coat and nice shoes, walking in the middle of the fields of France like this, people would wonder who we are if we carry on like this.

It was nearly daylight when we came near a small village and passed in front a house where we heard that they were listening to the BBC. We just knocked at the door. René was in front and I was behind with my revolver out. We decided to tell them we are two British officers, we've just been parachuted and we have to stay and hide during the day. There was one man, a woman, and a very nice little girl, two or three years old. They said we're not for the Germans, we're not for the British, we don't have opinions at all. We said well, we're not asking you if you have opinions or not, we just want to hide and even if you don't want, you'll do it anyway. So we went in and they became suddenly very nice. They gave us a place to sleep, to wash.

In the afternoon, we took a train to the village where the cousin of René was expecting us. We were seated in third class and suddenly I saw René looking at my chest. So I looked and I saw my revolver was sticking out of my pocket but nobody had noticed it.

We arrived the next day. The problem was – what are we going to do with the things we left in the field? René was very security-minded and he said we didn't hide them well enough so we just abandoned them. I didn't agree at all – I said if I don't have my wireless set I can't do anything, just tell me the way to the Pyrenees and I'll go back to England straight away. So we went by bicycle.

We found the spot quite easily and we went to the first place where we had hidden some of the parcels and there was nothing. I said let's get out of it quickly. I was sure we had been discovered. We took our bikes and were going away and suddenly a man came from behind a little house and made a sign to us to stop. He said what were you doing in that field? So we said well, nothing, we just stopped for a pee.

He said well, yes, but it's my field. He was very annoyed and I was wondering what was happening. In the end, as we were starting to drive off, he said to us, if you're looking for the parcels, I found them. They are all in my house.

He was a very, very nice old man and next day we came back with a truck and took all the parcels. He had seen everything. He had heard the plane. He had seen us while we were flying. He had seen what we had been doing in his field and after that he had gone back and picked up everything and hid them in his barn. Mr Pijon was very eager to serve, to help, but he didn't have consciousness of the danger. I think our despatcher must have let his gloves fall down from the plane. He found them in his field and they were in his house.

When I left England they had told me there we are not expecting news from you before at least a fortnight. When we arrived at that farm where the cousin of René received us, I found there was a barn just in the right direction for my aerial. So I thought, I'll make a message straightaway telling them we have arrived safely. I thought they would be astonished. I put my aerial in place; I connected my set; I tuned on the right wavelength and without searching more than that I heard them, QSA5 (loud and clear) London, calling me. I balanced it to transmission. I called them. They didn't hear me. I called them again and called them again. They didn't hear me. Then I realized that I had tried to transmit without my crystal – that piece of crystal you put on your set to determine the wavelength on which you are sending. What I was transmitting was going all over the place and not in the direction of London. That was my first mistake. I stayed about ten days in that farm and after that I was introduced to the brother-in-law of René, who was a young student exactly the same age as I was. He was the fellow who would be the angel who looks after me during all my stay in Paris. His name was Marcel Rougeaux.

We took the train; Marcel was carrying the set. On the train I saw German soldiers for the first time – that was a little bit of a shock. I said now I'm in an occupied country; in small villages you don't realize that the Germans are there. The way I looked at him, the way he looked at me, the way all these Germans looked at me, I found I wasn't something special. I was like all the other Frenchmen. I was very relaxed after that. Arriving at Paris, we got out of the train and we had to pass through the barrage at the railway station. I was carrying the crystals under my coat. My attitude was normal; people didn't think I was a spy. So that makes you more and more confident.

Marcel had a little apartment and I lived there for a while. After that I found a room of my own. A Belgian fellow who worked in our circuit had an apartment near the Avenue Foch with a room for a maid in the service stairs. He'd gone to an agency to say he wanted to rent that room. I went in to that same agency and asked them if they had a room to let. We knew very well that I was going to choose that room. Opposite of his building there was a very big palace made in rose marble. In here was living Von Stulpnagel, the German Commander of Great Paris.

One night, about one o'clock in the morning, I heard people coming up the service stairs. They were talking in German so I said, that's it, they are coming for me. I had time to look in my wallet and take a piece of paper where I had taken some compromising notes. I swallowed the paper. I was unarmed. I had hidden my code two storeys below my flat and apart from that I couldn't do anything. In the end they stopped at the flat under my room. They were Gestapo people. I heard them, they bullied a woman who was there. They beat her. I heard 'Your husband's a spy, your husband's a spy.' After that I don't know what happened because I think they took her away. So I always wondered if they had the wrong storey or the wrong flat or if that fellow was really a spy or something in the resistance. The next day I moved.

My life as a wireless operator was rather simple because, in theory, I was supposed not to interfere in actions other than my wireless operator's job. In fact I was often asked to help in different actions of our activities. Marcel was a student in chemistry and he introduced me to some of his fellow students. According to my cover story I was supposed to have been living in the south of France and have been sent to Paris to carry on my studies. With a touch of humour, I had entered the Sorbonne University for a degree in English Literature.

When I coded and decoded my messages, I endeavoured as much as possible not to remember the contents in order that, if I were arrested and interrogated, I should have the least possible things to say – because nobody knows if under torture, one could keep silent or talk. The safeguard of the circuit made it a duty for everyone to take all sorts of security steps, such as to always have a cover story to tell, wherever you were and whatever was the moment. For instance, if two or more of us were together talking shop, we were always agreed of a false version of what we were talking about, because the German police usually interrogated each one separately and, of course, if the subjects were not the same you became very suspicious.

All this was rather stressing. At the same time I was conscious to do the right thing, to take all the security measures I could take to protect myself and the others because when you were arrested the main thing was to protect the others. That's why I was very happy with my cover story, which was the double of a fellow who really existed in Antibes in the south of France. I knew that I had at least one day or half a day in order that the Germans could check my cover story. Very often when somebody didn't hear of you for one full day like this it meant that you were arrested. They had time to take measures. What would have happened if I had been tortured, would I have talked? Nobody can tell if when you are tortured if you could keep silent or if you could talk.

I remember one incident when I was cycling with my friend, Marcel, going to a place where I had to transmit. We had the coded message in the tubes of the bicycle and it was very hot. We just had gone up a hill and we came to a small village. We were very thirsty and there was a peach tree, showing nice peaches, outside the wall of a house. So we stopped and picked up a peach each and suddenly the owner of the house came out, an old man. He started shouting at us. He was the village policeman. On the other side of the road there was a bistro and in that café there were German soldiers. They heard that fellow shouting at us, came out, arguing with him and us. The Germans, of course, took the part for the policemen so we had to do as if we were small boys and say we are very sorry, we won't do it again.

One of the precautions I used to take was never to connect on the power of the town. I used to connect my wireless set on a car battery. The Germans, when they were trying to find a clandestine operator, used to cut the power of the different sectors, the different parts of the town. When they cut the power at the transmissions would stop so they knew that the operator was in that sector. The other precaution was not to stay too long on the air. The security rule was that you shouldn't send on the same wavelength for more than a quarter of an hour or twenty minutes maximum because this was the time which the Germans had to find you. The detecting stations in about five or ten minutes were able to determine a small triangle in which you were. They had time to call somebody in this triangle. They used to send a car with a direction finder – they used to come by car or by bicycle or even walking or with a baby cart. So if you stopped after a quarter of an hour they didn't have time to do all that. When I was transmitting it was such a concentration, anything can happen and I wouldn't have noticed it. That's the reason why I had always with me a friend, my bodyguard, who was watching if the Germans were approaching. Of course if my bodyguard was arrested, it was very bad for him and for his friends. But if I was caught it was very bad for the whole circuit. It's a pity to say, I used to tell him that he was worth much less than I was! He was laughing all the time. He has not only been my bodyguard but he's been my companion also, telling funny stories and he helped my morale very much.

One of the security rules was that the organizer, the head of the circuit, should never travel with the wireless operator and that the wireless operator never travelled with his set. One day René told me, I've got a car with a driver, I've got a set in my car. We go anywhere around Paris and you send that message very quickly. The fellow who was driving the car was in uniform; they were called at that time Groupe Mobile de Réserve, a kind of French police. They were helping the resistance. René was armed and I was behind in the car with the crystal and the message.

Suddenly the car broke down. It was the wireless set hidden under the bonnet on the engine that had disturbed the carburettor. So we took the wireless suitcase out; he repaired very quickly the carburettor. We had lost time for repairing the car so I said, listen, René, we won't be in time for the contact because as usual London was calling for quarter of an hour. So he said, then we have to take the main road, which was very dangerous. After a curve we fell on a real barrage of Germans. They had machine-guns in the middle of the road and on each side of the road; a car coming from the other side had been completely dismantled. A German made a sign for us to stop. I could see René taking his revolver and telling the driver to slow down when we reach the German, I shoot him, and we try to get out of it like this. One metre from the German, the driver said stop, stop, René. We won't get out of it like this. He stopped completely, got out of the car and said '*Französische Polizei*', French police. The driver knew what effect his uniform could make on a German. The German soldier told us, all right go through. Nothing happened and when you think that maybe two seconds later you could be dead...

We had two main missions. One was an attack on the prison of Fresnes, a combined attack by air and resistance troops. Bombers would bomb the walls of the prison. Inside we had everything ready to open all the cells and the prisoners would fly out. We would have taken in charge the agents and the French fellows belonging to the resistance, to our Spiritualist circuit or to other circuits. But that did not work because when we were ready, all the prisoners of Fresnes were evacuated somewhere else so that mission was abandoned. The other mission was to capture some French scientist in connection with the atomic research on the bomb and to send him to London. But both missions we couldn't do but we did all sorts of other things.

Near the end we had received, as all the other circuits in France, instructions to blow up all the communications the Germans could have. That was the time they were bringing reinforcements to stop the landing in Normandy. One day I was at St Pathus (near Meaux) and René told me, I have sent all my people on sabotage teams. I've got a double railway not far from here. There's only you and me left. So I said all right. We made our little charges of plastic as we had been taught in London. We went on our bicycles, each of us covered by one of the chaps with a Sten gun. There was a field and on the other side of the field were these two railways. We started each working on one of the railways. I had nearly finished mine when I looked up and saw a light a few hundred yards away. I thought it was a watchman but when it came near I heard it was a train coming very, very slowly. So I jumped to René who hadn't heard anything yet. I told him the train was coming on my railway and my charge was set. While we were running he asked me, are you sure your charge is well placed? I said, yes, you'll see in a minute.

We were about fifty yards from the railway when the train blew up. I think they saw us and they started shooting. That's the only experience I had of people shooting at me like this, by night. It gives the impression that the tracers are coming towards you rather slowly. We were hiding behind small haystacks until we got where we had left our bicycles and went back to St Pathus. The next day we sent a fellow to see what had happened: the train was going so slowly that it just derailed and it had only taken a few hours to put it back on the rails again, but never mind, some other people maybe ten kilometres later did the same thing, so that was very, very useful. Most of the communications of the Germans had been stopped at that time by action of the resistance.

When everything was finished and France liberated, I went back in the Army and was only demobbed in September 1946. Fifty-six years have passed since and from time to time I can hear in my head dit dah dah dit – dah dah – dit dit dit dit – PMH, the three letters of the Home Station calling me.

CHAPTER 12

BALKAN INFERNO

Barely six weeks after SOE's *coup* at the heavy water plant in southern Norway, and while Baker Street was still savouring the triumph of destroying the Asopos viaduct in Greece, an American Liberator bomber took off from a desert airfield outside Cairo. On board was an SOE mission of three men headed by Captain Erik Greenwood. He had been recruited in Cairo when he was working as an interrogation officer for prisoners of war. His first mission was to blow up the Russian oil fields in the Caucasus to stop them falling into German hands. He'd gone so far as to penetrate Azerbaijan before being withdrawn when it became clear that the Russians had their own preparations well in hand.

The Liberator headed north, crossed the North African coast, and five hours later was over north-eastern Serbia. The despatcher gave the order and the three men jumped into the blackness below. Several containers with their W/T set and supplies followed.

The date was 18 April 1943. Elsewhere, the Jews of the Warsaw ghetto were poised to launch their valiant but doomed uprising, British and American troops had cornered German forces in Tunisia, and in the Atlantic the battle against the U-boats was finally going the Allied way. Here, in Yugoslavia, Greenwood was to work tirelessly among the Chetniks until the spring of 1944. He had a clear vision of his goal: 'We wanted to stir them up into patriotic fervour and there would be a great uprising like Lawrence managed to achieve in the First World War with the Arabs.'

Greenwood's group was only one of a rapidly growing number of SOE missions sent into Yugoslavia that year. Guerrillas were causing havoc to the occupying Italians and Germans, tying down several divisions of enemy troops that might have been sent instead to Hitler's now crumbling eastern front. At last it appeared as though Churchill's hopes of setting Europe ablaze would catch fire in the Balkans. Mihailovich, leader of the Chetniks, had first emerged in the darkness of Fortress Europe as a courageous

symbol of heroic resistance and national liberation, polar opposite
to the treacherous Norwegian collaborator, Vidkun Quisling.

The very fact that Greenwood had arrived at all was a tonic to
the Chetniks. Even better, he'd arrived with some supplies, however meagre: 'I brought a few things, maybe a dozen rifles. It was
extremely welcoming…I was taken around and shown off as a
manifestation of the goodwill of the Allies and everything that was
going to turn out well for Yugoslavia.'[1]

That, at least, was the hope. The reality, as Greenwood was
quickly to find out, was markedly different. Far from a nation uni-
fied against the enemy, Yugoslavia was a seething cauldron of
ethnic turmoil and civil war.

The warning signs had been present ever since Captain Bill
Hudson stepped ashore from HMS *Triumph* in September 1941.
Even before meeting Mihailovich, he had stumbled on a resistance
group led by a Croatian revolutionary named Josip Broz, but better
known as Tito – General (later Marshal) Tito, a man destined to
lead Yugoslavia as its dictator for thirty years after the war. A hardened survivor of Stalin's purges of the 1930s, he was the undisputed
and charismatic leader of the Yugoslav Communists; he had also
launched his Partisans as a crusading army of national liberation.

Tito was friendly, and when he learned that Hudson was seeking Mihailovich helped him on his way. The Partisan and Chetnik
leaders were not yet bitter rivals and there seemed hope that
they might co-operate. But such optimism quickly faded and
Mihailovich, suspicious of Hudson's links with Tito, stopped
talking to him and refused him permission to use his W/T set.

For much of 1942 SOE thus remained in the dark about the
reality of events on the ground. Meanwhile, with little to contradict
it, the fame of Mihailovich spread and King Peter and the Royal
Yugoslav Government in exile even appointed him Minister of War
and Commander-in-Chief of the Yugoslav armed forces. British
policy still remained one of full backing for the Chetniks.
Eventually, after many adventures and severe hardship, Bill Hudson
managed to get back on air and re-establish himself with
Mihailovich. The reports he sent back to Cairo raised doubts about
the Chetniks. In the end it was decided a more senior SOE officer

should be sent to see for himself. On Christmas Day 1942, Colonel Bill Bailey parachuted in to Mihailovich's HQ in Montenegro.

Bailey, like Hudson, knew Yugoslavia well, having worked there as a metallurgist and been a mainspring of Section D's activities in Belgrade. So when he met Mihailovich he quickly sized up the man and his movement. Before him stood a slight, retiring figure, flanked by his staff. All wore beards, having followed the custom of the Serbian Orthodox Church in not shaving or cutting their hair during mourning – and until their country was liberated they considered themselves mourners. Most of them had abandoned formal uniform for homespun peasant jacket and breeches and traditional Serb slippers. They called themselves Chetniks after the Serb irregulars who had fought against five centuries of Turkish occupation that had ended less than a hundred years before. They were an essentially *Serb* movement committed to restoring the monarchy and the traditional, pre-war state of affairs in Yugoslavia – which meant Serb predominance through control of the monarchy and the armed forces.

This commitment to the Serbs also dictated Mihailovich's military strategy. German invasion had let loose the dogs of sectarian hatred and, in the fascist state of Croatia, hundreds of thousands of Serbs had already been massacred. Mihailovich was determined to keep deaths to a minimum, to protect his Serb people from reprisals, and to slowly build up a liberation army that would strike only at the moment of Allied victory – thus enabling the King and his government to return to Belgrade amid law and order. By contrast, the Partisans believed in constant harassment of the enemy at no matter what cost to the civilian population. They also wanted radical political change and the creation of a new federal state freed from Serb domination. These stark differences of political objectives and guerrilla strategy fuelled the growing civil war.

Mihailovich's strategy now posed an increasing dilemma for SOE. If their object was to set the Balkans ablaze, was he the right man to do it? Or were the Partisans, with their willingness to hit the Germans hard, not better suited to the task? Bailey found Mihailovich friendly enough. But he proved elusive and resistant to SOE's requests for action and the stand-off between him and Tito was obvious. Within a month Bailey reported back that it was hopeless to expect co-operation between the two men, and that it was time to meet Mihailovich firmly and make him do what SOE wanted. 'He must be made to realize,' Bailey insisted, 'that we can make or break him.'[2]

Meanwhile, Mihailovich was given every chance to prove his mettle, and Bailey arranged to send several sub-missions to help him. And so, Captain Erik Greenwood found himself parachuted to the Chetniks.

In Serbia, Greenwood's mind was still set on the kind of sabotage and demolition he'd carried out for SOE in Russia: 'The two real targets were the large copper mine in Bor which was then I think the only source of copper for the Germans [and] was certainly the largest copper mine in Europe. As for the Danube we needed a very small force to stop the traffic and move out.'

His plan for Bor was to persuade the local Chetniks to take control of the town with a small force long enough to destroy the physical plant extracting and processing the copper. For the Danube operation he proposed firing on one of the tugs towing its long convoy of barges to force it to run aground and block the main channel – the principal route for commercial traffic through south-east Europe.

It was a basic condition of his presence in Serbia that he was there merely to liaise with the Chetniks: 'I had no command over the troops at all. I certainly wasn't trying to stir them up (except by a general goodwill feeling) – that was the job of the Yugoslav officers...I talked really basically only to officers.'

This meant he could only use persuasion. He quickly found out that the Chetniks were lukewarm about both the operations that interested him. So far as the Bor copper mines were concerned:

We never got to that. They said that we'd need more troops than they could possibly arm to capture the town for long enough to bring that about. I didn't agree with that...in two hours we could have done a lot, but then they kept putting it off and said we want to have a big force to capture the town in the first place to give them time to do this and then to protect the town and the civilians from reprisals thereafter...They argued that they wanted to have a diversionary bombing attack on the town so that the whole thing could be disguised as a bombing attack.

But Greenwood had been sent *instead of* bombers and such an attack was impossible.

As for the Danube, the Chetniks kept inventing excuses about the difficulties of reaching it. As Greenwood had landed quite a distance away, he had no immediate way of finding out if what they said was true. What did strike him straight away was the deep hostility of the Chetniks towards the Partisans and their fixation on the massacres of Serbs that underpinned their military caution.

> The very first hour I was in Yugoslavia I'm sure the question of the million victims came up…they said all the Serbs in Croatia had been murdered…they were always referred to as the million victims. I suspect in fact there were maybe three hundred thousand, but that's a huge number of people, so I can understand the animosity of the Serbs towards the Croats and there was no limit the Serbs wouldn't go to kill a Croat – they'd much rather kill a Croat than a German, they really would.

As for the Communist Partisans, Greenwood observed that their dislike was largely ethnic: 'They didn't talk much about Communists. They talked about the Partisans and they identified them with Croats, so the real horror to them was a Croat-dominated Partisan whether he was a Communist or whatever he was. They [the Croats] were, in fact, mostly Catholic, so that was another thing. The Serbs were all Orthodox so that was another reason…'

Ethnic distrust surfaced in sometimes unexpected ways. From time to time Greenwood and the Chetnik officers – a ragbag collection of Royal Yugoslav officers, some air force, some army, and even one naval – would listen in to a BBC transmission in Serbo-Croat from London to catch up on news of the wider war in the Mediterranean or Russia: 'The transmissions from London caused unending trouble because they just couldn't imagine why it was that we had Croats speaking from the BBC…the Serbs positively hated these people and would have killed them willingly…On the

Partisan side of the operation I'm told that they objected to the fact that there were Serbian speakers from London.'

In practical terms little of this disturbed Greenwood's day-to-day existence, and he got on well with the Chetniks. The commanding officer, a professional infantryman in good command of his troops, immediately took care to give his SOE guest a personal bodyguard. The man took his job seriously, never got drunk, crossed himself religiously before anything happened, and always started or finished his sentences by saying 'If God grant it'.

He never left my side, he was marvellous and he carried my kit for me or arranged horses – all sorts of things. He was a professional soldier in the Gendarmerie in Bosnia. He was well-trained, he was literate and he looked like a picture of Mephistopheles in Faust so we started calling him Mephistopheles and that gradually became Mephistafolls and then Mr Folls…[eventually] he was referred to as Folls to his face. He didn't know a word of English of course but he was quite happy to be called Folls, or Seculo, which was his real name. He travelled everywhere I went and stayed with me until I boarded a plane to leave Yugoslavia and I gave him my revolver when I left. As I got into the plane I said, 'Here you are, Seculo, you've got a revolver now!'

In his early days Greenwood needed all the help he could get. Eastern Serbia was a remote place of scattered peasant villages and most of the Chetnik officers came from other parts of Serbia. So he invariably needed a guide. This had its perils: 'We would find a guide in the village and [say] we wanted to go to the next village, how do we get there? And he would say, "Oh, well, I know how to get there," and he would sometimes be offered money and sometimes not, but almost invariably before we set off he got drunk. I don't remember a move really where the guide wasn't drunk.'

Another problem was that guides, even if sober, were not very reliable. Most volunteered because they were anxious to please or eager for money. They would claim to be experienced travellers or to have relations in the next village. But Greenwood found this rarely to be true: 'He didn't have a cousin or if he did he didn't know who the cousin was and he'd never been there himself. It was quite frequent to find people who had never been two kilometres from the place where they were born.'

Eventually, as Greenwood got to know his territory, he dispensed with guides altogether. After several months he knew the terrain like the back of his hand and never got lost. There was one colourful character, however, whom he couldn't help bumping into from time to time and who proved useful:

> One of the people I happened to meet [through] some gypsies was the last surviving highwayman in Yugoslavia. I was quite interested. I had never in my life met a highwayman. His existence had rather ceased because of the war...He was a man, of course, who really did know the way everywhere and I used him subsequently as a guide because, if I could lay my hands on him, he at least knew where he was going. I met him maybe ten times...He was always drunk but not so drunk he got captured...I paid him and he was happy to have that; a gold sovereign was really a tremendous business for him and he was delighted to see me always. Occasionally he would go and get food for me as well because he was a man who knew how to look after himself and he looked after me if I paid him.

Greenwood himself came to appreciate the gold sovereigns, provided by SOE courtesy of the British Treasury, even more as time went by. Gradually, as he came to know the country and ventured further and further afield on his own, he needed access to ready cash simply to keep himself alive. He sent couriers into Belgrade who exchanged the sovereigns for the local dinars issued by the Serbian collaborationist government of General Nedic. With these he could buy almost anything he needed, from food to help for some small sabotage operations or other action he proposed.

It was not as though he was being kept well supplied with air drops from Cairo. SOE was still struggling with a shortage of aircraft, Greenwood was at the extreme edge of the range of Cairo-based planes, and as time passed the drops became less and less frequent. By the end of his time there they had practically ceased. In March 1944 he noted in his diary, 'Angrily signalled Cairo last night that we have stood by for over a hundred nights for this sortie, that we don't think it funny.'

Three months was a long and unsatisfactory wait by any count. But even when drops took place they often proved frustrating, as Greenwood soon learned: 'We spent a huge amount of time in ciphering lists of stuff and sending signals of what we wanted. Sometimes we'd decide we wanted enough uniforms to enable our troops to serve through the winter, for example, [because] they would have to go back to their peasant houses if they didn't have any clothing.'

Once, having requested such a delivery, he got up at five o'clock in the morning to unpack containers dropped that night. 'I started to unpack some stores,' he recorded at the time, 'a rude disappointment as they were appallingly bad, only seventeen pairs of trousers, forty tunics, fifty pairs of old and very small boots, and a few shirts.' He wondered why anybody had risked a plane and its crew for that. Stories also circulated about a mission that even though they had no electricity received an electrical standard lamp; another that received an entire load of onions, which could be still picked locally in the fields; and yet another sent a container of anti-snake bite venom when there were no poisonous snakes around.

On the other hand, drops could deliver welcome surprises. Not least were those that brought comfort and connected him to home: 'I got a lot of mail from my wife – thirty letters from her on one occasion all came together. I got copies of *The Times* reduced to one quarter size I think. It was on rice paper, very thin paper… I recall that I got a case of whisky on one occasion and it was very acceptable.'

The vagaries of air drops were irritating, but they did not – as might have been expected – seriously damage Greenwood's relations with the Chetniks: 'They grumbled about spending nights out in the cold and the rain waiting for some aircraft which didn't come but we didn't have real friction about that…because they realized that I could get no more supplies than they could. I was suffering just as much as they did.'

What did cause real friction was Greenwood's growing realization that – as Bailey and SOE in Cairo had long suspected – the Chetniks were determined to wage guerrilla war their own way and not as SOE required; this meant preserving their forces until the moment of liberation and in the meantime being extremely prudent. Greenwood put it this way: 'By the time we'd been there five or six months it was very clear they were unwilling to undertake anything...I would sometimes get quite angry and say, "Why can you not carry out the orders of the Supreme Headquarters?" and [someone] saying, "It's not orders, they're requests." They didn't regard themselves as part of the Allied armies.'

It was only by defying such Chetnik reluctance that Greenwood finally accomplished one of the two major goals he had set himself: disrupting the flow of traffic on the Danube.

In October 1943 he visited a local Chetnik commander, a Major Pilotic, who controlled territory close to the Danube, and persuaded him to co-operate. Then, with a handful of men lent him by Pilotic, he set off equipped with a dozen or so rifles and two light machine-guns. After two days of strenuous walking a courier caught up with them carrying a letter from Pilotic withdrawing his consent for the operation. Deciding that the Chetnik leader was simply trying to cover his tracks, Greenwood put the letter in his pocket and carried on as though nothing had changed.

Reaching the Danube under cover of dark, they positioned themselves carefully for the attack. One of the party was a former Danube pilot who knew the river channels well and told them exactly where to stop a tug so it would run aground with its convoy of barges. Action began at dawn when the first convoy appeared: 'We opened fire on the leading tug and the helmsman took evasive action and went almost immediately out of control and so did the second one...the barges behind them ran aground and that was the end of that really, that was exactly what I'd been trying to do for half a year...it cheered me up immensely.'

But as the Chetniks had feared and warned, German reaction was prompt and fierce. A few days later they announced the shooting of a hundred civilian hostages in Belgrade. The Chetnik response was also predictable.

The fact that they had these hostages shot, of course, was thrown in our faces by the local commanders. They said, 'There, we told you so, you can't do this sort of thing and have the poor civilians shot...and that was difficult to gainsay really...on the other hand you can't make an omelette without breaking eggs and we knew that it was customary when things went wrong with the Germans, they did shoot people. I not only felt responsible, I was responsible, but I felt it was how the war was being fought...I felt bad that they should be civilians who were dragged out of a cell and shot...anyone would feel bad about it.

The issue did not, however, poison Greenwood's relations with the Chetniks because by this time a far weightier issue had emerged to preoccupy them – the prospect that SOE support would be withdrawn altogether. Reports sent in by Greenwood and other SOE sub-missions in Serbia painted an expanding picture of Chetnik reluctance to engage the enemy. Cumulatively, they persuaded SOE that support to Mihailovich was not paying the hoped-for dividend. Reports reaching Cairo from Partisan territory also alleged that the Chetniks were even collaborating actively with the enemy. But whatever reservations Greenwood had about his Serb comrades-in-arms, this was not one: 'I had seen absolutely nothing to warrant that statement [re collaboration] at all, nor had any of my brother officers in Serbia, but I believe there was some truth in the fact of some accommodation between Mihailovich's forces in Montenegro and the Italians...I don't think they were collaborating, they'd agreed not to harm each other...'

The decision to abandon Mihailovich came early in 1944. After studying files in Cairo – including a photograph of a local Chetnik commander in Montenegro 'hobnobbing' with an Italian general – Churchill, once one of Mihailovich's strongest supporters, made his views plain. 'I have a policy which is perfectly clear,' he told the Foreign Secretary, Anthony Eden, 'namely, to persuade the King [Peter of Yugoslavia] to get rid of Mihailovich, who is hanging like a millstone around his neck and who is obnoxious to us...'[3]

When this news filtered down to Greenwood he worried how the Chetniks would respond. There was little need for concern, as he quickly learned.

The support they'd had was so meagre that it was almost immaterial, except that there was moral support and just to cut them off and leave them, that was going to be a disastrous thing and it worried us a great deal [about] what would happen to us when we said to them one day, 'Well, we're off.' In fact, nothing happened and they behaved remarkably well, we were astonished by it, not a hand was lifted against us...they said, 'Well, you know, you're a soldier and we're soldiers, you've nothing to do with this, you're doing as you're ordered...They took the view, 'We'll give you any help we can,'...they were entirely reasonable about it.

It took several weeks for Greenwood's departure to be arranged, but when it came he felt relieved to get out.

There were five British officers left and one radio operator and a plane came in to get us out. The Serbian troops were surrounding the area where the airstrip was but they weren't within sight. The only people actually physically with me was my Mr Folls and the servants of two other officers...We merely embraced them when we got on to the plane, we didn't hang about making speeches, and we were off and with rather a light heart than a heavy heart. I said, thank God I can get out of this...I'd spent six months doing nothing.

As support for the Chetniks dwindled and then died, so that for Tito's Partisans was born and flourished. From inside SOE's Yugoslav section in Cairo Basil Davidson had a front-seat view of the story.

By late 1942 intelligence was revealing that all was not what it seemed with the Chetniks and that Partisan resistance was causing the enemy greater problems. The source was top secret and known only to a few: intercepts of top secret enemy messages being broken by the codebreakers at Bletchley Park. One of those in Cairo briefed to receive it was none other than the man running SOE's operations there, Brigadier Mervyn Keble. An ambitious regular army officer, he left an indelible imprint on all those who encountered him. Davidson's memories remained pungent – literally: 'He was a strange man and this is in Cairo in the middle of summer, he wore nothing but a vest and if you wear the same vest for week after week it gets to be rather unpleasant and that was Keble all over, he was completely fixed on his work...he was very much authoritarian, he was a bully in short.'

Keble was receiving the intercept material because he had formerly been in intelligence and no one had taken him off the distribution list. What happened next is recorded by Davidson.

He came into my office one day and said that is a secret message. It was a little three lines of typescript in English, translated from the deciphering which they'd done...unique and wonderful information about what the Germans thought was happening...and Keble said 'Well, here you are, they're secret messages, you will not speak about them, you will not show them around, you will keep them locked up and you will draw up a map if you can of where you think these Partisans are.' So I drew up a map, put it on the wall, covered it up of course...this went on for some weeks until I got a fairly coherent map and could say to my superiors, if you want to contact these Partisans and if you want to drop people in to meet them, this is probably where you can do it.

Davidson worked on this with his number two, a young Oxford don named Bill Deakin, and together they decided there was a strong Partisan formation in western Croatia and another in central Bosnia.

Meanwhile the apparently inescapable conclusion from other supporting sources of intelligence – that help should be extended to Tito – had sparked bitter controversy in London and Cairo. A veritable civil war of competing factions broke out. Two sides took shape in SOE Cairo itself, as Davidson later wrote: 'Something like battle lines were drawn by the last weeks of 1942, and soon the opposing sides began to face each other with all the passion that set the Children of Light against the Children of Darkness. Fighting alliances were made, recruits were sought, morality wavered, truth lowered her head. Paper came into its own again. Squadrons of memoranda were loaded up and launched...'[4]

Decisive intervention in this civil war came with Churchill's arrival in Cairo in January 1943. By coincidence, Deakin had worked for Churchill before the war and knew him personally. Basil Davidson remembered: 'I heard that Churchill was coming to Cairo and Deakin immediately said that he would go and see him. The only thing I knew was that Deakin had been Winston's research man at Oxford when Deakin was a young historian and Winston was about to write the history of his great ancestor, the Duke of Marlborough.'

On Deakin's urging, Churchill agreed to see Keble, who told the Prime Minister about the Partisans. When he returned to London Churchill showed the evidence to Lord Selborne, the SOE minister, and ordered him to find out more about the Partisans. By April SOE was dropping exploratory missions and Deakin himself was parachuted in to Tito's headquarters. Later, Churchill sent in his own personal emissary, Fitzroy Maclean.

That summer, as head of a mission codenamed 'Savanna', Davidson himself went in: 'We were amazed at what we discovered…an effective resistance movement of people who were determined to fight and were perfectly ready to be our allies up to the point that their resistance would be respected of course. They weren't going to be anyone's stooges; they were going to be independent but they would be our allies.'

On greeting Davidson, Tito made it bluntly clear to him what he wanted.

He said, 'Oh, you've come, good, what do you want to do here?' 'Well,' I said, 'we've come to help you if we can.' And he said, 'How are you going to help…could we send in arms?' I said, 'Yes, we can up to a point.'…He was very pleased indeed and very friendly and I remained his friend after the war. In fact he was a man you couldn't help respecting and admiring. A dyed-in-the-wool Communist of course but I had nothing to say about that, we were not told you mustn't support the Communists…

Davidson himself, it should be emphasized, was not a Communist, and neither was Deakin or Keble, points worth emphasizing because certain hostile critics of SOE have pointed the finger at a Communist conspiracy in Cairo to explain the switch to Tito. Davidson, in fact, had worked as press secretary to Archibald

Sinclair, the leader of the Liberal Party immediately before the war. Sinclair and Churchill were close friends and allies in the fight against appeasement and neither was conceivably Communist.

By almost any count the Partisans were impressive, as Davidson noted.

First impressions were very good, they continued to be very good, it was a very fine movement and it was very combined, very solidified, very united, at least that was the product that I saw in northern Serbia. They were effectively all farmers, very decent people with a great tradition of hospitality and they took to us, to me and to others who were there in the measure that we accepted their standards and put up with the conditions which they put up with. They were physically very strong, very tough, but they were also morally tough. Any who were captured by the enemy were usually shot without question.

Davidson's Savanna mission was destined not for Yugoslavia itself, but for Hungary, his former stomping ground. The idea was to infiltrate the country through the Vojvodina, that part of Yugoslavia occupied by the Hungarians north of the Danube. Here, too, Tito's Partisans were active. Although Davidson succeeded in crossing the Danube, he never managed to penetrate into Hungary. Instead, for several months, he lived among them, experiencing the hardship, the perils, and the comradeship of guerrilla life.

The Partisans, who were mostly of peasant origin, were as tough in war as in peace. Hunger was a constant companion. Once, during a retreat from the Germans, Davidson witnessed how desperate it could be: 'Everybody was hungry, nobody had eaten properly for days and hunger's a terrible thing if you're really hungry and two of the Yugoslavs who were with me had got it into their heads that I was getting special food...unfortunately it looked and smelled like food [but] was plastic high explosive...small sausages which you could mould, very good for sticking on to tanks...it also smells like marzipan. They ate these sausages and they died in agony.'

They spent most of their active time in small-scale operations ambushing German convoys. They often used children: 'Little boys who might be eight or nine years old, you know, small nippy lads would creep up and throw their grenades over the parapet into where the enemy was and that would be an occasion to launch an attack.'

The perils were immediate and obvious. In March 1944 Davidson and the Partisans were driven out of Raca, a small village in Vojvodina that was solidly pro-Partisan and had been sheltering its local high command, by an SS unit of Bosnian Muslims commanded by German officers. After they'd left, Davidson went back in. What he saw was shocking. Altogether, almost 400 villagers had been slaughtered, women, old men, and children and babies. In detailed notes, he recorded that they had been 'slaughtered in the most fearful conditions, throats cut, bodies thrown into the woods or burnt...some cases of corpses being so mutilated and shot through that it's impossible to say how they were murdered.'

In one place, they found ten female corpses cut in pieces, and in a pile of ashes they found a baby's shoe, the flat disc of a baby's skull, and other charred fragments of bodies. In another village they found a young girl: 'I remember very well, she was eight years old and they had killed her mother by hitting her on the head and she fell on top of this child and the child, petrified, stayed there until we arrived two days later...The war was a dreadful business, don't let anybody suppose for a moment it was anything but horrible...the only thing was to fight it and make certain it didn't happen again.'

In June 1944 news reached Davidson of the D-Day landings in Normandy. It came as a great relief because the Partisans had been echoing Moscow's criticisms of the west for not launching it sooner. He retained a vivid memory of where and how he heard it.

I had been on reconnaissance north of the Danube [and we reached] a wooded forest on the southern bank and I remember there was a steep bank you had to climb...the river is 800 or 900 metres wide. When I climbed up [there] was a young Partisan commander who I knew very well and he said to me, 'You have made an honest man of yourself...the Second Front has opened up.' Climbing out of the ditch in wet weather I was rather cross...but the war was going to be won, there was no question about it...I stayed with that little group for a few days and that was a very happy time. By this time I could speak very good Serbian so they tended to forget I wasn't one of them so one could merge as it were into their companionship and that was very agreeable, in fact I've never forgotten it.

Tito, like Mihailovich, had his own plans for the postwar Yugoslavia that was now rapidly approaching. Despite his eager acceptance of arms from SOE, in September 1944 he flew to Moscow and made it plain he was no mere puppet of Churchill or the British. In October the Red Army, along with units of the Partisans, entered Belgrade. Davidson entered the Yugoslav capital a few days later: 'Once we'd taken Belgrade it was only a question of time, by mopping up parties of fascists left here and there, the thing was more or less over and there was a big banquet…they invited me, they said you'd better come too, you've been with us through all these months, come and share our joy and I wasn't averse to doing that, of course, so that is what happened, and nine or ten partisan generals and a lot of Russian generals were there…'

When the war ended Tito and the Communists were in full control of Yugoslavia. Mihailovich and a few loyal Chetniks took to the hills but were soon captured. In 1946, after a show trial, Mihailovich was shot. He had, he declared, wanted much and begun much but had been swept away by the whirlwind of history.

For Davidson, as for others SOE officers in Yugoslavia, peace delivered a different fate.

It's difficult to get adjusted to the idea that you're not going to die, that's the first thing, because in partisan war the great thing was that you passed the early part of the day until about twelve o'clock expecting to be attacked…you're not necessarily expecting to survive, this was the test of nerves and there's a point at which they cease to be resilient and peace breaks out and you find it hard to adjust. I can only put it that way, others might put it quite differently. In any case I was lucky, I survived…we were lucky, we survived!

NOTES
1 'Erik Greenwood', in *The Special Operations Executive: Sound Archive and Oral History Recordings* (Imperial War Museum), p. 95.
2 S. W. Bailey, 'British Policy Towards General Draza Mihailovic', in *British Policy Towards Wartime Resistance in Yugoslavia and Greece*, ed. Phyllis Auty and Richard Clogg, p. 72.
3 Churchill to Eden, 'Most Secret', 5 February 1944, Chartwell 20/152, Churchill College, Cambridge.
4 Basil Davidson, *Special Operations Europe*, p. 107.

CHAPTER 13

FIGHTING FOR FRANCE

There were two agents in the car as it pulled away from Baker Street and headed north up the Finchley Road. In the office they had collected the cases already packed and waiting for them.

Around them the humdrum daily routine went on. Telephones rang, doors opened and shut, secretaries hurried about with files. It was drizzling outside, a typically bleak winter afternoon. The car headed up the Great North Road towards Tempsford. In the front beside the driver one of the two agents, a young man, sat quietly reading a book of poetry. His companion, a woman barely in her twenties, sat in the back lost in her own thoughts. That night they stayed in a large country house close to the airfield. The next afternoon, checking the blackboard over the chimney piece in the drawing room, they read their names. It was time to leave.

A car came, they climbed in, crossed a railway line, and they were on the aerodrome. In a Nissen hut with a blazing fire, a final check of their clothing and personal possessions confirmed that none of them showed evidence of being made in Britain. They were handed bundles of bank notes, struggled into their parachutes, and collected their pistols. The woman, unlike her male companion, declined the cyanide pill offered her. Then they got back in the car, drove a couple of hundred yards, and clambered out under the wing of a Hudson plane. They shook hands with the pilot and the despatcher and climbed on board.

Inside it was cramped and they lay down on the cold metal floor. The propellers swung, the engines caught, the pilot revved, and the floor began to tremble. The wheels bumped beneath them as the plane taxied to the end of the runway. Then the engines opened up and in the gathering speed they suddenly felt the ground drop away beneath them. It was February 1944. Two more SOE 'Joes' were on their way. This time the destination was France.

France took up more of SOE's time and effort than any other

occupied country except Yugoslavia. It was close and relatively easy to infiltrate. But more important was its choice as the site for D-Day, the 1944 Anglo-American landings that hastened the end of the war in the west. This main strategic target defined SOE's mission in France for most of the war.

But it was never easy. Although its size and varied geography made it ideal resistance country, it was a politically and militarily divided minefield. The collaborating Vichy regime under Marshal Pétain, the hero of Verdun from the First World War, commanded the loyalty of most of the population. By contrast the Free French, under the command of General Charles de Gaulle in London, struggled at first to find their feet. The Germans divided the country into two zones and occupied the whole of the north and the entire Atlantic coastline. After the Allied landings in North Africa in November 1942 they extended this to occupy the entire country. The knowledge that France was destined to become a major battleground sharpened the vigilance of the Gestapo who found dangerous allies among ardent French collaborators.

SOE had several sections working into France but the two most important were its RF and F sections. The former worked exclusively with the Free French and for this reason was often called the 'Gaullist' section. The latter worked quite independently of de Gaulle: it was by no means clear how much support he enjoyed in France and British strategic interest did not always coincide with his. He was furious when he found out about it and never reconciled himself to its existence – as F section agents were to discover at the end of the war.

The RF section had many successes and one of its most famous agents, Forrest Yeo-Thomas – better known under his codename 'The White Rabbit' – personally convinced Churchill in one memorable face-to-face encounter to order more supplies to the Maquis.[1] To RF section too can be credited two of SOE's earliest successes in France. While Operation Savanna of March 1941 failed to achieve its target of eliminating a German pathfinder force in Brittany, it conclusively demonstrated at a critical time for SOE that agents could be dropped into the country, move about unobtrusively, and then be safely extracted. Two months later Josephine B, an RF section sabotage operation, severely damaged an important power station near Bordeaux. Both gave heart to Baker Street and helped convince Dalton and the Chiefs of Staff that it could fight a plausible war.[2] But until November 1942 SOE was hampered by a Foreign Office ban on sabotage in the unoccupied zone.

Among the first wave of F section agents parachuted into France was Jean Le Harivel, a twenty-three-year-old wireless operator. He was also a trained saboteur, as were the other three members of his mission, codenamed 'Corsican': Daniel Turberville, Jack Hayes, and the leader of the group, only ever known by his surname, Jumeau. Like many SOE agents Le Harivel was of mixed nationality. His father was British, his mother was French and he was born in France. But he grew up in Edinburgh and got his degree from Glasgow University before joining the Royal Corps of Signals in 1940 and becoming a wireless operator. SOE soon spotted him and he volunteered to go to France after a friendly and persuasive interview with Lewis Gielgud.

His reason was simple, and potent. The humiliation of French defeat burned as deeply into his soul as that of Charles de Gaulle: 'We were patriotic, we really believed in this fight against Nazism and the fact that France had been invaded hurt terribly. My mother was very upset but we were all upset to think of the German army reaching Paris, it was unheard-of that Paris should be occupied. That picture of Hitler dancing in front of the Eiffel Tower was really deplorable.'

The Corsican mission was typical of many operations into France in 1941–2. Coming soon after the first special duties squadron was formed, it further demonstrated the potential for dropping agents behind enemy lines. Yet its fate when it got there revealed how difficult and treacherous the terrain could be. It took place at a crucial moment in France. That same month – October 1941 – the Germans shot forty-eight French hostages in reprisal for the assassination of one German colonel, an event that sparked the birth of a proper nationwide resistance. But this remained a minority and dangerous choice and the vast majority of the population preferred to lie low or else support the Vichy regime. As for SOE, by this time it had succeeded in sending only twenty or so agents into the country and there were a mere couple of W/T sets in operation. Gubbins even admitted to Dalton that they had more arms than resistance to give them to, through 'insufficiency of agents abroad'.

After standard training in England and Scotland Le Harivel's group was parachuted into the Dordogne, near the town of Bergerac, in October 1941. Their plane was a Whitley and they were seen off by Thomas Cadett, the former BBC correspondent in Paris who was now working for F Section. Their mission was to create a network using Marseille as a focal point. Le Harivel remembered the flight as tense and uncomfortable: 'Our emotions were a bit mixed, glad to get off at long last but thinking what the devil is going to happen to us once we get there. The plane was most uncomfortable because it was stripped of everything inside, so very cold. I remember feeling cold, the RAF escort officer was very kind and he had a Thermos of hot coffee which helped.'

The discomfort soon turned to brief euphoria. Over the dropping zone the pilot circled a couple of times before spotting the agreed signal being flashed by torch from the ground, switched the light in the fuselage from red to green, and Le Harivel jumped into the night: 'I can still remember as if it were yesterday the drop because it was a full moon, beautiful scenery. There was a large field and trees all around, the countryside was absolutely wonderful, and I remember for a few seconds just admiring the countryside, not thinking about the actual jump. You could hear dogs barking.'

But harsh reality descended almost as quickly as the ground that sped up towards Le Harivel as he vainly struggled to avoid landing among the trees. One of the team, Daniel Turberville, landed several kilometres from the main group and was almost immediately arrested. Worse, Le Harivel's wireless transmitter, which was packed into one of the several containers dropped by the same plane, also went astray and neither he nor the waiting reception committee ever found it. He was finally behind enemy lines. But without his wireless set his mission had got off to a disastrous start and SOE in southern France was little better off than it had been before.

Far worse was to follow. Having hidden for a few days in a nearby barn they set off by train for Marseille where they had been given the name of a safe house, the Villa des Bois. They travelled separately, passed safely through all the documentary checks and personal searches, and after lying low in a small hotel for a few days Le Harivel made for the agreed rendezvous. The door was opened by an attractive young woman with a small child at her side who told him that unfortunately her husband was not there but that he should meet him the next day at a café on the bustling Boulevard Canebière. Le Harivel scrupulously and unsuspectingly followed her instructions.

> The next day as agreed I went to the café on the Canebière and as I approached I saw on the terrace the lady I'd met the night before and a man whom I supposed was the husband. Pleased, I walked up to them, sat down and chatted for a while, but a very short while, because two plain-clothes policemen arrived with their cards, with the tricolour flag on them, and arrested me, without any fuss, no handcuffing or anything like that. My heart dropped, my stomach dropped, it was an awful moment of my life. I couldn't understand what had gone wrong, I was meeting a 'safe' contact. I was completely shattered. The first contact had been the last contact. It was an awful moment, you know, everything collapses at that time and in a flash everything's finished.

While the police took him back to his hotel Le Harivel did some rapid thinking because he was still carrying his codes and broadcasting schedules. Fortunately the police inspector appears to have been half-sympathetic to his captive's plight and as he searched the hotel room, 'he turned his back on me for quite a while, a minute or two, and during that minute or two I was able to swallow my little card with all my wireless codes and times of broadcasts. I swallowed with difficulty but I swallowed so that they didn't find that at least.'

But what the French police *had* found were the other members of the Corsican team who had walked into similar traps after visiting the Villa des Bois. So had several local members of the resistance. Le Harivel found this out when he arrived at the police station and encountered the pro-Vichy commissar of police: 'He was raving and ranting and shouting and saying, "Ha! I've caught another one." My heart dropped another time and he was so happy because he'd been able to capture several people. I thought, several people, whatever's happened? At the prison not only did I find Hayes and Jumeau but finally there were twelve of us, twelve who'd been caught.'

Le Harivel still wonders what lay behind the disaster of the Villa des Bois. Was it treachery or careless security? The latter seems more likely. Several people had been given the name of the Villa des Bois and once the Vichy police had their eyes on it the fate of the SOE agents was sealed.

At least they were facing the Vichy police, not the Gestapo, and their conditions of imprisonment were relatively benign. From Marseille they were transferred to Périgueux prison and then, after several weeks, to a Vichy internment camp at Mauzac in the Dordogne some fifteen miles from Bergerac, where they were treated reasonably well. Here the wife of one of the internees managed to smuggle in a camera with which they took a picture of themselves that constitutes a unique record of an SOE team behind enemy lines. On the wall behind them they wrote *Les causes qui meurent sont celles pour lesquelles on ne sait plus mourir* ('The causes which die are those for which we no longer know how to die'). Later, the same woman also made possible their escape and in the summer of 1942 Le Harivel made his way back to Britain and Baker Street via Spain and Gibraltar.

Safely home, he became an escort officer for F Section agents training in Britain. He noticed that in the months he'd been away things had changed. Apart from new faces at the top he discerned a far more confident and professional atmosphere at work: 'The organization had changed. It had become bigger, the staff was more aware of what was happening, the objectives were more clearly defined, and credibility was gaining in the circles surrounding our activities. Experience had been gained and they had learned from our mishaps. The staff were more aware of the situation in France because information was being sent back all the time on the state of mind of the French.'

France by this time had also changed. The shock of defeat had worn off and two years of occupation had exposed the harsher realities of collaboration. The comforting illusion of freedom created by the huge non-occupied zone was shattered in November 1942 when the Germans marched in after Anglo-American forces invaded North Africa. Soon after, the demand for conscripted French labour to work in the factories of the Reich sent thousands of young men fleeing into the countryside where eventually they formed the Maquis, an important element of the resistance provided it could be fed and armed. Another milestone was the Red Army victory at Stalingrad in February 1943 that further gave heart to the occupied and injected new militancy into the resistance.

But by the same token the collaborators became more desperate to save their skins and in early 1943 created the Milice, a brutal paramilitary force that worked hand in glove with the Germans to hunt down the resistance. Allied victories thus proved a mixed blessing for SOE agents in France.

Into this turbulent scene arrived Roger Landes, who after his interview with Lewis Gielgud had joined SOE as a radio operator. He was to survive in France for almost two years and even to make a successful return trip to Britain in the middle of it. His career as an agent bridged the crucial period between the North African landings and D-Day when SOE moved decisively from its formative stage to delivering its massive dividend for liberation.

It was no less dangerous for that. It almost failed at the start when Landes had the miserable experience of three failed flights from Tempsford before he was finally able to parachute over the Loire and make his way to Bordeaux. Here, taking the codename 'Aristide', his mission was to act as wireless operator for the 'Scientist' circuit led by one of F Section's most capable operators, Claude de Baissac. Both were acutely aware of how careless security had damaged SOE's work, and de Baissac had deliberately cut links with a huge but deeply flawed network straddling southern France known as 'Carte' on which many of SOE's early hopes had been pinned. Lack of security and German penetration were to characterize some circuits in 1943, too, and de Gaulle's personal representative with the resistance in France, Jean Moulin, was to be arrested and tortured to death by the Gestapo in Lyon. But for SOE the overall picture was one of slow but steady success.

Landes was a careful man. By and large he kept himself to himself and always observed a cardinal principle of never letting anyone, not even his boss de Baissac, know where he kept his wireless set (or sets, because he kept four hidden around the city), or where he transmitted from, or even where he slept at night. By now SOE knew much more about German radio detection methods and Landes tried whenever he could to use a car battery rather than mains electricity for his power source.

This did not, however, save him from at least one narrow escape.

He had been transmitting once a week from a set hidden in the bedroom of a house owned by a woman on the outskirts of the city. To enter the house he walked through a garage which to a casual observer looked as though it belonged to the house next door. Arriving on his bike, he followed the usual procedure. But then he received a shock.

> When I arrived the daughter, who was about sixteen years old, said, 'Mummy has been arrested. The Germans were looking for a transmitter but didn't find it.' She said she'd tried to dispose of the set through the septic tank but it was too big. I said, 'Well, I didn't see anyone when I came to your house,' and she said, 'No, because they left someone from the Gestapo to watch the house and from time to time he goes to the café next door.' Then I said, 'Well, I will take the set and put it on the back of my bicycle and when you see that fellow go into the café let me know.' Then I put my revolver in my pocket and as I came out from the house the fellow from the Gestapo came out of the café and my set fell from the bicycle. I put my hand in my pocket but he lifted up the set and helped me put it on the bicycle and I said, 'Thank you very much,' and at the next corner took another road.

Only after the war did Landes learn that the Gestapo agent had later filed a report saying that a small man, obviously not a British agent, had come out of the garage of the house next door to the one he was watching and ridden off on a bicycle with a package on the back and was obviously of no relevance to the case. Careless security was no side's monopoly in the underground war.

But how did the Gestapo suspect he had a set in the house in the first place? At the root of this episode lay treachery that forced Landes to take brutal action he had never contemplated, despite his training.

De Baissac had recruited for his Scientist circuit a retired colonel named André Grandclement, a member of the OCM (Organisation Civile et Militaire), a resistance grouping of conservative army officers and civil servants. The son of an admiral, Grandclement himself was on the political far right but had proved invaluable to de Baissac in finding recruits and organizing reception committees for drops of agents and equipment. In July 1943 the Germans carried out mass arrests around Bordeaux and from someone got hold of Grandclement's address. He was not there, but his wife was, and she was immediately arrested. Her husband had carelessly left a card index of all his contacts and besides arresting many of them the Gestapo was able to track Grandclement himself to Paris where he, too, was picked up and immediately returned to Bordeaux for interrogation by the local Gestapo chief.

This was a man named Dhose, and by subtly playing on Grandclement's right-wing views – as well as exploiting fears of what might happen to his wife – he convinced Grandclement to help the Germans, as Roger Landes later told the story: 'I always feel but could not prove it that Grandclement betrayed us after his wife was arrested. The chief of the Gestapo told Grandclement the Germans are losing the war but the Communists will take over in France and you've got to collaborate.'

After this, and following his close brush with the Gestapo watcher on his bicycle outside the house, which had originally been recommended as a suitable hideout by Madame Grandclement, Landes returned to England via Spain while SOE took stock of the disastrously changed scene in Bordeaux. He returned by parachute in March 1944 to build a new circuit in time for D-Day. He was also determined to deal with Grandclement, who was causing considerable damage to the resistance cause.

The opportunity came when a local resistance group managed to capture Grandclement and his wife and summoned Landes to help with the interrogation. After it was over the outcome was clear. Convincing the couple they were being taken back to London where they could plead their case before fellow Frenchmen, they drove them out to a Maquis stronghold in the country. Here, Landes told Grandclement that the plane from England was on its way and for security he had to be separated from his wife. As he walked ahead, a member of the group shot him in the back of the head. This was the sign for Landes, who put the muzzle of his .45 automatic to the back of Madame Grandclement's head and fired once. The blood spouted from her forehead and she fell to the ground, killed instantly. The bodies were then hastily buried by the Maquis and Landes and his men returned to Bordeaux.

Later, after the war, Landes learned from the Gestapo chief Dhose that Madame Grandclement had never agreed with her husband's actions and was unlikely to have provided him with information. But in 1944 Landes felt he had no other choice; he simply couldn't take the risk of letting her go even if he'd known then she was innocent, as he explained.

> We were discussing with the other men from the Maquis who is going to kill the woman, me being in charge of the group, well, it is my duty to do it. We couldn't let her go, you see, because if I had been arrested all my group would have been arrested. I was responsible for the lives of my men, I'd got to protect my men and unfortunately in a war sometimes you've got to kill innocent people. I didn't sleep for a week after that because it was the first time I used my pistol and I had never shot anybody before.[3]

Few SOE agents had to face such awesome choices, and not all worked in such treacherous territory as Bordeaux. Francis Cammaerts, for example, who established a circuit in south-eastern France in mid 1943, felt himself on surer ground and remembered with affection the support he received from ordinary Frenchmen and women:

> I was never lonely because the welcome and protection I received from my French friends who were my hosts and looked after me was so warm and so profound. It was the modest homes, the housewives and the husbands and their families who looked after us, who helped us, who hid materials, who carried messages. In all the cells there were people like this and I would say the most important element was the housewife who fed us, clothed us and kept us cheerful.

A particularly vivid example was provided by his own reception when he parachuted back in early in 1944 after returning to London for a briefing.

> I had to jump in an area I didn't know. I landed in a potato field not far from the farmer's house and knocked at the door and he poked his head through the window and said, 'What do you want?' I said,

'I've had an accident,' and he said, 'Well, you're five kilometres from the road, how does that happen?' I said, 'You may have heard the aeroplane,' and he shouted out to his wife, 'Get the bottle of wine out – we've got an airman.' That's the kind of reception I would have had in nine out of ten farmhouses in rural France.

Yet Cammaerts owed his survival and success to scrupulous security. He originally arrived in France by Lysander with a mission to repair the damage done to SOE in southern France by the collapse of the Carte network. Immediately he sensed that all was not right. 'My own personal experience on arriving was shock and horror because I was put with members of the reception committee into a petrol-driven car and driven through Paris. This was after the curfew and I didn't feel happy about it and it was just the beginning of severe criticism on my part of the failure of proper security on the part of the people who were meeting me.'

His instincts were confirmed when the very next day his principal contact was arrested. Leaving quickly for the Riviera he found much the same there. 'These people,' his French wireless operator told him, 'money is too important a part of their life, we want to go to people for whom living and politics are more important than money.' So he moved on again, north up the Rhône, and for the next eighteen months exhibited what one historian has described as 'extraordinary gifts as a clandestine operator'.[4]

But even here he always remembered the cardinal rules of security. He never slept more than three or four nights in the same place, selected his personal cover with great care – posing as a doctor got him through many a German curfew – and recruited supporters only after rigorous inspection.

You had to be certain that the people you were working with had the same understanding of security as you had yourself, you had to work through trusted leaders, every cell had to have someone whom you knew was loved and trusted by the people he was working with. They had to accept your basic principles of security which meant a whole lot of things including not using the telephone and not going into the black market cafés.

Such care paid off. When a sub-agent's careless talk led the Gestapo to round up thirty members of one of his circuits, including its second-in-command, none of them could lead the Germans to Cammaerts because they had no idea where he was – he always used couriers to contact them; and even when they circulated a description of him throughout southern France, no one turned him in.

All across France organizers like Cammaerts patiently constructed networks throughout 1943 and early 1944 in preparation for D-Day. By this time F section had received its detailed directive for the landings: in advance to increase the tempo of sabotage and then, when the landings took place, to launch 'an all-out attack on roads, railways and telephones, and the harassing of occupation troops wherever they could be found by any available means'.[5] Throughout the country circuits prepared for liberation and SOE agents arrived in increasing numbers.

One of them was Yvonne Baseden. After boarding the Hudson that cold night in February 1944, she suffered the all-too-common frustration of having to return to Tempsford when the pilot failed to satisfy himself that the landing ground was safe and had to wait for another attempt.

SOE was unique among wartime organizations in allowing women to join the front line as equals with men. The decision was made in 1942 after intense discussion in Baker Street about the urgent need for wireless operators and couriers to build up networks in France. It was felt that women, who could move about more freely than men, would be especially suitable. As a result F section sent in thirty-nine women agents over the next two years. All received the same training as men including unarmed combat, the use of pistols and Sten guns, and the handling of plastic explosives. They proved fully equal to the more numerous men. Fifteen were captured by the Germans and sent to concentration camps. Of these, twelve were murdered, one died and only two survived the horrors. Yvonne Baseden was one of those caught who lived to tell her story.[6]

After being contacted by SOE, she trained as a wireless operator. Early in 1944, aged twenty-two, she parachuted into France on her second flight from Tempsford with her poetry-reading companion, a young French nobleman named Gonzagues de St Genies, codenamed Lucien. As his wireless operator she was to help him build up 'Scholar', a circuit in eastern France close to Dijon and the Swiss border. Their job was to prepare for D-Day. This involved locating and preparing landing grounds for drops of arms to be stored for action later – hoarding was not always welcome to the local resistance, which was keen for immediate action.

The biggest and most dramatic of these drops was Operation 'Cadillac', the first ever mass daylight delivery of small arms and explosives to the resistance by American Fortress bombers in July 1944. This came after D-Day but before the American landings in southern France. Baseden was in radio contact with the thirty-six planes even before they left the ground. The sight left an indelible memory: 'This was an extraordinary day, a Sunday, and a very nice afternoon when the planes came over. We could hear the roar of the engines and we had lots of lorries gathered all around that particular area. The sight of all these parachutes dropping the containers was an amazing sight in the middle of the day. There were about 500 containers. We needed probably 800 people there to move the material as quickly as possible.'

But exhilaration turned quickly to disaster. In advance of the huge German sweep they knew would follow she and Lucien quickly went to ground. Unfortunately they were unable to reach their planned hideout because of German road traps and so returned to the base they had previously been using, a cheese depot on the outskirts of Dole. She took the normal security precaution of not travelling with her wireless set. But the man who did was caught and tortured. Believing that Baseden and Lucien were elsewhere, he finally revealed the location of the depot.

Here the two agents and several resisters were sitting down to a meal to celebrate the historic drop with the concierge and his wife, both Swiss, who had long helped with SOE escape routes. What happened next scarred Yvonne Baseden's memory for life.

We sat down to lunch keeping someone on watch of course at the window because the depot was surrounded by a lot of spare land and there was a big entrance and one could observe the approach. Within half an hour or so the chap at the window said, 'The Boche!' We swept up the table, left two places, and dispersed as quickly as we could to various hiding places within the depot.

I happened to be on the ground floor where I could hide immediately and Lucien went up and hid between the floor and the ceiling of where we were. The first part of the search was not very extensive because the Germans couldn't quite follow why they'd been brought to this huge depot and left one man on duty.

The hours went by and we were all anxious that maybe with the approach of darkness some of us might be able to escape until unfortunately the sound of a water cistern meant that the man on duty decided there must be someone there and called the Germans back to do a proper search. There were at least twenty of them and they started to shoot randomly. Eventually we were found one by one. I was one of the first. They shot through the floor in exasperation and it's only because blood came through the ceiling that they realized there was someone there and they eventually found Lucien. I saw his body being brought down handcuffed to another man. We were all put into horse-drawn carts and taken to Dole.

Lucien almost certainly swallowed his suicide pill after being wounded. This was an option he had insisted with Yvonne he would follow in order to protect the other members of his group – which was why, unlike her, he had picked up his pill in the Nissen hut at Tempsford. Still traumatized by his death and the events of the day, Baseden was eventually transferred to prison in Dijon.

We realized that this was going to be a very difficult time. We were put into individual cells. The only thing that kept us going was the thought that probably the job that had been the day before had been a success. I was on the top floor, cell number 111. I could peer out of the window which was giving some sight of the outside road. We knew D-Day had happened of course but we visualized the armies advancing more rapidly than they really were. But it did give us some hope and we also heard that there had been a plot to kill Hitler. There were cheers. I always talk in the plural because I visualized what the others were doing! Everyone was interrogated separately and there was no idea that they had found my radio or thought I would have been the radio operator so there was nothing much pinned to me except being with a group of resistance.

The failure by the Germans to identify her as an SOE agent undoubtedly saved her life. Like thousands of Frenchmen and women caught in the resistance she was put on a train and sent east, to Germany and a concentration camp. En route to Ravensbrück she was kept for two or three days at a camp in Saarbrücken. There, to her horror, she saw three fellow SOE female agents whom she recognized from her training – Violet Szabo, Denise Bloch and Lilian Rolfe – who were also destined for Ravensbrück: 'I thought it's incredible, they've got the whole of SOE. I hesitated about speaking to them and they naturally reacted in the same way until I realized it was safe to speak with Violet and I thought I would love to be with them, if only I could get into their group. But fortunately, as circumstances worked out, it was just as well that I was not able to do this. I saw them just to see that they were OK and they were on their way before us.'

It was a poignant moment, for the three young women were already doomed. Unlike her they were identified as SOE agents and were shot together at Ravensbrück in February 1945.

Yvonne Baseden followed them to this notorious camp, crammed for two days with dozens of others into a cattle truck with its doors firmly locked and no food or water. Fifty years later she still remembered her block number – 26 – and her individual number – 62,947. Over the winter, sick with TB, she was transferred to the hospital wing. Here, by some miracle, a guardian angel appeared under the name of Mary Lindell, a fellow prisoner and escape-line worker whom she had already met in Dijon who was also a qualified Red Cross nurse. Lindell managed to get Baseden into a small group of the sick who were evacuated by the Swedish Red Cross in April 1945, just days before Hitler's suicide in his bunker in Berlin. After brief hospitalization in Malmö she was put on a plane to Leuchars, in Scotland, and from there made it back to London and a year-long recovery from her ordeal.

For SOE in France, D-Day and its aftermath was the pay-off for three hard years of perilous preparation. On 1 June 1944 hundreds of coded warning messages to resistance circuits went out over the BBC alerting them to the impending invasion, following them up on the evening of 5 June, as the massive Allied invasion fleet sailed across the Channel, with a general call for action. The next two months, until the Allied armies broke out of northern France and the Americans – with seven French divisions – landed in southern France in mid-August, saw the resistance deliver the long-planned-for dividend. In Bordeaux Roger Landes, who by now had built up a force of some 2000 men, launched massive sabotage attacks on road and rail routes north out of Bordeaux towards Normandy. Cammaerts and others in south-eastern France opened doors for the Americans advancing from the south. Here, as one historian has put it, 'So thoroughly had the termites of resistance eaten away by now the pillars of German authority that the whole structure crumbled to powder in days.'[7]

A huge army of agents descended on France at this time. Arriving in Dole shortly before Yvonne Baseden's capture was a tough and rambunctious Scot, George Millar, who parachuted in from an American Liberator bomber on the night of 1 June 1944 to form the 'Chancellor' network. Already familiar to him during an earlier escape from a German prisoner of war camp following his capture in the North Africa desert while fighting with the Eighth Army, the local Maquis formed the backbone of his mission. As with others, it was to obstruct German reinforcements rushing into the Normandy bridgehead. Making Besançon, the capital of the Franche-Comté, his focal point, Millar quickly warmed to his task of getting to know his men.

They proved to be very much to my taste, they were young men, very keen indeed. One of them, Maurice, had been in the hands of the Gestapo when they knocked out four of his teeth. He was a tough young man obviously, probably had been a Communist, he was really good. I started straightaway on sabotage with them. In marshalling yards you had turntables. I'd been taught in SOE school that these were prime targets so I sent two chaps the first night I was there in the Maquis to blow up these two turntables. We waited in sleeping bags in the woods until in the end I heard two explosions. The next night, thinking that people don't strike on successive nights, I took the whole lot of the Maquis into Besançon station, positioned the men on guard, and I put sixteen charges inside the crook of each set of points. We marched away and were perhaps half-way back to the forest and the explosions were sounding one after another, pretty well all in a real clump together as we'd put half-hour time pencils on all of them and they thought in Besançon that an air raid was on so they left the marshalling yards severely alone.

As a result of Millar's action the RAF decided against bombing Besançon, a city of stately seventeenth-century architecture, another of many examples where well-targeted sabotage by SOE did a better job than destructive mass bombing. Elsewhere, by dint of similar action, he played a significant part in post-D-Day sabotage throughout his region and after the war he wrote up his experiences in three classic books.[8]

Paris was liberated on 25 August and by mid-September de Gaulle had established a provisional government. For SOE's F Section agents this was a difficult time, as Roger Landes discovered painfully when de Gaulle arrived personally in Bordeaux to accept the plaudits of his liberated countrymen. The SOE agent, whose small army of resisters had by now grown to some 20,000, was introduced to de Gaulle wearing his British army uniform. But the gesture received a frigid and brutal response. 'You are British. Your place is not here,' said the general, and gave him two hours to leave the city. Later that day Landes was summoned to the prefecture to meet de Gaulle's Minister of War. Landes described what happened when he got there.

I came with one of my bodyguards and at the top of the staircase was someone in civvy clothes who started shouting at me, 'What are you doing here, you've been ordered to leave.' My bodyguard put a machine-gun on his stomach and said, 'If you don't shut up we're going to shoot.' He said, 'Do you know who I am?' I said, 'No, you didn't introduce yourself.' 'I'm the Minister of War.' I said, 'Monsieur le Ministre, if you've got something to say you have to tell me privately.' He took me to the room next door and said, 'You've done your duty, you go back.'

Similar dismissals took place across France. George Millar even left Besançon the day before official celebrations of the liberation, although in this case the summons came from Baker Street which sent a Hudson to pick him and several fellow British agents up. But Millar knew that de Gaulle was behind the move. In the circumstances his attitude was remarkably forgiving and perceptive. 'I was simply told that de Gaulle had expelled me. He saw himself as Joan of Arc. He hated Englishmen being in charge of fighting the war in France. I can understand that. He was fiercely patriotic. France had disgraced herself in the first part of the war and he was eager to redeem her.'

De Gaulle's abrupt termination of SOE's work was caused less by ingratitude and more by wounded national pride. He and his followers, not to mention those in Baker Street who had toiled endlessly to mobilize resistance in France, knew full well that without SOE their history might have been very different. Undoubtedly France would eventually have recovered from defeat and rejected Nazi rule, while de Gaulle and Free France rejected the capitulation of 1940 spontaneously and independently. But it was SOE that made possible the links that de Gaulle forged with the resistance at home by providing him with transport, arms and supplies, and thus enabling him to speak for France as a whole. And the country that eventually embraced him owed much to the men and women of SOE who risked their lives to keep hope alive and make resistance possible.

NOTES

1 For Yeo-Thomas and Churchill see the biography by Mark Seaman, *Bravest of the Brave*, pp. 124–6.
2 M. R. D. Foot's magisterial official history, *SOE in France*, is the best source on the subject.
3 Roger Landes's SOE career has been described in *Aristide: Warlord of the Resistance*, a biography by David Nicolson. An earlier account may be found in E. H. Cookridge, *They Came from the Sky*, pp. 81–160.
4 Foot, op. cit., p. 253.
5 Ibid., p. 350.
6 The story of women agents in SOE has often been told, most recently in *Flames in the Field*, by Rita Kramer, the collective biography of four of those who died.
7 Foot, op. cit., p. 412.
8 See his *Maquis, Horned Pigeon* and *Road to Resistance*.

CHAPTER 14

BEHIND THE LINES

Guido Zembsch-Schreve was born in Switzerland, the son of a Dutch neurologist. He was working in Antwerp when the Germans invaded Belgium, and ended up in Canada. Here he joined the Dutch army-in-exile and was sent to England where he joined the commandos and then SOE. He was dropped 'blind' into France from a Tempsford-based Halifax on the night of 22/23 July 1943 to run the SOE escape line 'Pierre Jacques'. He used the alias Pierre Lalande and was captured in Paris in March 1944. He spent time in Buchenwald and the notorious Dora slave labour camp in the Harz Mountains, where V-2 rockets were built, before escaping from Ravensbrück in the last month of the war.

Zembsch-Schreve wrote a detailed account of his exploits in his book *Pierre Lalande: Special Agent*. Like Henri Diacono (Chapter 11), he is here a compelling eyewitness of the life of an SOE agent.

In Thurso Lord Lovat was training for a small operation in Norway. The training was tough; I was there just under one month. We were disbanded and I went to Number 12 Commando which was located at Dunoon. In London, with my friends the Stubbing family, I met the banker Charles Hambro who at that time was the bigwig in SOE. He asked me if I was ready to do something out of the commando unit. I said, yes, gladly, because I was a little bit fed up with climbing up a church tower or going shooting in early morning behind the moors.

Coming from the commandos I did not have to do the classical training; more time was given to learning the job of being a secret agent – how to react in case of arrest, how to manoeuvre people to build up from scratch a whole organization. At the end, I had not less than 349 people who were working for me, which taken with a family factor made about 1000 people who eventually might be in jeopardy if something would happen to me and I would talk.

In the commandos I had no parachute training. I went to a short course near Manchester; I think I jumped a total of nine times there. There is nothing more beautiful than to hear the light swish of the air when descending with a chute and you overlook everything, it's a marvellous feeling.

The tuition at Beaulieu was something very special. They knew that I spoke five languages. So they said immediately, if ever you are arrested, tell them that you don't need an interpreter, get interrogated in German. It's a thing which helped me a lot I can tell you, later on.

I don't feel very proud about it but I was given a training exercise, a mission to go to Liverpool and find out about a suspected person who was getting people to Northern Ireland, then to Cork. I knew she was a teacher from Aintree and I knew which pub she was going to. I took the cover of walking round in the uniform of a Pioneer and I went into the pub and let it be known that I was an escaped PoW. Fiona, because that was her name, caught the bait and she caught it so well that we got very intimate. On the tenth day she said, tomorrow there's a guy who will come with a kitbag. You'll don other clothes and you are going to Birkenhead with him. I managed to call London and they said, just go along, the worst which can happen is that you find yourself in Cork.

Early the next morning there was a guy with a duffel bag and clothes with a sailor's cap. When we were boarding the gangway police in civilians caught us. When we were being transferred back to the police station there at the harbour was Fiona.

As the manacles were taken away from me she realized what had happened and she spat at me. I can understand that. Though I am not very tall I was not a bad-looking boy. She had beautiful green eyes and black hair. Under special circumstances once you get to the pillow, things are much easier and that is why afterwards I felt like a heel. I took advantage of her. She was an IRA sympathizer, she was an IRA girl up to the end of her nails but just that type of person where it is so difficult to condemn because so persuaded of the rightness of her cause. She believed in Ireland, she did not believe in Germany. Me going over was a part of the war effort against the UK which she hated but I had a certain respect for the girl. She ended her war on the Isle of Man, and she served time in prison. It was part of the job and I do believe that it's one of the reasons why afterwards such a very heavy and difficult mission was given to me.

My cover story was a very simple one. I had received papers in the name of Pierre Lalande, born on the 17th of May, 1916 and as place of residence, Arras. Why Arras? Because the whole town hall was burned down by the Germans in 1940 so they couldn't find any trace of my activity. I was first a student, which was far too dangerous, but later on I became an inspector of an insurance company who was working simultaneously in the north of France and Belgium. Nothing special in that cover story, always a part of the truth because that's very important if you get interrogated to be able to fall back on things which are real.

We left from one of the places on the Thames, in a car. We were already in the civvies we were to be parachuted in. There are two things which came to my mind. One was that Vera Lynn song, 'Don't know where, don't know when but I know we'll meet again some sunny day'. I was sure I could come back. The other one was from Jean Sablon. He was living in the States but he was a very well-known French actor. The song is a very old one the troubadours used to sing in medieval times, 'I take my bow and go at random over the roads of France and Navarre'. For me it meant the idea of going back in that country which I cherish very much, France. Though I was raised partly in Switzerland and partly in Belgium, France was always the place where I went in the summer.

We had a lovely reception at Tempsford and then we went to the hut to don our chutes. I had a piece of chewing gum which I placed on the aircraft saying I'll come back. I remember the aircraft's letter, it was Q. We turned a while in circles, joining craft which were going into France for bombing raids. There was the usual flak when passing the Channel. In order to throw out leaflets, the hatch was opened and we sat with our feet and legs dangling. It was a beautiful night, moonlight, of course, and going down the Loire valley, then the forest of Fontainebleau. The red light on, followed by the green light. The despatcher saying, go, go and jumping into the unknown.

There was a problem. The packages which we had were thrown a good two miles further up and in the high corn. It was too dangerous to try to find them because to walk through the corn would have been noticed immediately. Having seen a farmhouse, I decided to climb the gate and to wake the farmers. Of course that was just like throwing dice because they could have been good, could be bad. But the peasant was not sure about me because the gun I had chosen in England was not a Colt, it was a small German Walther. I felt in my pocket and produced two pills which I had received to make water drinkable. I said to him, if Gerry catches me, here are two pills. They are cyanide. Do you want me to give them to your cats? He believed me then. This man was what one calls an occasional resistant. He would never have thought about retrieving the parcels and helping me but I felt the warmth of the deep spirit which was still prevailing here and there in France. He gave us two rucksacks and changing a little our clothing we went to the main road from Fontainebleau to Paris. We arrived there at a fork in the early morning looking like young people who had passed the night in the forest, not being able to catch the last bus.

After a while, one car having passed, a second car having passed, I said to my W/T operator, well, the next car, I shall stand in the middle of the road and stop it. A small open Mercedes with two airmen, non-coms in it, stops. I speak to them in German, explained that we are expected at our work place early morning in Paris and that unfortunately we got lost the previous night. We boarded the German car. They gave us chocolate. I talked about how beautiful München [Munich] was, which I had visited before the war. They dropped us off just before Orly at the place where normal Paris buses go and we got into Paris having by-passed all controls because we were in a German car with German personnel. Should they have realized that only a few hours before we had left Tempsford airfield, but, well, under those special circumstances you have to dare. Occupied Paris was a very painful thing, everywhere the signposts in German.

The first priority was to establish a little nucleus in Paris itself, from where I could operate. It was easier for me because I had one contact, who was a manager of a section of the Gaz de Paris, of the gas company, and through relations, one built up a first network. At the start there was far less pressure but once travel had become a part of what I had to do, into Holland, through Belgium, in Switzerland, it was very exhausting. I lived on black coffee and

Maxiton pills to remain awake and other pills to be able to sleep. It is lonely because it is too much of a risk for other people to be involved with you. If I go out with a girl, well, it is just because I have to go out with a girl in order that other people see me. That's a normal thing, otherwise people might start to think.

Anything can be dangerous if you aren't alert the whole time. Near one of the apartments which I used was a police station. I used to pass there, sometimes after curfew. One day a policemen comes up to me. He says, you are a military man, because of the way you walk and the heels you have on your shoes. I hear you passing often. Be careful. Take those metal plates off because the German police pass here to see if everything is all right. They might also be aware of that and wonder. I had not thought about it, a little detail. I don't know his name, but there were good policemen also.

I was paymaster for a number of organizations, money which was coming from the UK, a large amount of money – 6 million French francs. That money was stored at one of my other apartments; the largest part had to go elsewhere. I go down at the Gare de Lyon, take the next Metro, sit down. I was wearing a hat. Two German non-commissioned officers enter. They had already had something to drink and they were with two whores, boasting. They say to the girls, you see that fellow sitting there? You'll see what we'll do to him. When he gets angry we'll get him arrested by the *Feldpolizei*.

They start elbowing my hat, once, twice and of course, I was sitting there with my little suitcase with 6 million. The only thing is to bluff your way out. So I turned around and called in German, 'You, you come here. Have you never seen a Frenchman who works for the great Reich? Give me immediately your military books.' They are obedient because I bark at them. They give their military books. I look into them and let one station pass, let another station pass and I say, 'Hans, I see that you are on leave from the Leningrad front, and you are wearing the Iron Cross, so you must be a good soldier. Let not two whores get you sent back, because tomorrow your military books will be on the desk of Von Stulpnagel' – who was the commandant of Paris. But then I say, 'Well, here are your two books, you both get off at the next station but those two women remain on the train. I will see to it that they are handed over to the military police at one of the next stations.' They go out with great 'Heil Hitler's. I answer with a great 'Heil Hitler'. I let the two women off, each one at another station. But when I arrived at the Porte des Lilas I was shivering. There was a café still open. I drank two cognacs which helped me a lot. I had all my 6 million and I delivered the parcel.

In between Christmas and the New Year I had to go to Marseilles where very good friends of mine lived. I proposed to stay a few days with them because I was really tired. Of course the train was late. I had in my suitcase a goose for the belated Christmas dinner. In Marseilles, when out after the curfew hours, you had to remain in the carriages and be screened very slowly which in itself was dangerous. Though I had papers which could pass a normal control, deep control would have been very bad. But there was also German personnel in the train and I go with them out through the front. I come to the guard; it was a *Feldpolizei* who says, what do you have there and where are you going? I said, I'm going to the Hotel Splendide. I knew that the Hotel Splendide was a hotel for non-coms and I say to the man, in my suitcase I have a goose. I called that goose Mrs Goering because she is fat like Mrs Goering. I'm going to the Splendide because I promised so and so that I would bring him a black market goose. The guard let me through. I didn't show one paper because he found that story of Mrs Goering hilarious.

I cannot say that I had bad luck in getting arrested. I should normally have left the contact to another man, but in certain ways I was soft-hearted. He told me that his wife was in a fix because the baby was sick and could he go home. So I go myself to the place – the Tao Bar. The password goes off all right but I feel that something is not right. The barmaid says to me, Monsieur, attention, beware. I look at one side; there is one of those faces one can recognize immediately – police. I go to the toilets and there is another one who follows me. So I sit down and make contact with somebody from the French Ardennes – but a thing not known was that that organization was entirely penetrated. So I played a game. I left the things which were compromising where I was sitting. Going out of the bar, I said to the barmaid, there are papers and my keys which are there, will you make sure that they disappear. She did. I went out of the bar, turned the corner. Two cars, black Citroën cars were there. I was manacled, pushed into the car. I don't even think that many people saw that I was arrested, so quickly did they do it. I have to say it was French personnel, in civvies but they were French.

I was captured by the Abwehr, the military counter-espionage service. Their chief was Canaris who was murdered by the Gestapo. They bullied but never did they do something which was against the rules of clean warfare. The Abwehr interrogators were all non-coms, Feldwebel, so no SS rank. I said that I was a black marketeer who off and on did a job and that I hated people who were active from the resistance. The story is hilarious. I said I have to meet the man who gave me the order at the station. If everything is all right I have to take a red handkerchief, blow my nose three times and that will show when the coast is clear. The interrogator did not go into my proposal of going with them and they decided to go on their own, my first victory. They came back and bawled me out saying we didn't see anybody. So I said well, sure my contact has seen me before so when he has seen another fellow blowing three times his nose with a red handkerchief, he knows immediately that something is wrong and he skedaddled off. So I bawled them out that they didn't take me with them.

The fun was the idea of having that fellow blowing three times his nose with a red handkerchief. That's what makes survival possible – the feeling which you have then that you have had the upper hand somewhere, that you as a prisoner have to bawl out your jailers. I pitied them when a month after my arrest it was the Gestapo who took over and they were pushed entirely in a corner. You see, they were people out of the regular old army, the Junkers army, the nobility. They had a code and they held to it.

Entirely different were the Gestapo who also interrogated me. They took everything over and where I still have the traces on my fingers…but let's not go further in that matter. Today I can't understand yet how people can be without any feeling. The *baignoire* was one of their favourite games. It consisted of putting your head under water, sometimes the whole body, and just keeping you under the water until your lungs were practically bursting. One gets so exhausted I simulated fainting. They went so far as reviving their own bodies by one or two glasses of schnapps in order to be able to go on. But the *baignoire* is meant to break you physically and morally at the same time. You have that feeling then, let me give up. Very often have I been close to that feeling of it is enough, let happen whatever may happen, it's finished. But don't give in on something, my father always told me, go on. Dutchmen, they have a very hard skull and they don't give in. May I frankly say that SOE training helped me more in interrogations by the Abwehr than the type of interrogations from the Gestapo who were just ruthless. There was little help to be found in the teaching when you realize that for these people a human being was worth nothing.

Before the war I weighed 62–3 kilograms which corresponds to how tall I am, which is quite normal. When I came back from Dora labour camp, well I weighed a mere 39. When I arrived at Croydon airfield Colin Gubbins was awaiting me. He said, well, you son of a gun, we never expected you back. I haven't much time but I wanted to be here today. That was for me one of the greatest rewards I could get, just that man acknowledging the fact that I had come back. Later he brought me to Pall Mall to one of his clubs and who was there? Winston Churchill. He introduced me, said who I was, what I was and we had a short meal together.

CHAPTER 15

MAKING MAYHEM

Two days after D-Day, on the night of 8 June 1944, three men para-chuted from an Allied plane near the town of Aurillac, in the Massif Central of southern France. The first man who met them on the ground was a member of the local Maquis. Excitedly he ran to the waiting reception committee announcing that a French officer had arrived bringing with him his wife. He was right about the French officer but not about the 'wife'. She was in reality Major Thomas Macpherson of the Cameron Highlanders wearing his kilt.

Thus arrived one of the earliest 'Jedburgh' teams into post-D-Day France. These were three-man teams drawn from SOE, the American OSS and the Free French and sent into France, in uniform, at the time of the Normandy landings. Their task was to co-ordinate local resistance with the work of the Allied armies, provide them with a wireless link, arrange the supply of arms and equipment, and train them in small arms and sabotage. Ninety-three Jedburghs arrived in France from D-Day onwards, mostly from the UK but also from North Africa. Nearly all went in by parachute to receptions organized by SOE. Each team (most were bi-national) had a sergeant wireless operator with W/T set and two officers.

Colin Gubbins, SOE's executive director from 1943, had a para-military rather than civilian background and considered D-Day the litmus test of SOE's success. The Jedburghs were his idea in the first place and this, plus the fact that they required close co-ordination with the Americans and the French – and thus had a significant political dimension – meant he attached more than usual importance to their missions.

From February 1944 Jedburgh training was concentrated at Milton Hall, near Peterborough, with wireless and parachute instruction at the usual SOE training centres. Teams selected themselves during training. The first one parachuted into France in the early hours of D-Day and the majority followed throughout July and August. No Jedburghs were captured although some twenty-one of them were killed.

Jedburghs were not supposed to take command of local resistance groups but instead to encourage them and help plan attacks on German communications, fuel and ammunition dumps, enemy convoys and Wehrmacht units isolated by the Allied advance. A handful of SOE agents more used to clandestine life found the Jedburghs' fairly public operations disconcerting. And although most Jedburghs concluded that they should have been sent in earlier, nearly all considered their missions worth while.

Thomas Macpherson was one. Captured by the Italians in North Africa and making three daring escapes in Italy and Germany, he made his way via Sweden back to Britain. In November 1943 Gubbins, a family friend, recruited him for SOE and the Jedburghs. Here is his own story, in his own words.[1]

The Jedburghs were a unique organization. They were one of the few operations of the European campaign that really worked smoothly on a basis of co-operation between the Allies. The idea was to parachute into France, around the time of an invasion, uniformed teams of a tri-partite nature – French, British and American. It didn't always work out that way. My own eventual team had in fact two Brits and a Frenchman, but they were in principle mixed. This was obviously a high-level political decision; it had arisen from political pressure by both the Americans and the French who wanted to be in on an act which had been British in conception. In the combination of nationalities, SOE was the senior partner and the controller of who, which mission went where, and when.

Milton Hall was an exceptional place as a training school because the French somehow procured a certain amount of wine of a very drinkable sort for the mess and the Americans had copious rations of the sort that British households wouldn't have seen for years during the war. We had our standard rations which were good enough if somewhat predictable, but mixing the three together produced a standard of food which gave us a good deal of pleasure. There were some elements which didn't entirely accord with the British taste. The Americans seemed to enjoy the British breakfast of bacon and eggs and sausage, on which they spread maple syrup and waffles. This early in the morning after a night exercise was a little bit off-putting to the more sensitive of us.

Part of our training programme gave us some briefings on the operations that had been going on in France up to that date and these were, of course, clandestine. They were agents dropped in or ferried by Lysander or boat in civilian clothes to take their place in the civilian society whether for intelligence-gathering or for urban sabotage, but it was a secret operation. They kept themselves under cover – the last thing they wanted to draw to themselves was publicity. The idea of the Jedburghs was absolutely the opposite. Our job was to create the maximum amount of disruption to transport, power supplies and telephone lines, but we were to do this in uniform throughout. That was not just for our own protection. It was to give a message to the French that the armies might have been a long time in penetrating the defences in Normandy, but that uniformed help was there on the spot in their own piece of the countryside. That was the objective of the mission and that was an enormous difference between the clandestine and the Jeds. The Jeds wanted not to be caught, but to draw attention to their presence.

The Jedburgh school at Milton Hall completed its training on schedule by the end of April. We were on standby to go into France at any time because, of course, none of us knew when D-Day would take place. The team was broken up in two ways. One was that the individual parties that were going into France were designated. The second was that about a quarter of the total were at very short notice embarked in a rather jolly ship called the *Oriana* and sent off to Algiers. There we completed our training, not so much in the technical side as being sent up into the mountains for physical tests and endurance exercises designed, I fancy, to bond the teams together, which they did very successfully.

The Jedburgh team would contain three people: an officer commanding, a second officer who was his backup and could undertake certain missions for him, and a radio operator. Now the radio operator was the most valuable possession you had. He, obviously, was your communication with London or Algiers. He also was your authority in dealing with the disparate types of French resistance groups that you came across. An overseas officer, coming in like that, had no authority with the structure of the resistance. In spite of the fact that you carried American and British General Staff authority and even a letter signed by General de Gaulle, you had to create your own authority by what you did and who you were. Now half of that authority was created for you by the fact that your radio contact was there and you could call up a drop of arms or explosive or an air strike, and generally create in the resistance mind a feeling that you were important and indispensable.

My team was called Quinine – that followed a pattern of medical names for the Jedburgh teams. I was appointed the leader of the team and was one of the relatively few Jedburghs that had prior active service or experience; my second-in-command was a French lieutenant who had actually enlisted in the United States Army and been transferred and commissioned in the French Army. He was called Michel de Bourbon. My sergeant was Arthur Brown of the Royal Tank Regiment, from which most of the radio operators came because they had to have in their own regiment considerable basic skills of signals and communication. We were one of the youngest teams. I was twenty-three at the time; de Bourbon was twenty or twenty-one and Brown was nineteen or twenty. We were summoned with all speed to the airport, briefed to go on board a Halifax on the night of the 4th of June. While we were in the air heading for our dropping zone, we heard on the aircraft's radio that Rome had fallen to the Americans that day. However, because the aircraft either missed its target or got counter orders and turned back, we found ourselves back in Algiers instead. We were re-embarked four days later on the night of June the 8th and sent forward to France. Either by bad luck, mismanagement or change of order, we came in after D-Day. I myself think that was a mistake. We could have prepared the delaying of the movement of German forces towards the Channel much better if we had had a few days in there to find our feet and see what resources we had.

We had a remit of the most general nature: we were to go in there; liaise with the French Forces of the Interior (FFI); assess what potential they had; arm them at our discretion; prepare for the liberation; and more generally to create what mayhem we could occupying the attention of the German forces on the ground. We had been given some briefings by one or two SOE clandestine agents who had returned and told us about urban life, the danger of travel; but we were totally unaware of the political nuances. We were totally unaware of the limited number of people in France who were active supporters of the resistance and the serious danger of French people betraying their own countrymen or any British officers who turned up.

We arrived at about two o'clock in the morning of June the 9th. It didn't take me long to assess on waking up from a brief sleep that we had an inactive group, which was inactive from lack of knowledge, equipment and really leadership. So I made up my mind that we were going to show we had arrived and give them confidence by carrying out a sabotage immediately that first night. It was the only operation that we carried out where I did not personally, or through Michel de Bourbon, carry out a reconnaissance first. But I just felt it was so urgent that I had to take the local people's view that we could get undetected to this relatively nearby target, which was a railway bridge. We loaded up with what I thought was an adequate amount of plastic explosive which I had already primed. It was prepared to go off the moment I put in the detonators and activated them. We got to the bridge. I set out some perimeter guards. The work on the bridge took about ten minutes. I set the things off with a five-minute delay. To my delight and to the morale boost of my French companions, we heard this enormous bang as we moved off.

Our arrival in France somewhat depressed us in that we came in to a well-organized dropping zone which had been in operation since 1942 under the management of the local mayor and garage proprietor who was a remarkable chap. His entire team consisted of two or three neighbouring farmers who turned up in the black night with their carts and their oxen to pull the containers to safety, and a group of about seven resistance members of ages from fifteen to sixty-odd who were not to be considered an active body at all at that stage.

Later we were able to enlarge our zone of operations and to make contact with a number of bodies of the resistance, some active, some frankly just hiding from the Germans, some preparing to be active at the moment of liberation. We dropped in the

Department of the Cantal in the Massif Central which had two or three little pockets of resistance – five to ten people. Over the borders in the Lot a different situation prevailed. There was a group called the FTP who were an overtly Communist group. They fulfilled my requirement of being prepared to be very active against the occupying forces. They had, of course, a private agenda of their own, because they were considering in their timetable not only a defeat of the occupying forces, but a political takeover of France for the Communist cause after the war. The leader of FTP in the Department of the Lot was a very strong character who went under the name of Commissar Georges. He actually held indoctrination classes as well as his military operations and exercised a degree of almost forced recruitment among the young people of the area, threatening their families. But once he got them on board, he did operate against the Germans. So he and I got on with a degree of friendship and a degree of mutual suspicion. As a practical partnership it worked quite well. They were certainly the largest organized force in the area of about four departments that I eventually spread into.

The acquiring of transport was one of the very early priorities. The group that I went to had only one vehicle when I arrived. This was a lorry of about two-ton capacity, driven by a boiler with carbon gas at the back of it, literally a boiler that you stoked. It made its own gas and the most appalling smell and appalling noise. It went along rather slowly, so I had to get our French friends to commandeer some vehicles. The first one I had that was any use was a tiny little bubble car, called at that time a Peugeot 202. I rapidly discovered that the quality of the wartime tyres was quite appalling. We had to carry three spare wheels, and we, rather like Formula One, got down the changing of a wheel to about three minutes.

The final triumph was where we captured two cars from the French Milice, the armed part of the collaborating French police. They were the best cars of the day, long, sleek, black Citroëns, front-wheel drive. They were extremely roadworthy and probably the fastest vehicle around. Because of the air raids, the Germans and the police cars had shielded headlights with only a pinpoint of light coming through at night. We left our headlights open, so that if we ran into trouble we'd blaze away with full headlights which could blind an ambush. We did have one occasion where at night we ran into a road block. I think they were a bit somnolent because it was in the early hours of the morning and we simply crashed it. They hadn't properly blocked the carriageway. There was a light barrier across and we switched on our full headlights which dazzled them so that their shooting was not very good and crashed straight through. Some forty miles later we came to a 'fut-fut-fut' stop because we found they had holed the petrol tank and it had leaked away.

That car covered a good few miles for me. The wife of the garage proprietor and the wife of his brother made two pennants which I put on each wing for propaganda reasons. One was the Union Jack and one was the French flag with the Cross of Lorraine, both of them surrounded with gold tassels. It was very smart indeed. I hadn't been there very long before they put up posters in various towns offering enormous rewards for my apprehension. That I took as a compliment. I thought it was good news, the message was getting out.

In the Peugeot 202 there was really only room for the driver and myself. As we upgraded the car there was generally the driver, myself, and a chap who acted as messenger/bodyguard. We were all armed, of course, but that was the team. There was no point in having more. The whole essence of guerrilla activity is speed of movement and ease of disappearing.

The most common acts of sabotage were ambushes on soft transport, that's German communication vehicles. The next type was the railway – almost every second night, it was simply blowing up the rails over a quarter of a mile or so in a series of explosives at the junction of two rails. That was extremely economical. We had white rectangular gun cotton slabs which actually fitted into the rail, so you just taped it on with a hole for the primer and the detonator. It was a very quick operation indeed and it kept them repairing all the time. The third was the cutting of telephone lines – a very easy thing for which you used the most junior of people. You gave them a franc or two for each they'd cut. Then there was the bringing down of electric pylons. This was something I took quite seriously because an immense amount of the electricity of France is carried through or on the edge of the Massif Central to the factories. The most notable one was the night of July the 14th, Bastille Day; we thought it'd be one of the jollier little celebrations. The two pylons you've blasted fall towards each other and there is a splendid noise of crumbling metals and sparks flying in every direction as the wires whip about. I used to enjoy that very much indeed.

The second morning after our arrival, I was tucking into our meagre breakfast which was local peasant brown bread and some chestnut purée on top of it. There arrived an immaculate, middle-aged French officer in the rank of captain in full cavalry uniform. He requested my assistance either personally and physically, or by arranging a drop of weapons, for an assembly of the FFI. I listened to him and then refused completely. I said to him that the best thing you could do is disperse these people immediately; it is the absolute antithesis of guerrilla warfare to group people together, because then they're located, they're identified and it's easy meat for regular forces to mop them up. He went away down-hearted, assuring me that the British weren't pulling their weight. About what I'd predicted occurred. They were surrounded by regular forces, they were routed, happily the loss of life was not very great; but they lost all the weapons, ammunition, equipment that so many people had risked their lives to bring in to them. It was quite wrong.

He had hardly gone when a ragged but impressive chap came in on a bicycle from the east of us with the news that there was heavy German movement going north; we immediately deduced to the Normandy Front. I didn't know what the divisions were – it was only subsequently that I learned it was the Das Reich and the Second SS Motorized Infantry Division. We put together our plans; it was a great help having the chap who had come in from there because he was able to give us ideas of how we could approach in a vehicle. We got there in the late afternoon. He had taken us to one of these many dust-covered tracks that ran parallel to the main road and went from farm to farm. We parked up at one of the farms with our gasogen vehicle hidden in the byre.

I did not on that first reconnaissance see any tanks, but there were trucks and half-tracks and armoured cars and supply vehicles. I thought they would probably continue all night and that would be the time to hit them. But in fact they had decided to camp because about two hours after dark the movement absolutely ceased. So we rethought. It was obvious that firing a few sten guns was not going to bring the column to a halt. We conceived the idea of blowing heavy trees from the woods close to the road in such a way that they fell across the road as an obstacle, which, over a certain distance, had a cumulative effect on the delay.

The first barrier just had the trees. When the Germans came up, as I heard later from the man we had left, they drove up to this barrier which at first they thought was just trees that had fallen across the road. The column was led by an armoured car, followed by a half-track which had some troops in the back who got out with a non-commissioned officer, walked up to the barrier, scratched their heads and talked to the armoured car chap. He tried to push it out of the way but it was much too heavy. This caused a long delay. A vehicle came forward and proved to be the type of tank that is used for engineering work; it had a bulldozer and a scoop. It came up and with some difficulty cleared the trees. The whole thing must have taken well over three hours. Then the tank was told to go in the front of the column. The men, who had been watching this operation with interest, walked back to get in their half-track. At that time the man I'd left behind opened up with his Sten gun. That created some alarm and despondency. They weren't at all sure where it was coming from, so the chap was able to skip out of cover, down the hill and disappear.

What I did at the next barrier was to use the same technique, putting down two trees across the road. But well camouflaged with dust and gravel underneath them, I put our only two anti-tank mines. The tank came along and this time they paused because they realized there might be a chap with a gun somewhere behind them. So they swept the area in around each side of the road for about half a mile in front of the road block and for about a quarter of a mile behind. All this took a nice lot of time. Then they gave the all-clear and the tank ploughed forward and there was a nice big bang. If you lose one track on a tank it slews round and blocks the road. That was an illustration of the extreme rarity of things going to plan. It meant a very long delay while they sent for another heavy vehicle.

None of this I saw because we hadn't left any personnel there at all. We had gone on to make a third one about three miles up. We again blew an almost identical pair of trees down across the road. This time in a crude and elementary way we booby-trapped it. Not on the ground, because I envisaged that they would see this, stop and send engineers up to see if there were mines on the ground, which there weren't. There was a lot of leaf above head height lying across the road and in those leaves, very precariously balanced, we left a couple of standard hand grenades with their pins out, so that the moment they were dislodged, the pins would fly off and in seven seconds the grenades would blow. That we thought would serve as a degree of discouragement and I believe it did. It was some hours before they got their column on the move again and got this tank out of the way.

During that time we did our last fling, which was purely dummies. We blew a couple of light trees but did nothing else on the grounds that we thought they would be sufficiently cautious to sweep the sides, look underneath and all the rest and we legged it. We left one man from the area who had tipped us off and I'm sorry to say he became the only casualty. I think he must have got a bit carried away and stayed too long.

Our contribution to the Das Reich and the Second Motorized Divisions going north to Normandy was in essence trivial; but cumulatively, if you could imagine this in various degrees going on the whole 800-mile length of France, it contributed to about a ten-day delay in the projected arrival of these heavy reinforcements and it must have had a considerable effect in allowing us to stabilize our bridgehead.

Much later on, near the time of Liberation, the Germans who had garrisoned the south-west of France, headquartered in Bordeaux, decided the moment had come to make the quickest possible evacuation and head up towards the Loire Valley to try to break out between the two Allied armies before they met. At the same time General de Gaulle and General Koenig, his deputy for the FFI, had sent in a mass of staff officers to take charge of all the resistance in the south and south-west, based on Toulouse. There had been a degree of pre-organization going on in that area for some time, but I had not been aware of it and had been operating independently. However, Commissar Georges of the FTP and I decided jointly we'd better head for Toulouse and try to keep these sudden visitors of high rank on the right sort of rails.

There was bedlam going on in Toulouse, but eventually a substantial force was put together but very light in equipment and most of them pretty light in either discipline or experience. They headed up in a miscellany of vehicles towards the point where the Loire and another big river called the Allier join, which, if held, would block the passage of this substantial force of some 23,000 Germans which was coming up from the south-west. The French Army lent a troop of Sherman tanks to reinforce this position and it looked to me as if it could be held. Then a prisoner from the advance guard of the retiring Germans made me doubt this possibility in the extreme. The German prisoner indicated that the advance force of about 7000 Germans were quite good fighting troops. They would certainly have made mincemeat of what we had at our disposal, although we were much more numerous. Behind that was their substantial tail of occupying troops of second calibre and transport of third calibre including some horse-drawn vehicles. Obviously what was needed was to make sure that the 7000 valid troops couldn't mount an attack and drive their way through. It would have been difficult anyway with the final bridge blown, but it was a risk to avoid.

I was able to persuade the incoming nominee of the FFI that we should send myself and a uniformed French officer in a captured German Red Cross car with our own driver, but with one of the captured German doctors with us to vouch for the fact that we were on a peaceful mission. We drove at night across the bridge with our headlights full on and drove straight through the German lines. I had a telephone call earlier that morning from a Captain Cox, also a Jedburgh, who said, 'Look, these chaps are in a mess here, but they're going to try to drive you out of the way. If they can't, they will surrender. You need to come and persuade them.' We drove an exciting drive through at very high speed. I must say we owe our lives to the French driver, because we went through two lines of Germans who both fired copiously on us. When we arrived we were met by Captain Cox and the local French resistance leader, and the mayor who gave us an excellent meal, washed down by very good Loire wine.

We made our plan for the morning. Major General Elster, the Commander of the Germans, had, through the French, contacted the Americans of General Patton's Army who were some distance to the north. His prime concern was that if he surrendered to the French, they would hang or shoot all his officers. He was also procrastinating so that his forward people could have one more try at breaking out. The plan was that I should appear in full uniform with my hat on, which was something I rarely wore, and make it quite clear that I had my battalion and a force of tanks and some guns across the river and that he was welcome to come. We sat down at ten o'clock the following morning in either the school hall or the town hall, on a long table with the Mayor, the local FFI, Captain Cox, and myself at one side and General Elster, an interpreter, a staff officer, and his colonel commanding the forward troops on the other side. Clearly I must have given the right impression of force in front of him, because he agreed to sign a surrender document, on condition that his men could keep their arms until the Americans took them over. I agreed this on condition they made no move but stayed precisely where they were. He accepted that. As the document was being signed, two American officers, a colonel and a lieutenant, appeared and that solved the rest of the question because they said, 'Oh gee, yes, we'll take them over we'll look after them.' And indeed they did and that was the end of the war for 23,000 Germans and really the end of the resistance operation for most of the centre of France.

NOTES

1 Macpherson's part in attacking the 'Das Reich' division, as well as the anecdote about the kilt, is recounted in Max Hastings, *Das Reich*, pp. 149–62. For an account of the Jedburgh divisions in general, see Ian Dear, *Sabotage and Subversion*, pp. 181–96.

CHAPTER 16

DOUSING THE FLAMES

After 1944 SOE's wartime task in Europe was largely over. De Gaulle's abrupt dismissal of its agents meant that Baker Street's mission in France was at an end. The politics of peace had returned with a vengeance and de Gaulle made a triumphant walk down the Champs Elysées greeted by thousands of cheering Parisians. Soon after, as witnessed by Basil Davidson in Belgrade, Tito made clear that he and his Communists were now the masters of Yugoslavia.

They were poised to take power elsewhere. In August 1944 the Polish underground Home Army rose in revolt against the Germans but after eight weeks of heroic fighting was forced to surrender while Soviet forces stood by and watched. Warsaw lay in ruins and Poland was open to Communist takeover. SOE had done its best to supply the Poles but was defeated by distance and politics – Baker Street's early talk of supporting a secret army had been quietly dropped after the Soviet Union entered the war. John Debenham-Taylor was a witness. Slated to parachute in as a liaison officer to the Poles, he found his mission that summer had been scrubbed. The whole affair, he recalled, 'opened the eyes of people to just what postwar dealing with Stalin was going to be like'.

In Greece 'Monty' Woodhouse experienced a bitter liberation. After the brilliant success of Operation Harling he'd stayed on to persuade the different factions of resistance to unite behind Allied strategy. Given the Communists' political goal of postwar power, this proved difficult. When the Italians surrendered in 1943 most of their arms ended up in the hands of ELAS, and Woodhouse bent his efforts to ensure that when the Germans left they did not turn them against the British. It seemed at first as though he had succeeded, but events quickly changed. British troops, along with the Greek government-in-exile, arrived by sea in Athens in December 1944. Woodhouse went on board to welcome them.

I went to greet them and told them that things looked all right. ELAS were somewhere in the background but were not attempting to be a tiresome nuisance in any way. We all went ashore and we drove in grand cars through the streets and we were cheered and everything seemed very happy and satisfactory. And then a few days later ELAS started marching on Athens with obviously hostile intention. I thought this was raving mad, because if they were going to stage a *coup* why did they leave it until after the Royal Navy and the British Army units had arrived? They were bound to be defeated.

Checked they certainly were. Churchill, who considered ELAS no better than bandits, personally flew out to Athens that Christmas to sort things out. He exhibited all his natural combativeness, riding through the streets in an armoured car carrying a pistol and presiding over a conference dimly lit by hurricane lamps and punctuated by the sounds of rockets being fired against the guerrillas by RAF planes. Fighting stopped but it proved little more than a ceasefire in a civil war that dragged on until the final defeat of the Communists five years later.

While all this was going on Hitler's Reich was fighting a bitter rearguard action that extended the war into 1945. The Allied breakout from the Normandy beachhead inspired optimism in London and Washington that the war would be over by Christmas. Yet setbacks such as Arnhem revealed that the Nazis could still fight back. Was there a role here for SOE in shortening the war?

The German heartland had never been a top priority for the Baker Street warriors who viewed it as mostly barren territory not worth much effort – although minor campaigns of sabotage had been mounted from adjacent countries such as Switzerland. Then, on 20 July 1944, Hitler was almost killed by a bomb planted by a group of dissident army officers headed by Count Claus von Stauffenberg at his east Prussian headquarters at Rastenburg. SOE played an indirect part in the plot because the plastic explosive and timer pencil in the bomb came from Britain after being dropped to a circuit in France and then captured by the Abwehr – elements of which were in on the plot.

The attempted assassination did, however, prompt a turnaround in Baker Street's policy towards the Reich. 'Germany must now be the first priority target for SOE,' declared Gubbins ten days after Stauffenberg's bomb, 'and all our energies and resources must be concentrated on the penetration of the Reich itself.' To this end he appointed an old friend from MI(R) days, the energetic Brigadier Gerald Templer, as head of a new German directorate. In the final months of the war about thirty anti-Nazi German prisoners-of-war were despatched on sabotage missions to their homeland and SOE continued to support left-wing railway workers in southern Germany in attacks on marshalling yards and rolling stock.

But many in Baker Street remained sceptical about the existence of any real resistance in Germany. So a plan to create an entirely fictitious anti-Nazi movement deep within the Reich garnered some enthusiasm. This was Operation 'Periwig', planned jointly with the Political Warfare Executive. Through black radio transmissions and other deception techniques it was hoped to persuade Hitler and his minions that they faced serious internal resistance and sow panic and confusion as the Wehrmacht fought its rearguard action against the advancing Allies.

Periwig prompted one of SOE's most controversial operations. To work, it had to appear real, and this involved creating dummy radio traffic and codes. Templer asked Leo Marks to take care of this and revealed a plan to drop an agent into Germany carrying a code book and one-time pads. Only this would be no normal dropping operation. It would be arranged for an accident to happen with the parachute so that it failed to open. The Germans would then find the hapless agent's body with the code book and hence believe in the deception. The victim was carefully chosen. He was a German, his name was Schiller, and he had originally been sent to Britain by the Abwehr as a spy before being captured and turned as a double agent. 'If you've got any qualms about this,' Templer told Marks, 'he's betrayed as many British agents as he has German.' Marks duly briefed Schiller on codes, as he did with other SOE agents. A week later Templer told him that Schiller, as planned, had met with his 'fatal accident'.[1]

Did SOE really send an agent to his death this way? It is only fair to say that others' recollections differ from Marks's and that

Peter Wilkinson, for one, the biographer of Gubbins, declared that all the agents despatched to Germany survived.[2] Until historians have thoroughly mined the records, and perhaps not even then, the truth may never be known.

What *is* certain is that SOE generated a plot of its own to kill the Führer – Operation Foxley.

Assassination was part of the SOE agenda. Baker Street experts trained and transported the Czech agents who killed the much-feared SS General Reinhard Heydrich, a principal architect of the Holocaust and bane of European Resistance, in Prague in May 1942, and they played a still murky role in the assassination of the Vichy French Admiral François Darlan in Algiers a few months later.

As early as 1941 Churchill and the Chiefs of Staff gave SOE permission to study the possibilities of killing Hitler and later that year the Polish Resistance almost succeeded in blowing up his personal train when he was travelling through West Prussia. It still remains a mystery what happened to the plan over the next three years. But soon after D-Day it was revived by the German section (Section X). It involved finding a sharp-shooting assassin, infiltrating him into Hitler's Bavarian mountain retreat at Berchtesgaden, and shooting him while he was taking a walk. Churchill gave SOE the green light to develop the plan but from the first it was controversial.

In Baker Street there was a split of opinion. Some strongly supported it. SOE's Air Adviser, Air Vice-Marshal Ritchie, argued that the only thing keeping the German Army going was its faith in Hitler's genius. 'Remove Hitler,' he argued, 'and there is nothing left.' Others, including the head of the German section, believed that Hitler alive was better than Hitler dead because of his irrational and self-destructive command of the German armed forces. 'As a strategist,' declared Ronald Thornley, 'Hitler has been of the greatest possible assistance to the British war effort...to remove [him] would almost certainly canonize him.'[3]

Despite the doubts, planning went ahead. A key condition was finding a suitable assassin, a skilled and resourceful sharpshooter with fluent German prepared to accept what was certainly a suicide mission. Section X spent months on this task and it was early 1945 before a potential candidate was found – an intelligence officer working in the Defence Attaché's office in Washington DC. In March General Templer asked for more details about him and he was carefully sounded out – without revealing precise details – by Sir William Stephenson's office in New York. But days later Baker Street signalled they were no longer interested. American troops had entered Frankfurt, the Red Army was poised for its final advance on Berlin, and Hitler moved his headquarters from the Chancery to the complex of underground bunkers beneath it. A month later, on 30 April 1945, he achieved Foxley's goal himself by committing suicide.

As the Third Reich crumbled, thoughts in London increasingly turned to the perilous peace ahead and what SOE might do to protect it. Many of Baker Street's agents in western Europe did an about-turn from sabotage and subversion to protecting industrial plants and communications from last-ditch destruction by the Germans. In the chaos of liberation political disorder and unrest could only help the Communists. Far from setting Europe ablaze SOE was now dousing the fires of revolution. In central and eastern Europe a new occupation was tightening its grip. As the Cold War took shape was there still a place for SOE to wage war behind enemy lines?

Talk about a peacetime role for SOE began as early as the spring of 1944. Even before that Selborne had warned Churchill of the growing power of the Communists in European resistance movements. Although the Prime Minister shared Selborne's anti-Communism he was also a realist who had to deal with Stalin and he didn't reply to his SOE minister. But he had already initiated a purge of known Communists in Whitehall. Baker Street itself experienced the nightmare of discovering one of its own officers handing information to Moscow.

His name was Ormond Uren. Born in Australia, he was educated in Edinburgh and recruited for SOE from the Highland Light Infantry. A *New Statesman*- and *Daily Worker*-reading idealist, he was a square peg in a round hole among his stuffier conservative Baker Street colleagues in the Hungarian section. He was due to take part in a mission in which he had little faith and even received a briefing from Leo Marks on the codes being used by SOE's Hungarian agents.[4]

At the same time he admired the Red Army. The Soviet Union was an ally, tanks were rolling off production lines with 'Another One for Uncle Joe' written on them, and to Communist friends he confided he would like to join the Party. In a greasy-spoon café on Charing Cross Road he met surreptitiously with Douglas Springhall, one of its leading recruiters, and told him where he worked. At a second meeting in a mews behind Baker Street Uren then handed him an envelope in which he described his work in SOE.

But Uren was far from being some hard-bitten Soviet mole. On the contrary, he was naïve, uncertain and confused. The night before handing the envelope to Springhall he walked around Regent's Park arguing the pros and cons to himself and was greatly relieved when Springhall was arrested on a secrets charge: 'I was in a highly nervous state over all this period actually so that when he was eventually arrested I felt an enormous relief, I thought, Oh thank God, I don't need to go on with this any more.'

His relief was unwarranted. MI5 had been keeping Springhall under surveillance and had noted his meeting with Uren. They kept watch on him, too, and in October he was arrested, charged under the Official Secrets Act, and sentenced at court-martial to seven years in prison. Uren appears to have been overwhelmed by the whole affair and stunned when MI5 accused him of spying: 'I hadn't thought of what I was doing as spying and I was quite sincerely shocked by his use of the word spying because I hadn't seen that as being what I was doing.'

The affair did little damage to SOE although Leo Marks took care to change the security checks of every agent known to Uren. The heavy sentence was mostly a deterrent to others, as Uren suspected: 'I've heard somewhere or another on the grapevine that Churchill was very concerned about Soviet espionage in high places and I rather suspect that this was meant to be *pour encourager les autres*, that they insisted on a very heavy sentence.'

If Churchill was clear-eyed about Communism he was far less certain about a postwar role for SOE. Although he'd made it independent of SIS he'd grown weary of the in-fighting between Broadway and Baker Street and worried about the burgeoning secret

bureaucracies and the power they held. This ran counter to
Gubbins's firm belief that Baker Street had a major mission to fulfil.

For the last few months of the war he toiled hard to guarantee
its future. An important stimulus was the effort after D-Day by
'Wild Bill' Donovan, the buccaneering head of OSS, to break free
of SOE and make his American agency independent. Gubbins
agreed that national independence was the way ahead. A visit to
Washington in October 1944 strengthened his resolve. 'It would
be foolish to ignore the strength of OSS,' he declared, 'provided it
survives into the peace it will undoubtedly be used by the
American government as an instrument of policy. Of the Big
Three, is Great Britain going to be the only one without such an
instrument?'[5]

His efforts were in vain. Selborne, the SOE minister, agreed
that special operations had a future but knew that his Ministry of
Economic Warfare would not survive the war and was content to
have either the Foreign Office or Ministry of Defence take charge.
More important was the view of Clement Attlee, the Labour Party
leader and Prime Minister-in-waiting. A sympathetic midwife to
SOE's birth when Britain had its back to the wall and Dalton's
heady talk of a 'people's war' and revolution in Europe was in
vogue, it was radically different now and SOE was under fire in
left-wing quarters for supporting reactionary monarchs in such
places as Greece. The events in Athens in December 1944 added
fuel to the flames and Attlee set his face against anything resembling a 'British Comintern'. The Chiefs of Staff and Foreign
Office were equally determined to get rid of Gubbins.

In Baker Street the staff smelled the whiff of impending dissolution. Many thought SOE, or at least Gubbins, deserved a postwar career. Leo Marks was one.

There was unease at this time, late '44, early '45, there was an
unease about the power of Russia, we weren't all that happy
about relationships with America either, there were new enemies, possibly unknown enemies, and the job as we knew it
wasn't quite finished, we were finished but the job wasn't. We
all knew in Baker Street that SOE's days were numbered but I
learned from my commanding officer, Nicholls, that if SOE in

some form continued in peacetime Gubbins would not be part of it, Gubbins was not acceptable to 'C', to SIS. He was too brilliant, too much of a menace, they might have been afraid of the power he would exert and they were formidable enemies with long memories and Gubbins had long fought them. This was a bitter moment because he was a great leader and he was being ignored, rejected, and humiliated, that's how Nick [Nicholls] saw it.

The death blow was administered by Attlee after he won the 1945 general election and he and his Foreign Secretary, Ernest Bevin, agreed that SOE should be dissolved. The final decision was made in January 1946 by Sir Alan Brooke, Chief of the Imperial General Staff, and 'C' – Sir Stewart Menzies.

But it would be misleading to say that SOE was abolished. Instead its tasks were returned to SIS which had controlled them before Churchill's order to Dalton in 1940. Officially, as recorded by the Chiefs of Staff, the two services were now 'amalgamated' on 15 January 1946 when 'C' took control of the new Special Operations Branch of the Secret Intelligence Service.

SOE was dead but special operations lived on. Many Cold War operations were run by what were virtually revamped SOE units using ex-Baker Street personnel. In 1953, to mention but one example, 'Monty' Woodhouse found himself spearheading a joint SIS/CIA 'dirty tricks' operation against the Iranian nationalist leader Muhammed Mussadeq that ousted him in a *coup*. In Southeast Asia SOE survived well into 1947 where Mountbatten demanded their use in counter-insurgency operations in Burma, Malaya, Indochina, and Indonesia.[6]

Defeated, nonetheless Gubbins went down fighting. A new weapon of warfare had been forged and he hoped that he might still persuade his superiors to accept his views. He also felt a powerful obligation to discover what had happened to his agents who had fallen into Gestapo hands. This meant sending missions to Germany which also had the hidden agenda of attempting to get an SOE foot in the postwar world.

The search for the missing agents began almost as soon as the Allies liberated France. Angus Fyffe was deeply involved from the beginning. In September 1944 he was assigned to an evaluation unit which, for various reasons, did not get off the ground until May 1945. As part of Templer's German directorate it was known as ME42 (Military Establishment 42). Its head was Ernest van Maurik, recently returned from Switzerland. Angus Fyffe recalled its mission.

> Over the years, SOE lost a lot of agents, inevitably, and in some cases we'd no idea what happened to them, whether they were shot, transported to Germany to camps where they were held. We had no idea of their fates. It became an essential feature of SOE to try to uncover what had happened to these poor souls. Security decided to set up an evaluation mission to tour the camps in Germany and Austria, in particular, to search out whatever possible information from records could be obtained. The Germans kept the most meticulous record of individuals entering their camps. The mission was ready to move in September 1944 but didn't get off the ground until May 1945 when we set sail. It was headed by Major Ernest van Maurik. We became very close friends. I headed the Security side; we then trained and landed in Holland.

With him Fyffe carried detailed lists prepared by the country sections of all their agents still missing. To track them down meant contacting the military authorities in the various zones of occupation into which Hitler's Reich had been divided – French, British, American – and then asking for records seized from the many prisoner and concentration camps they had liberated. Fyffe found the Americans especially useful, and they lent him some staff to cope with the work. Sometimes this involved going into the camps and searching through the often detailed records the Germans had kept.

> The entries in the camp records were absolutely meticulous. All the details, gold teeth, the progress of the man or woman through the camp, when they were ill, what illness they had. Sometimes there was an entry which meant that he had disappeared into the night, into the mist. The implication was they had managed to escape but didn't escape death. The other little

entry was shot while trying to escape. Of course, there again, it didn't really mean what it said on the paper. The man or woman was just shot.

Sometimes he was able to mobilize the help of camp officials who had compiled the records in the first place. What he uncovered was sometimes grim.

We tried all sorts of sources – in Karlsruhe there was a woman who had been a wardress in a transit camp. She turned out to be an intelligent woman and was the first source of information about some of our girls who were transhipped by train from Avenue Foch in Paris. They were held in detention for a brief period in Karlsruhe and they were shipped elsewhere – some of them died in Ravensbrück concentration camp. I was told about one of the guards from Ravensbrück. I was able to get his name and we tracked him down – it turned out he had been on duty when three of our girls were put to death. One was conscious, one was ill and only semi-conscious and the other was unconscious. Their bodies were placed on the rollers. When they reached the incinerator, there was a flash of flame. This man threw up on the spot. Suddenly it seemed to have been borne in upon him the horror of the whole thing. He got away, he absconded and managed to hide himself in this little village further south.[7]

Ernest van Maurik had an even more horrific experience when he traced a former guard at Buchenwald.

One of the most unusual and really rather horrifying experiences I had with ME42 was when Joe Thomas came out to visit us and wanted me to help him interview the man who had saved his life in Buchenwald. He was one of the German privileged prisoners who was giving inoculations, typhus inoculations to lots of prisoners for so-called medical research, killing them one by one. Joe Thomas had persuaded him to give him a fake inoculation and save his life by substituting his so-called corpse for somebody that this man had actually killed. Although Joe could speak a little German he was not prepared to utter one word of what was to him a horrible language, so he asked me, as an old friend, to take him to this man's house and to act as his translator. When we got to see this chap, he was really very unprepossessing, completely bald head, little rat-like eyes. We started questioning him because Joe had come out on behalf of the war crimes people and he wanted to save this man's life, as he had promised. So we went through all the details.

I ended up in an absolute daze. I couldn't believe the things I heard. I didn't know all this story because when he was rescued or liberated and got back to London, I was already in Germany so it was all new to me. We started off and the first question was, now tell me, how many people do you think you inoculated with typhus and who died? When the answer came, it was obviously several hundred. I began to think I was perhaps dreaming. It went on like this from one horror story to another. Eventually we were served some ersatz coffee by the woman he had married, who had been a member of the brothel in the concentration camp. I can't say I actually enjoyed the cup but at any rate I thought they were all out of their minds. I discovered later that that was exactly the truth of what had happened and I must also tell you that when I first saw Joe Thomas after his experiences I didn't recognize him, he looked so absolutely dreadful. When Joe got all the information he then went off and saved this man from the worst – he went to prison for twelve years but he did not get executed.

At other times the news they uncovered was more heartening, as Fyffe recalled: 'I heard of a man who was important to us, a Hungarian man, and I knew that he was being held in camp 92 and within four weeks we were actually able to contact this man, and a Pole, also an agent of ours, and deliver them to London, to their respective country sections, which was quite unexpected.'

Fyffe and the ME42 mission were not alone in a concern about vanished agents. Vera Atkins, F Section's intelligence officer responsible for bidding personal farewells to many agents at Tempsford, badly wanted to know what had happened to those who had not come back and to help war crimes investigations.

Some 200 SOE agents in France had been captured by the Gestapo and nearly all had been liquidated – a mere thirty survived to tell the tale. Fyffe heard one night that she was due to arrive in Berlin for what turned out to be a memorable visit.

I dashed up to Berlin. We had a safe house – 14 Kronprinzenstrasse – under one of our officers. I met Vera who had teamed up with Francis Cammaerts, one of our main French agents. She said she had a particular interest in one of her agents. She understood that he had been hospitalized in the East of Berlin. She wanted to try to trace this man, to see if he was alive or dead. I said, 'Look, Vera, the Russian zone is not the best place to go, you know. It's forbidden to go into the Russian zone.' 'Oh,' she said, 'but I must go and see this man. I must find out now that I'm over here.' So we set off by car. We passed through four control points. They were usually held up by a man with a machine-gun who didn't speak anything but Russian. Occasionally they knew the phrase '*papier, papier*', and so you handed out your pass which was only the ordinary British officer's pass. These chaps looked at it, sometimes upside-down. They just looked at it kind of puzzled, handed it back and waved us through. But in one case he motioned with his hand against his ears that he was going off to telephone. I thought, 'My God, that's the end of it.' I said, 'Now, Vera, I think I can get myself out of here because I have certain contacts in the military government in Berlin, but a woman officer is a novelty to the Russians.' I'd no guarantee that she would come out with me. But this chap was hardly in the office when another face looked out and waved us on.

So we go to this small hospital in a wee suburb, to find it was run by an English doctor but he was on leave so we spoke to someone else. Vera explained that this British officer had fallen ill, and she thought he may have died, and asked if he would be buried around here. This chap said there were no burials in any of these camps around here. He suggested a main hospital a little further on. They couldn't give us any details but suggested we go to the Bürgermeister's office and were directed to find it exactly opposite the Russian Kommandatura. I said to Vera,

'We are not stopping here in a British military vehicle, we're not even stopping, we're going right on.' So we found some small lanes and back streets and managed to get a place to put the car and walked back to the premises of the Bürgermeister. We were admitted by a young woman who listened to our story, brought down a man who indeed confirmed the fact that no burials were taking place in any of the camps. He took details of this man and said he would contact the English doctor when he got back from leave. He said, 'Can I have an address for you?' I thought I can't compromise ME42 in the safe house on Kronprinzenstrasse. So I said to Vera, 'I'm going to give them your name and rank and an address through the British Public Relations Office at the British Military Government in Berlin.' He took all that down but whether he ever contacted Vera or not I can't tell you. But we got out, and had a wild dinner that night.

As head of ME42 van Maurik soon realized there was more to the mission than met the eye and that Gubbins was pinning post-war hopes upon it.

When I got back from Switzerland, I was posted to the German section. About the same time General Templer joined SOE and took over the German section. The object of Military Establishment 42, of which I was appointed to be the acting head, was to follow the British Army into Germany. When they got established there, to try and find the very many SOE agents who had been arrested, captured by the Germans, and who were either in concentration camps or prisoner of war camps. In actual fact, we were not permitted to go until the war was nearly finished. Most of the people had either liberated themselves or had been liberated by the American or British Armies. Many others, we could wipe them off our card index before we even got there but I know that General Gubbins and the bosses of SOE were extremely keen that we should go because they looked upon this as an extension of SOE's work.

The army intelligence division were very pleased to have us because twelve people who spoke good German were not easy to find. They soon started giving us jobs which were more intelligence jobs than resistance jobs but that didn't matter. We were happy to do whatever we could to be of use with our language qualifications because we knew that SOE in the guise of General Gubbins was keen that a presence should continue to be felt in Germany. Therefore we were as it were keeping the flag flying for them.

ME42's work did not, as Gubbins hoped, save SOE from dissolution. But its intelligence efforts in Germany did pave the way for some of its members to enter the postwar intelligence community. The Iron Curtain was already descending and those with former resistance contacts behind enemy lines now proved to have valuable assets in the battle against the Soviets, as van Maurik recounted: 'One of our agents had a lot of contacts in what was now the Russian zone. I arranged for him to come to our headquarters in Germany. I gave him the facilities to visit his political allies in the Soviet zone and bring back very good intelligence reports as to what was happening inside the Soviet zone. That was snapped up by the Army.'

Meanwhile, back in London, the work of winding down Baker Street went on. This involved laying off staff, emptying the offices, and getting rid of the mountains of files that had accumulated during five hectic years. Officers sat in Baker Street haphazardly throwing files away, often competing with each other to fill a wastepaper basket, and not even bothering to read them. Overseas missions were ordered to send surviving files home after first weeding them thoroughly of ephemeral material. Many had not even survived the war, having been burned along the way by security-minded agents. The files of British Security Co-Ordination in New York were burned over several days at Camp X in Canada, and all the Beaulieu Training School papers, as well as those of the Massingham Mission in North Africa covering southern France, likewise went up in flames.

Then, in February 1946, just a month after SOE was merged with SIS, a fire broke out on the top floor of Baker Street. It gutted the entire top floor and destroyed nearly all the FANY records and many operational files including details of the field activities of the

SOE female agents and various blown (i.e. enemy-penetrated) circuits. Speculation has raged ever since that there was more to the conflagration than met the eye and that sensitive material had been deliberately sent up in flames.

Perhaps. But in the frantic atmosphere of the day who knew what was in half the files anyway? If there was some deliberate attempt to cover up deadly secrets it could only have been random at best. Angus Fyffe expressed doubts that still prevail.

> That was a great blow to me. I'd sent records to London, week by week, and when I heard that all these records had been lost that was the end of SOE as I had known it and it was one of the most tragic things I heard. I couldn't believe that these papers were destroyed deliberately and yet at the same time some of these papers I know about myself were time bombs waiting to explode. Perhaps there was a reason for a fire breaking out, I don't know, but it wouldn't surprise me if there was a deliberate destruction.

But deliberate or not, the Baker Street fire was perhaps a fitting finale to the story begun five years before with Churchill's order to Dalton to set Europe ablaze.

Some time after the fire Leo Marks, now back in civvies, went back to take a nostalgic look at the last office he'd worked in for SOE in Montagu Mansions. He recalled it as a melancholy moment.

> It was for sale and in the hands of the agents and I wondered what it was going to be like to go inside for the last time. The office was derelict, there were bars across the windows and I felt them across my chest, it had been gutted by experts. It was in this room that I'd had to write so many poems for agents to use for their messages. I hated doing it but they had to have poems to give them a little bit of extra safety. I had resolved I would never write another and suddenly I felt one coming on and the more I suppressed it the more it insisted on its right of way. I had no pencil, no paper, but there was a blackboard and a piece of chalk.

This was the poem Leo Marks wrote.

> We listen round the clock
> For a code called peacetime
> But will it ever come
> And shall we know when it does
> And break it once it's here
> This code called peacetime.
>
> Or is its message such
> That it cannot be absorbed
> Unless its text is daubed
> In letters made of lives
> From an alphabet of death
> Each consonant a breath
> Expired before its time.
>
> Signalmaster, Signalmaster
> Whose Commandments were in clear
> Must you speak to us in code
> Once peacetime is here?

NOTES

1 Leo Marks, *Between Silk and Cyanide*, pp. 566–75.
2 Peter Wilkinson and Joan Bright Astley, *Gubbins and SOE*, p. 211.
3 Denis Rigden, *Kill the Führer: Section X and Operation Foxley*, pp. 53, 56.
4 Marks, op. cit., p. 398.
5 Wilkinson and Astley, op. cit., p. 216.
6 Richard Aldrich, 'Unquiet in death: the post-war survival of the Special Operations Executive, 1945–51', in *Contemporary British History 1931–61: Politics and the Limits of Policy*, ed. Anthony Gorst, Lewis Johnman and W. Scott Lucas (Institute of British History, 1991), pp. 193–217.
7 He may have been thinking of Natzweiler, not Ravensbrück, where four female SOE agents were killed in such a manner in July 1944.

EPILOGUE

SOE peaked in size at the time of the D-Day landings when some 10,000 men and 3000 women worked for it around the globe. Of these, about half the men and perhaps a hundred of the women had also served as secret agents behind enemy lines or in neutral countries. While the leadership was British, many of these men and women came from countries occupied by the enemy and little could have been achieved without them or the local resistance. By trial and error they helped forge a new way of warfare. What are we to make of their achievements?

Strategically, SOE was a valuable bonus to the regular forces. General Dwight D. Eisenhower, the Supreme Allied Commander in Europe, recognized that the disruption to German forces by the resistance, much of it organized by SOE, played a 'very considerable' part in the Allies' final victory. In the Balkans guerrilla forces kept several German and Italian divisions tied down; throughout Asia SOE administered constant pinpricks to the Japanese; and nowhere could the dictators ever truly relax and believe their conquest final. In neutral countries SOE agents toiled deviously to optimize British interests.

Baker Street made mistakes, some deadly – the *Englandspiel* was the worst, and there were others. This was hardly surprising given that SOE was built virtually from scratch in 1940. More extraordinary is that within a mere five years it grew into a professional and effective organization that left a powerful mark on history. Some critics have taken it to task for lighting fires in Europe and encouraging populations to revolt before they were ready and thus provoking terrible enemy reprisals. But this forgets that Europeans themselves helped set the pace for SOE and that Baker Street spent much of its effort discouraging premature action. Without its guiding hand things may have been very much worse.

As it was, the presence of SOE agents behind enemy lines demonstrated that Britain fought on, that all was not lost, and that there still remained hope. In the darkness of Nazi occupation SOE fanned the flames of hope and kept alive the flag of freedom. For this alone it deserves remembering.

But let us leave the last words to some of those who took part, whose stories have been told in the preceding pages.

Angus Fyffe, training instructor at Arisaig
'I suppose it could be said that SOE invented a new form of warfare. Call it what you like, it was something that had never been done before on that scale.'

George Millar, organizer of the Chancellor circuit, France
'I think it was an important part of the war against Hitler's Germany. It had some magnificent agents.'

Francis Cammaerts, head of Jockey circuit, France
'I don't know what SOE achieved throughout the world. There will be many views on that. What it achieved in the Alps of France is quite straightforward. The troops that landed on August the 15th on the Mediterranean coast got through the Alps to Grenoble in seven days, whereas their plan had been to spend nine weeks gathering materials together on the beaches. Now that was because there was no fighting. They went through the Alps because the Alps had been taken over by the resistance. The Alps had been taken over because the Germans couldn't operate there. That to my mind is an enormous achievement, an achievement which saved tens of thousands of lives.'

Noreen Riols, staff member at Beaulieu
'I think without it D-Day would have been very much more difficult because these people went ahead and they prepared the ground. They'd been able to say what was happening on the coast, on the two coasts because after all there was the false D-Day on the Calais coast which the Germans imagined. They could give all sorts of information about troop movements and what was happening and also do a little bit of sabotage beforehand. I think if it only achieved that, it achieved a great deal.'

Thomas Macpherson, leader of Jedburgh team, Quinine, France, 1944
'I have no doubt that while we made very little difference to the

French uprising at the moment of liberation itself, if there had not been Jedburgh officers and similar in France in the gap between June and mid-August, nothing would have happened at all that would have had any significance on the result of the war. Whereas I believe the cumulative effect of these officers and their relatively small actions had a real effect in tying down occupying troops.'

Hugh Verity, SOE air operations
'I don't think there's any doubt about it, that SOE made a very great contribution to the success of the liberation of France and other countries. The Allied troops, the regular forces of the British and Americans, and in the south the French army coming in across the beaches very soon found that they were sort of punching into hollow cheese because some of the areas were already being administered by the resistance. The Germans couldn't continue to enforce their systems. People much better placed than me to judge thought that the SOE operations really knocked six months or more off the length of the war.'

Henri Diacono, W/T operator for Spiritualist circuit, France
'I heard for the first time of SOE after the war. We didn't know what we were; we thought we were only on a mission as agents to help the French resistance, to provide them with arms, ammunition, money and also to reassure all small groups of resistance that they were depending on the high command of the Allies. Most French people wanted to help, wanted to do something. SOE has really organized, helped French people to organize their resistance. We were amateurs but who was not an amateur – and we won the war anyway!'

Ernest van Maurik, SOE, Switzerland, and ME42, Germany
'I think of the effect it had on all the occupied nations because we supported them. SOE supported them and enabled them to gain self-respect. In Denmark, for instance, they became with SOE's help a fighting ally; they were no longer just an occupied nation.'

Guido Zembsch-Schreve, agent in France
'There were some theatres which were really a success; there were theatres where the action was a pure flop. It is not to me to judge. History will judge but as what concerns myself and the people I worked for, it was a great thing. It was a venture, something splendid.'

BIBLIOGRAPHY

Auty, Phyllis and Clogg, Richard (eds), *British Policy Towards Wartime Resistance in Yugoslavia and Greece*, London, Macmillan, 1975.

Beevor, J .G, *SOE: Recollections and Reflections 1940–45*, London, The Bodley Head, 1981.

Berkeley, Roy, *A Spy's London*, London, Leo Cooper, 1994.

Braddon, Russell, *Nancy Wake*, London, Cassell, 1956.

Butler, Ewan, *Amateur Agent*, London, Harrap, 1963.

Cassidy, William L., *Quick or Dead*, Boulder, Paladin, 1978.

Clark, Freddie, *Agents by Moonlight*, Stroud, Tempus Publishing, 1999.

Cookridge, E. H., *They Came from the Sky*, London, Heinemann, 1965.

Cruickshank, Charles, *SOE in Scandinavia*, Oxford, Oxford University Press, 1986.

Cunningham, Cyril, *Beaulieu: The Finishing School for Secret Agents*, London, Leo Cooper, 1988.

Dalton, Hugh, *The Fateful Years: Memoirs 1931–1945*, London, Muller, 1957.

Davidson, Basil, *Special Operations Europe: Scenes from the Anti-Nazi War*, London, Gollancz, 1980.

Deakin, F. W. D., *The Embattled Mountain*, London, Oxford University Press, 1971.

Dear, Ian, *Sabotage and Subversion: The SOE and OSS at War*, London, Cassell, 1996.

Escott, Beryl E., *Mission Improbable*, Yeovil, Patrick Stephen, 1991.

Foot, M. R. D., *SOE: The Special Operations Executive 1940–46*, London, BBC, 1984.

SOE in France, London, HMSO, 1966.

Hastings, Max, *Das Reich*, London, Papermac, 1993.

Haukelid, Knut, *Skis Against the Atom*, Minot, North American Heritage Press, 1989.

Howarth, David, *The Shetland Bus*, London, Thomas Nelson, 1951.

Howarth, Patrick, *Undercover: The Men and Women of the Special Operations Executive*, London, Routledge and Kegan Paul, 1980.

Imperial War Museum, *The Special Operations Executive: Sound Archive and Oral History Recordings*, London, Imperial War Museum, 1998.

'J. E. A.', *Geoffrey: Major John Geoffrey Appleyard*, London, Blandford Press, 1946.

Kramer, Rita, *Flames in the Field*, London, Penguin, 1996.

Lorain, Pierre, *Clandestine Operations: The Arms and Techniques of the Resistance 1941–1944*, New York, Macmillan, 1983.

Marinos, Themistocles, *Harling Mission 1942*, Athens, Papazisis, 1993.

Marks, Leo, *Between Silk and Cyanide: A Codemaker's War 1941–1945*, London, HarperCollins, 1998.

Messenger, Charles, *The Commandos 1940–46*, London, William Kimber, 1985.

Millar, George, *Horned Pigeon*, London, Heinemann, 1946.
Maquis, London, Heinemann, 1947.
Road to Resistance: An Autobiography, London, The Bodley Head, 1979.

Nicolson, David, *Aristide: Warlord of the Resistance*, London, Leo Cooper, 1994.

Pimlott, Ben, *Hugh Dalton*, London, Cape, 1985.
The Second World War Diary of Hugh Dalton 1940–45, London, Cape, 1986.

Richards, Brooks, *Secret Flotillas*, London, HMSO, 1996.

Rigden, Denis, *Kill the Führer: Section X and Operation Foxley*, Stroud, Sutton, 1999.

Seaman, Mark, *Bravest of the Brave*, London, Michael O'Mara, 1997.

Stafford, David, *Britain and European Resistance 1940–1945*, London, Macmillan, 1980.
Camp X: SOE and the American Connection, London, Viking, 1988.
Churchill and Secret Service, London, John Murray, 1997.

Sweet-Escott, Bickham, *Baker Street Irregular*, London, Methuen, 1965.

Tickell, Jerrard, *Moon Squadron*, London, Hodder and Stoughton, 1960.

Verity, Hugh, *We Landed by Moonlight*, Wilmslow, Airdata Publications, 1995.

West, Nigel, *Secret War: The Story of SOE*, London, Hodder and Stoughton, 1992.

Wilkinson, Peter, and Astley, Joan Bright, *Gubbins and SOE*, London, Leo Cooper, 1993.

Woodhouse, C. M., *Something Ventured*, London, Granada, 1982.
The Struggle for Greece, Hart-Davis MacGibbon, London, 1976.

Zembsch-Schreve, Guido, *Pierre Lalande: Special Agent*, London, Leo Cooper, 1996.

ACKNOWLEDGEMENTS

The publishers would like to acknowledge the following for their permission to reproduce copyright material. Every effort has been made to trace copyright holders but in a few cases this has proved impossible. The publishers would be interested to hear from any copyright holders not here acknowledged.

Quotations from Crown Copyright material appear with the permission of the Controller of Her Majesty's Stationery Office: Brooks Richards, *Secret Flotillas* (HMSO 1996); M.R.D. Foot, *SOE in France* (HMSO, 1966); Churchill to Eden, 'Most Secret', 5 February 1944, Chartwell 20/152, Churchill College, Cambridge; Godfrey, 'Special Operations Executive-a Review', 27 December 1941, in ADM 223/481, Public Record Office; 'Relations between SOE and the Foreign Office', Annex 1 to Hanbury-Williams/ Playfair report; DO (44)2, in CAB 69/6, Public Record Office.
John Hanbury-Williams and W.E.Playfair to Lord Selborne, 18 June 1942, in SOE file HQ 60. Advance copy prior to public release kindly provided by Duncan Stuart, CMG, SOE Adviser to the Foreign and Commonwealth Office.
'Erik Greenwood', in *The Special Operations Executive: Sound Archive and Oral History Recordings*, reproduced by kind permission of the Imperial War Museum Sound Archive, 11374, July 1990.
'J.E.A', *Geoffrey: Major John Geoffrey Appleyard*, (Blandford Press, 1946).
Peter Wilkinson and Joan Bright Astley, *Gubbins and SOE*, (Leo Cooper, 1993).
Harris to Portal, 28 March 1942, in AIR 20/2901, quoted in David Nicolson, *Aristide*, (Leo Cooper, 1994).
Bickham Sweet-Escott, *Baker Street Irregular* (Methuen, 1965)
Patrick Howarth, *Undercover* (Routledge and Kegan Paul, 1980)
Ian Dear, *Sabotage and Subversion: the SOE and OSS at War* (Cassell, 1996)
Charles Messenger, *The Commandos 1940–46* (William Kimber, London, 1985)
The Second World War Diary of Hugh Dalton 1940–45, Ed. Ben Pimlott (Cape, 1986)

Basil Davidson, *Special Operations Europe: Scenes from the anti-Nazi War* (Gollancz, 1980)

C.M. Woodhouse, *The Struggle for Greece* (Hart-Davis MacGibbon, London, 1976)

C.M. Woodhouse, *Something Ventured* (Granada, 1982)

Themistocles Marinos, *Harling Mission 1942* (Papazisis, 1993)

Hugh Dalton, *The Fateful Years: Memoirs 1931–1945* (Muller, 1957)

Gubbins, introduction to Knut Haukelid, *Skis Against The Atom* (North American Heritage Press, 1989)

Knut Haukelid, *Skis Against The Atom* (North American Heritage Press, 1989)

Leo Marks, *Between Silk and Cyanide* (Harper Collins, 1998)

Quoted in Freddie Clark, *Agents By Moonlight* (Tempus Publishing)

Hugh Verity, *We Landed By Moonlight* (Airdata Publications, 1995)

Pierre Lorain, *Clandestine Operations* (Macmillan, 1983)

S.W. Bailey, ' British Policy Towards General Draza Mihailovic', in *British Policy Towards Wartime Resistance in Yugoslavia and Greece*, edited by Phyllis Auty and Richard Clogg

Denis Rigden, *Kill the Fuhrer: Section X and Operation Foxley* (Sutton Publishing Limited, 1999)

PICTURE CREDITS

Credits in order of appearance:

Special Forces Club, Special Forces Club, Popperfoto, Special Forces Club, Hulton Getty Picture Collection, Special Forces Club, Special Forces Club, Public Record Office, Museum of Defence Intelligence, Imperial War Museum, Public Record Office, Public Record Office, Public Record Office, Public Record Office, Public Record Office, The Orion Publishing Group, The Orion Publishing Group, Imperial War Museum, Special Forces Club, Special Forces Club, Special Forces Club, Special Forces Club, Special Forces Club, Norwegian Industrial Workers Museum Vemork, Norwegian Industrial Workers Museum Vemork, Special Forces Club, Noreen Riols, Special Forces Club, Jill Price, Patricia Jones, Imperial War Museum, Herr Rudolf Staritz, Imperial War Museum, Imperial War Museum, Topham Picturepoint

INDEX

abrasive grease 48
Adlington, Bert 50–6
Admiralty 20
Africa,
  East 89-90
  North 70, 74, 83,
    96, 170, 181, 199,
    203, 204
  West 75–81
ageing 54–6
Air Liaison Section
  133, 140, 145–6
Alexander, General 97
Aosta, Duke of 90
Appleyard, Geoffrey
  72–3, 75–6,
  79–80, 83
Arisaig 25–7, 46, 73
Army 20
Asia 252
  East 82
  South-east 243
Asopos viaduct 109
Atkins, Vera 170, 172,
  246-8
Atlantic 23, 74, 181
  Charter 74
atomic research/bomb
  110 see also
  Norway
Attlee, Clement 167,
  242, 243
Australia/Australians
  17, 74
Austria 11, 84–7
  passim, 244
'Auxiliary Units' 13
Aviemore 32-33, 111
Azerbaijan 181

Bailey, Col. Bill 183–4,
de Baissac, Claude
  204, 205

Baker Street HQ 15,
  20, 23, 24–5 and
  passim
Balkans 12, 23, 73, 84,
  85, 87, 88, 91–5,
  181–96, 252 see
  also individual
  entries
Barnes, Major Tom
  105–7 passim
Baseden, Yvonne
  18–19, 209–212
Beaulieu 33–46, 153,
  217, 249
Beevor, Jack 12
Berkeley Court 24–5
Besançon 213–14
  passim
Bevin, Ernest 243
'Bigots' 147
Bletchley Park 74, 191
Bloch, Denise 212
Bordeaux 204–7, 213,
  214
Bosnia/Bosnians 192,
  195
de Bourbon, Michel
  227
bribery 87,93
Brickendonbury 37,66
Briggens (Station XIV)
  50
Bright, Joan 17
Brittany 61, 66–70,
  199
Brockies, Pauline 19,
  50, 59–60
Brooke, Sir Alan 131,
  243
Brooker, Major R.M.
  ('Bill') 38–9
Brooks-Richards,
  Francis 63

Brown, Arthur 227
Broz, Josip see Tito
Buchenwald 216, 245
Buckmaster, Col. 33,
  173
Bulgaria 91–22

Cadett, Thomas 201
Cadogan, Sir
  Alexander 133
Cammaerts, Francis
  16-17, 26, 33, 37,
  46, 207–9, 213,
  247, 253
Canada 17, 94
  Camp X 39, 249
capture, of agents 128,
  148, 150–1, 153,
  166–69, 210–214,
  221–3, 243–9
de Chastelain, Gardyne
  84
Chiefs of Staff 25, 131,
  135, 166, 168,
  200, 239, 242,
  243
Churchill, Odette 59
Churchill, Winston
  9–11 passim, 71,
  73, 74, 82, 83,
  93, 94, 109, 128,
  131, 132, 133,
  146, 167, 168,
  190, 192–3, 199,
  223, 237, 239–42
  passim
circuits 172, 178, 204,
  209, 212, 249–50
  see also networks
'Scholar' 210
'Scientist' 204–5
'Spiritualist' 170,179